THE CATHOLIC UNIVERSITY OF AMERICA

STUDIES IN ROMANCE LANGUAGES AND LITERATURES

VOLUME XVII

THE BLESSED VIRGIN MARY

AS MEDIATRIX

AMS PRESS
NEW YORK

THE BLESSED VIRGIN MARY AS MEDIATRIX IN THE
LATIN AND OLD FRENCH LEGEND PRIOR
TO THE FOURTEENTH CENTURY

The Blessed Virgin Mary as Mediatrix in the Latin and Old French Legend prior to the Fourteenth Century

BY

SISTER MARY VINCENTINE GRIPKEY

THE CATHOLIC UNIVERSITY OF AMERICA
WASHINGTON, D. C.
1938

TABLE OF CONTENTS

v

Contents

PREFACE

The purpose of the present study is to examine the theocentrism of the rôle of the Blessed Virgin Mary as Mediatrix in the Latin and Old French legends. It also seeks to establish the status of the Virgin Mary in the Marial *miracula* more definitely than has been heretofore attempted. It is already the opinion of various scholars that at the time of the Crusades the Blessed Virgin of the legends began " to overshadow the Trinity itself," [1] to be given a " dignity equal or superior to that of Christ," [2] to be exalted " practically into a fourth person of the Trinity," [3] in short, to be deified. Such statements imply that the theocentric tradition which held during the first eleven centuries that God alone can perform miracles, was gradually lost sight of, and that the Virgin performed them by her own power; that the attribute of God's mercy was comparatively dimmed by her charity toward the unfortunate; finally, that in the Marial *miracula* she was elevated above the status of creature, accorded to her during the period prior to the twelfth and thirteenth centuries.

Speculation as to the improbability of such assumptions do not solve the problem. This study is neither apologetical nor theological. Its purpose is to investigate the theocentric aspect and not to offer specific refutations of charges of mariolatry. It is limited to the consideration of the following questions. Is there evidence that Mary is a mere instrument of the divine power? As the main protagonist in the Marial legends, does she, nevertheless, occupy a secondary position as a suppliant Mediatrix? Are the attributes of God in the background? May objective evidence be obtained concerning her status as creature?

Many scholars have treated the cult of the Virgin from an historical point of view. Ahsmann traces the evolution of the devotion

---

[1] H. Adams, *Mont-Saint-Michel and Chartres* (New York, 1913), p. 90.

[2] D. Schaff, *History of the Christian Church* (New York, 1907), V, Part i, 833.

[3] G. G. Coulton, *Five Centuries of Religion* (Cambridge, 1923), I, 139. MacCulloch writes: " To the average Christian the Trinity was expressed as Father, Son, and Virgin." *Medieval Faith and Fable* (Boston, 1932), p. 110.

from its earliest manifestations in the catacombs and then proceeds to show the "reflet de ce culte dans les poésies profanes du moyen âge en France." [4] He devotes only one chapter to the Marial legend and places no emphasis on the idea of mediation. Heinrich Becker [5] makes a survey of the cult of the Virgin in the entire field of Old French literature. Although his citations include Gautier de Coincy and Adgar, the scope of his dissertation is too broad to treat them more than summarily. Maurice Vloberg presents a brief sketch of the evolution of the legend in the introduction to his *Légende dorée de Notre-Dame* [6] but he is not concerned with the theocentric aspect of the *miracula*.

Scholarly research in the Marial legend dates from the appearance of Mussafia's monumental work, "Studien zu den mittelalterlichen Marienlegenden," [7] which is the result of a painstaking examination of manuscript collections in Europe. Besides listing at least seventy collections in Latin and several in French, he gives his conclusions concerning their origin and relationship. Necessary additions to the *Studien* have been made by Ward in the *Catalogue of Romances in the Department of Manuscripts in the British Museum*. [8] The present writer is particularly indebted to Albert Poncelet's *Index Miraculorum* [9] and to the more recent study of J. Morawski [10] who lists all collections in French verse and supplements the work of Weber [11] and Schwan [12] by his investi-

---

[4] *Le culte de la sainte Vierge et la littérature française profane du moyen âge* (Paris, 1930).

[5] *Die Auffassung der Jungfrau Maria in der altfranzösischen Litteratur* (Göttingen, 1905).

[6] Paris, 1921.

[7] *Sitzungsberichte der kais. Akad. der Wissenschaften in Wien* (phil.-hist. Cl.), CXIII (1886); CXV (1887); CXIX (1889); CXXIII (1890); CXXXIX (1898). These articles are here designated as *Studien* I, II, III, IV, V.

[8] Vol. II (London, 1893).

[9] "Miraculorum B. V. Mariae quae saec. VI-XV latine conscripta sunt Index postea perficiendus," *Anal. Boll.*, XXI (1902), 214-360.

[10] "Mélanges de littérature pieuse," *Romania*, LXI (1935), 145-209; 316-350.

[11] *Handschriftliche Studien auf dem Gebiete romanischer Litteratur des Mittelalters*, I (Frauenfeld, 1876); "Zu den Legenden der Vie des peres," *ZRPh*, I (1877), 357-65.

[12] "La Vie des anciens Pères," *Romania*, XIII (1884), 233-63.

gations in the *Vies des Pères*. Research in the subject has likewise
been facilitated by Crane's reprint of the Latin collection published
by Bernhard Pez in 1731.[13]

Monographs and dissertations, tracing the history of the more
popular legends, have been written by Eugen Wolter,[14] Heinrich
Watenphul, Gédéon Huet, Hjalmar Lundgren, Theodor Pelizaeus,
Robert Guiette, and Erik Boman. Adolf Mussafia[15] and Carl
Neuhaus[16] have investigated the sources of Gautier de Coincy and
Adgar, while Hilding Kjellman[17] in his edition of MS *Old Royal
20 B XIV* of the British Museum, includes the Latin originals as
well as the corresponding variants in MSS *Bibl. nat. fr. 818* and
375.

These scholars have not been primarily concerned with an interpretation of the position of the Blessed Virgin in Marial legends.
Although it is not the main purpose of the writer to trace the
evolution of the *miracula*, it is believed that a survey of the background and sources of the vernacular collections will establish a
firm basis for conclusions which may be drawn concerning the
status of the Virgin Mary in the miracle stories of the twelfth and
thirteenth centuries. Special attention has been given the Latin
local collections, for their appearance created the vogue of the
miracula in France.[18]

I wish to acknowledge my great indebtedness to the late Very
Reverend Romanus Butin, S. M., S. T. L., Ph. D. I owe much to
his kindly assistance and inspiring guidance during the preliminary stages of this dissertation. I also desire to express my sincere
appreciation to Reverend David Rubio, O. S. A., Ph. D., Head of
the Department of Romance Languages and Literatures, for his

---

[13] *Liber de miraculis Sanctae Dei Genitricis Mariae* (Ithaca, 1925).

[14] See bibliography.

[15] "Ueber die von Gautier de Coincy benützten Quellen," *Denkschriften
der kais. Akad. der Wissenschaften in Wien* (phil.-hist. Cl.), XLIV (1896),
Abh. i, 1-58.

[16] *Die Quellen zu Adgar's Marienlegenden nach der Londoner Hs.*,
Egerton 612 (Aschersleben, 1882). Also *Die lateinischen Vorlagen zu den
altfranzösischen Adgar'schen Marienlegenden* (Aschersleben, 1886).

[17] *Deuxième collection anglo-normande des miracles de la sainte Vierge
et son original latin* (Paris and Upsala, 1922).

[18] Vloberg, *op. cit.*, p. 4.

direction and encouragement, to Dr. Harry Austin Deferrari for his able criticism of the study, and to Dr. William J. Roach for his many excellent suggestions and careful revision of the manuscript. Acknowledgments are also due to the Staffs of the Library of Congress and Mullen Library for their courtesy and efficient service. Above all, I am deeply grateful to Mother Mary Josepha and the Sisters of Charity of Leavenworth for the opportunity of pursuing graduate study at the Catholic University of America.

SISTER MARY VINCENTINE.

Washington, D. C.
May, 1938

CHAPTER I

Origins of the Marial "Miracula"

Many of the miracles of the Virgin, which were assembled in great collections during the twelfth and thirteenth centuries, have as their source the legendary accounts scattered in the works of Latin writers who frequently related them as *exempla* for the edification of the people. They derive from an age in which their authors, more or less explicitly, place the miracle on the same plane as natural events, considering both in their essence to be equally marvelous and due to the providence of God.[1] As a written literature they begin in the West with Gregory of Tours (d. 594), but undoubtedly they circulated among the people in Gaul[2] before the sixth century.

Gregory of Tours

In the *incipit* of his *Libri Miraculorum* Gregory asserts, in imitation of Jerome[3] and the apostle Paul,[4] that he would relate nothing except " ea quae Deo digna et eclesiae aedificationem oportuna iudicarentur."[5] This first writer of Marial legends does not give exclusive treatment to the miracles of the Virgin. He first presents those of Christ:

> Dominus igitur noster Iesus Christus in adsumpta carne de virgine multa populis miracula est dignatus estendere.[6]

In one sentence he passes in brief review the miracles of the Gospels,[7] and then recounts in more detail the wonders wrought

---

[1] A. Michel, " Miracle," *Dictionnaire de théologie catholique*, ed. Vacant et Mangenot, X, 2 (Paris, 1929), 1803.

[2] J. Th. Welter, *L'exemplum dans la littérature religieuse et didactique du moyen âge* (Paris, 1927), p. 89.

[3] *Epist. ad Eustochium*, xxii, § 30 (*PL*, XXII, 416).

[4] Rom. 14: 19; Eph. 4: 29.

[5] *Liber I Miraculorum: In gloria martyrum*, § 1 (ed. W. Arndt and B. Krusch, *MGH*, *SS. rer. Merov.*, I [Hannover, 1885], 487).

[6] *Ibid.*, § 2 (p 488).

[7] He writes: " Haustos enim latices in vini sapore convertit, caecorum oculis, depulsa nocte, lumen infudit, paralyticorum gressus, ablata debili-

1

through the cross, the nails, and other relics of the Passion.[8] Just as he prefaces this with excerpts from the Gospel of St. John referring to the divinity of Christ and to His Incarnation, so he introduces the Marial legends with a proclamation of Mary, Virgin and Mother, in a brief but suggestive description of her Assumption:

> Maria vero gloriosa genetrix Christi ut ante partum ita virgo creditur et post partum, quae, ut supra diximus,[10] angelicis choris canentibus, in paradiso, Domino praecedente, translata est.[11]

Three of his eight narratives present her as Mediatrix, and of these the legend of the Jew boy appears with greatest frequency in later collections.[12] According to Gregory's version, the child tells his father that he has received the Eucharist in a church of the Christians. He is thrown by his angry parent into an oven, but is miraculously saved by the Virgin Mary. It is a Eucharistic miracle, for the child goes to Mass with his Christian playmates and approaches the altar with them " ad participationem gloriosi corporis et sanguinis dominici." [13] For this deed the father, whom Gregory describes as " Christo Domino ac suis legibus inimicus," throws him into the fire. He is saved by the mercy of God:

tate, direxit, febres aegrotantium, fugato ardore, restinxit, ydropicum, conpraesso tumore, sanavit, lepram discedere sacri oris virtute mandavit, mulierem daemonio inclinatam, . . . erexit; super aquas vero, non dehiscentibus aquis, incessit, profluvium mulieris tactu fimbriae salutaris avertit. Multa quidem et alia fecit." *Ibid.* (pp. 488-89).

[8] He adds: " De lancea vero, harundo, spungia, corona spinea, columna, ad quam verberatus est Dominus et redemptor Hierusolymis." *Ibid.*, § 6 (p. 492).

[9] *Ibid.* (p. 488).

[10] *Ibid.*, § 4 (p. 489).

[11] *Ibid.*, § 8 (p. 493). As Krusch indicates, Gregory used the *Libellus Pseudo-Melitonis de transitu Mariae, Bibl. Max. Pat.* II, 214.

[12] For the influence of Gregory of Tours upon later versions, see Theodor Pelizaeus, *Beiträge zur Geschichte der Legende vom Judenknaben* (Halle, 1914), pp. 18 ff.

[13] Gregory of Tours, *loc. cit.*, § 9 (p. 494). For several quotations within the same legend page numbers are given in the footnotes only for the first reference. Titles of the legends are those made standard by Ward in his *Catalogue of Romances*. The writer has italicized significant Latin words.

Sed *non defuit illa misericordia,* quae tres quondam Hebraeos
pueros Chaldaico in camino proiectos nube rorolenta resper-
serat. *Ipsa* enim et hunc inter medios ignes, prunarum moles
iacentem prorsus consumi non patitur.

The visible agent or Mediatrix, according to the boy's testimony,
was the " woman " whose picture he had seen in the church where
she was depicted as holding a little child. Those who are present
are deeply affected by the miraculous occurrence. Their shouts, he
says, fill the place " et sic *Deum* omnis populus benedicit." Many
Jews, besides the mother and child, are converted:

> Agnitam ergo infans fidem catholicam, credidit in nomine
> Patris et Filii et Spiritus sancti, ac salutaribus aquis ablutos
> una cum genetrice sua denuo sunt renati. Multi Iudaeorum
> exemplo hoc in urbe illa salvati sunt.

The two other miracles, related by Gregory of Tours, presenting
Mary Mediatrix, have been used by the author of the earliest specimen of this genre in the vernacular, the MS of Orléans.[14] One
describes Mary as an active agent, instructing three children how to
raise the columns of a church which is being constructed in her
honor. They easily accomplish what the workmen are unable to do.
The legend makes no mention of God;[15] the other which tells of the
plight of a monastery in Jerusalem because of famine, indirectly
implies the exercise of her intercessory power. The abbot counsels
the monks: " Oremus, fratres dilectissimi, et *Dominus ministrabit
nobis cibos.*"[16] His next statement is an implication of Marial
mediation: " Nec enim potest fieri, ut deficiat triticum in eius
monasterium, quae frugem vitae ex utero pereunti intulit mundo."
Their barns are miraculously filled with wheat and in gratitude
" gratias egerunt *Deo.*" Again there is a famine and the abbot
advises: " Vigilemus ac *deprecemur Dominum,* et forsitan trans-
mittere dignabitur alimenta." An angel places a quantity of gold
upon the altar. Gregory terminates the legend with a remark from

---

[14] Paul Meyer, " Notice sur un manuscrit d'Orléans contenant d'anciens
miracles de la Vierge en vers français," *Notices et extraits des manuscrits
de la Bibliothèque nationale,* XXXIV, 2 (1895), 39-50.

[15] Gregory of Tours, *loc. cit.,* § 8 (p. 493). Cf. *infra,* p. 14.

[16] *Ibid.,* § 10 (p. 495). Cf. *infra,* pp. 15 and 206-207.

which one may infer that the monastery was dedicated to the Virgin [17] and that the monks had had recourse to her intercession:

> Nec mirum, si beata virgo sine labore suis protulit victum, quae sine coitu viri concipiens, virgo permansit et post partum.

One other legend is not Marial, but appears in later collections.[18] Gregory relates that an image of Christ is pierced by a Jew who then takes it home in order to burn it:

> Sed res mira apparuit, quae de *virtute Dei* non potest ambigeri. Nam de vulnere, ubi imago transfossa fuerat, sanguis effluxit.[19]

The expression, *virtus Dei*, which often appears in the works of Gregory,[20] is an indication of the theocentrism of his stories which, however, must be judged in the light of his other writings, as the miracles of the Blessed Virgin constitute such a small part of his hagiographical works. Nevertheless, it is quite obvious that the more signal benefits conferred by Mary Mediatrix in his legends— assisting the workers in the building of the church or covering the Jew boy with her mantle—are, in the opinion of Gregory of Tours, on a much lower plane than the divine mercy manifested in the Incarnation and Redemption. He writes:

> Insignia divinorum beneficiorum carismata, quae humani generi caelitus sunt indulta . . . cum praepotens inmorta- lisque Creator mortalis carnis patitur amictu vestiri, mortem pro hominis peccato mortui reparationem adire victorque resurgere.[21]

Later in the thirteenth century, this contrast between Marial charity and infinite mercy is again found.[22]

---

[17] Paul Meyer, *loc. cit.*, p. 41. This is definitely stated in the version in MS *Bibl. nat. fr. 818:*

> El nom de la Virge Marie
> Estoit fondée l'abaïe.   (9-10)

Ibid., p. 65.

[18] E. Galtier, " Byzantina: L'image blessée par le Juif," *Romania*, XXIX (1900), 517-23. Cf. *infra*, p. 35.

[19] Gregory of Tours, *op. cit.*, § 21 (p. 501).

[20] *Ibid.*, § 5 (p. 490) ; § 24 (p. 502) ; § 25 (p. 503) *et passim.*

[21] *Liber Vitae Patrum*, 19 (ed. Arndt and Krusch, *MGH, SS. rer. Merov.* [Hannover, 1885], 736).

[22] Cf. *infra*, p. 89.

Gregory the Great

In his *Dialogues,* written late in the summer of 593,[23] Gregory the Great (d. 604) relates the prophecies, miracles, and visions of holy men who had lived in Italy. However, these supernatural phenomena occasion no astonishment on the part of the author, for he has a theocentric explanation [24] for even the more common wonders of nature which are no longer regarded as marvels because of their frequency: " Mira *Dei opera* humanis oculis usu viluerunt." [25] One need not be surprised if a man return to life after death:

> Unde fit ut si mortuus homo suscitetur, in admirationem omnes exsiliant, et quotidie homo qui non erat nascitur, et nemo miratur.[26]

Later writers hold the same belief as one finds in the popular legend [27] concerning the two brothers of Rome, Peter and Stephen, in which the latter is rescued out of Hell and restored to life for thirty days penance—a tale which Ward [28] believes to be derived from the vision of the knight who saw Peter in torment and Stephen crossing the Bridge of Dread, as related by Gregory.[29]

In describing the passing of the dying, he tells how Christ, " Auctor ac Retributor vitae," [30] appears to the maiden Tharsilla

[23] M. Manitius, *Geschichte der lateinischen Literatur des Mittelalters* (Munich, 1911), I, 103.

[24] Miracles are a proof of the presence of God who animates all things: ". . . omnipotens Deus aspirando vel implendo, ea, quae rationi subsistunt, et vivificat et movet invisibilia." *Dialogi,* ed. Umberto Moricca (Rome, 1924: " Fonti per la Storia d'Italia, LVII "), iv, 9 (p. 238). The wonders of the universe are the " omnipotentis Dei mirabilia." *Moralia,* vi (*PL,* LXXV, 738).

[25] *Moralia, ibid.*

[26] *Ibid.*

[27] For the popularity of this legend see variants listed by Crane in his reprint of Pez, *Liber de miraculis Sanctae Dei Genitricis Mariae,* p. 86.

[28] Ward, *Catalogue of Romances,* II, 607 (16).

[29] *Dial.* iv, 37 (pp. 286 ff.). According to Gregory, it is a supreme manifestation of God's mercy when a soul, who disbelieves in the existence of Hell, is restored to life for the purpose of amendment. *Ibid.* (p. 284). He introduces his account with the theocentric statement: " *Suprema* enim *pietas ex magna misericordiae suae largitate disponit,* ut nonnulli etiam post exitum repente ad corpus redeant. *Ibid.* (p. 285).

[30] *Ibid.,* iv, 17 (p. 254).

to console her departing soul. This account is followed by the
story of Musa, the sister of Probus, who sees Mary and her virgins.
Her desire to share their innocence and to live in the service of the
Blessed Virgin will be fulfilled, she is told, if she abstains from
childish levity and laughter for thirty days. She does so and at
the expiration of the time of trial, she has a similar vision:

> Cui se etiam vocanti respondere coepit, et, depraessis rever-
> enter oculis, aperta voce clamare: ecce, domina, venio; ecce,
> domina, venio in qua etiam voce spiritum reddedit, et ex
> virgineo corpore, habitatura cum sanctis virginibus exivit.[31]

One other legend which reappears in a thirteenth century MS
Cornell B. 14 [32] is contained in the *Dialogues*. Gregory relates
that Bonifacius, Bishop of Ferenti, is so moved to compassion by
the miseries of the poor that in virtuous violence he breaks open
the money-box of his nephew and takes out twelve gold crowns.
Later to quiet the fury of his relative, he enters the church dedicated to the Virgin Mary:

> Et elevatis manibus extenso vestimento, stando coepit exorare,
> ut ei redderit unde praesbiteri furentis insaniam mitigare
> potuissit . . . repente in sinu suo duodecim aureos invenit,
> ita fulgentes tamquam si ex igne producti hora eadem
> fuissent.[33]

Nowhere does Gregory exhort that a particular devotion be rendered to the Mother of God.[34] Even in the legend of Bonifacius in
which he refers to her invocation, he concludes this and other
accounts of the miracles of the holy man with the remark of his
interlocutor Peter: " Valde mirum quod *exaudire praeces* in se
sperantium etiam in rebus vilibus *dignatur Deus.*" [35]

---

[31] *Ibid.*, 18, p. 256. For variants, cf. Mielot, *Miracles de Nostre Dame*
(Westminster, 1885), p. xvii.

[32] The legend is of infrequent occurrence. Cf. T. F. Crane, " Miracles of
the Virgin," *RR*, II (1911), 274-75, no. xxvii.

[33] *Dial.* i, 9 (p. 55).

[34] F. Homes Dudden, *Gregory the Great* (London, 1905), II, 372-73.

[35] *Ibid.* (p. 58).

Adamnan

The miracle of the " Virgin's Image Insulted " occurs in the *De locis sanctis* of Adamnan, Abbot of Iona (d. 704). A French pilgrim, Arculfus, visited various places of pilgrimage and saw the image of the Virgin at Constantinople which emits a miraculous oil. It is upon his authority that Adamnan tells how a Jew attempted to defile the picture and oil flowed when the image was restored to a place of honor:

> Mirum dictu, ex eadem beatae Mariae imaginis tabula uerum ebulliens distillat semper oleum, . . . Hoc mirabile oleum honorem protestatur Mariae matris *domini Iesu,* de quo pater ait: In oleo sancto meo linivi eum (Ps. 88: 21).[36]

The account is theocentric in that the writer considers the miraculous oil a reparation for the dishonor shown to God as well as to the Mother, since the Jew had defiled the picture " ob Christi ex Maria nati dehonorationem." [37]

Cixila—Roderic Cerratensis

Cixila, Bishop of Toledo (770-783), in his *Vita S. Ildefonsi,* narrates only a few of the many legends of the Saint which he claims to have heard from Urbanus, an old cantor of the cathedral of Toledo, and from Evantius, an archdeacon of the same see.[38] He includes, however, an account of the apparition of the Virgin who presents Ildefonsus with a chasuble in reward for his treatise, *De Virginitate,* and which she says is from the " thesauro *Filii mei.*" [39] For continued faithfulness in her service and in that of her Son she promises Ildefonsus that " in futuro in promptuariis meis *cum aliis servis Filii mei* laeteris." The Virgin in Cixila's

---

[36] Ed. Paul Meyer (Vienna, 1898: " Corpus Scriptorum Ecclesiasticorum Latinorum, XXXIX "), iii, 5 (p. 295). This miracle sometimes forms a part of the legend " Saturday," as in the Salisbury MS (53) and the Toulouse MS (67). Ward, II, 611-12. For variants see Kjellman, *Deuxième collection anglo-normande,* pp. lxviii-lxix.

[37] Adamnan, *op. cit.* (p. 294).

[38] *Continuatio Isidoriana Hispana* (ed. T. Mommsen, *MGH, Auct. Ant.,* XI [Berlin, 1894], 358).

[39] *PL,* XCVI, 48.

account makes no threat if the vestment is worn by another. This detail is included in the *Vita S. Ildefonsi* by Roderic Cerratensis [40] who narrates that Siagrius had the presumption to don the chasuble and was struck dead.

This miracle becomes the first of a series of seventeen legends and is contained in the earliest of the Latin collections. [41] The *De Virginitate* was brought to France by Godescalcus, Bishop of Aquitaine. [42] It was found at Chalons-sur-Marne by Herman of Tournai who refers to the legend in his prefatory epistle to Bishop Bartholomaeus. [43]

Hatto

In 824 Wettin, a German monk, [44] had a vision which is related by Hatto, Bishop of Reichenau, afterwards Bishop of Basle (d. 836). A potion of medicine produces a visionary phenomenon in which Wettin is first visited by a troop of devils. However, " subito adfuit *divina miseratio*," [45] and an angel appears to frighten away the evil spirits. Wettin pleads with the angel for further protection, and in his petition, his conception of the interest of the church triumphant in humanity is apparent:

> Nam patriarchae, prophetae, et apostoli, omnisque dignitas caelestis sive terrestris *pro genere humano laborabant.* Et *vos* modo *magis laborare debetis,* quia istis temporibus fragiliores sumus.

The angel disappears but returns a second time to conduct him

[40] The Blessed Virgin, in the thirteenth century account of Roderic, adds: " Si quis autem post te praesumpserit hoc vestimentum induere, et in hac cathedra sedere, non carebit ultione." *Ibid.* (col. 50).

[41] The many variants are listed by Crane in his notes to Pez, p. 82.

[42] Mabillon, *Acta Sanctorum Ordinis Sancti Benedicti* (Venice, 1733), saec. II, p. 498.

[43] Manitius, III, p. 532. Herman writes of the chasuble " quam beate Dei Genitrix S. Hildefonso Toletanae civitatis archiepiscopo dederat, ob remunerationem trium libellorum quos de Virginitate sua composuerat." *De miraculis S. Mariae Laudunensis (PL,* CLVI, 961).

[44] Carl Fritzsche, " Die lateinischen Visionem des Mittelalters bis zur Mitte des 12. Jahrhunderts," *Romanische Forschungen,* III (1887), 337.

[45] *Visio Wettini,* § 2 (ed. Ernst Dümmler, *MGH, Poetae latini aevi Carolini,* II [Berlin, 1884], 268).

through Hell and Purgatory. Wettin is then led into the celestial regions where he beholds God in all His majesty surrounded by the saints:

> Tunc processit *rex regum* et *dominus dominantium* cum multitudine sanctorum, *tanta gloria et maiestate fulgidus,* ut homo corporeis oculis iubar tanti luminis et dignitatem gloriae sanctorum, quae ibidem apparuit, sufferre nequiverit.

Too much awed to beg for mercy, he seeks those who will intercede and, prompted by the angel, he approaches the order of priests " apud deum meritis operum bonorum coronati," to ask that they be mediators. " Prostrati ante thronum, misericordiam postulabant," and although the great saints Denis, Martin, Anianus, and Hilarius are among them, a voice answers: " Exempla aedificationis aliis facere debuit sed non fecit." He then appeals to the multitude of martyrs " quos . . . sine ulla dilatione ad thronum divinae maiestatis tendentes, prostrati veniam . . . poposcerunt." Again the voice replies that he must lead back to the way of truth those whom he has misled by bad example. The angel now urges him to approach a multitude of virgins, who are resplendent with an " incomparabili dignitate et splendore corusci luminis," that he may ask for longevity so as to amend his life:

> Antequam vero solo ad preces prosternerentur, apparuit maiestas domini obviam et *elevans eas,* dixit: ' Si bona doceat et exempla bona agat et eos, quibus mala exempla praebuit, corrigat, erit petitio vestra.'

Here God shows a deference to their petition. The Virgin Mary is not absorbed in the collective group in the abridged account of the vision of Wettin by William of Malmesbury,[46] nor in the versified legends by Adgar and the author of MS *Old Royal 20 B XIV*.[47]

---

[46] The legend by William of Malmesbury in MS *Salisbury 97* presents the Virgin Mary, courteously received by her Son who does not allow her nor her company of virginis to prostrate themselves: " At vero beatissimam matrem suam non tulit domini Jhesu dignatio ante se prosterni cum sociarum virginum." Mussafia, *Studien,* IV, p. 46.

[47] *Ibid.* For purposes of comparison Mussafia (*loc. cit.*) publishes the three texts in parallel columns.

Paul the Deacon

From the Greek of Eutychianus [48] derives one of the earliest extant Latin translations of the legend of Theophilus, that of Paul the Deacon of Naples who flourished in the ninth century.[49] According to his narrative, Theophilus is deposed from his office of Vicedominus of the Church of Adana in Cicilia, and to regain his former honors makes a compact with the devil. However, he repents and after prayer and fasting, he is assured of his forgiveness by the Virgin Mary who also obtains for him the charter.

In this relation the grace of repentance is a direct gift of God:

> *Creator omnium ac redemptor noster Deus* qui mortem peccatorum non uult, sed conuersionem et uitam, recordatus priorem eius conuersationem et in quibus sancte Dei ministrauerat ecclesie, quod uiduis, orfanis et egenis optime ministrauerat, non despexit creaturam suam, sed *dedit ei conuersionem penitentie.*[50]

After a penitential period of forty days, the Virgin Mary appears to him but is reluctant to plead his cause:

> Quali fiducia possum postulare eum, cum tu apostataueris ab eo? Quoue modo adstabo tribunali illi terribili et presumam aperire os meum et petere clementissimam illius bonitatem? Non enim patior filium meum derogari iniuriis.

---

[48] Eutychianus was an eye-witness to the events in the life of Theophilus, as he himself testifies: " Ego autem Eutychianus humilis et peccator, qui fui natus in aedibus hujus beatissimi Theophili, et deinde clericus hujus Catholicae Ecclesiae, cum [sum] secutus meum Dominum, ei inservissem in afflictione, quae vidi oculis meis et auribus audivi a beata ejus lingua, secure et certo scripsi, quae ei contigerant, et exposui fidelibus amicis et piis viris, *ad gloriam Dei omnipotentis et Domini nostri Jesu Christi, qui glorificatur in Sanctis suis.*" *Acta SS.* 4 Feb., 487.

[49] Concerning the attribution of the translation to Paul the Deacon, cf. *ibid.*, pp. 487-88. Wilhelm Meyer maintains that the legend of Theophilus has been influenced by the story of Proterius in the *Vita Sancti Basilii* (*PL*, LXXIII, 302-305). See " Radewin's Gedicht über Theophilus," *Sitzungsberichte der k. Bayer. Akad. der Wissenschaften zu München* (phil.-philol. und hist. Cl.), III (1873), 58. See also Henri Strohmayer's review of " Un drame religieux au moyen âge: Le miracle de Théophile " (by Marius Sepet), *Romania*, XXIII (1894), 602; G. Gerould, *The North-English Homily Collection* (Oxford, 1902), p. 76.

[50] Robert Petsch, *Theophilus* (Heidelberg, 1908), p. 3.

Theophilus is not discomfited but recalls the pardon of the Ninevites, the harlot Rahab, David, Peter, Zacchaeus, Paul, the incestu-
ous Corinthian, and Cyprianus, and begs that she obtain his forgiveness " per filium." Then the Virgin " que sola habet facun-
diam *apud eum, quem genuit, Christum,*" demands that he make
a profession of faith:

> *Misericors enim est* et suscipiet lacrimas penitentie tue et
> eorum qui puriter et sinceriter accedunt ad eum. Propterea
> enim Deus existens carnem ex me accipere dignatus est, . . .
> ut saluum faceret genus humanum.

Here Paul applies to Mary, because of her rôle of intercession, the
title Mediatrix,[51] the earliest specific use of this appellation in the
legends. When Theophilus has finished his *credo*, the " sancta Dei
genitrix . . . que intercedit pro peccatoribus . . . *mediatrix Dei
ad homines,*" says:

> Ecce ego propter baptismum, quod accepisti per filium meum
> Iesum Christum et propter nimiam compassionem, . . . rogo
> illum pro te *prouoluta pedibus eius,* quatinus te suscipiat.[52]

She returns in three days to announce that his penance has been
pleasing to the " Saluatori omnium et creatori Deo." Theophilus
is not yet satisfied and he pleads that she obtain the contract, " quia
te habeo *post Deum* protectionem et patrocinium." The docu-
ment regained, he takes it to the Bishop who invites all to share in
his exuberant joy:

> Uenite, omnes fideles, glorificemus *Dominum nostrum!* . . .
> Uenite, Christo dilecti, et uidete illum qui non uult mortem
> peccatoris, sed conuersionem et uitam eternam.

---

[51] Anselm Salzer, *Die Sinnbilder und Beiworte Mariens in der deutschen
Literatur und lateinischen Hymnenpoesie des Mittelalters* (Linz, 1893),
pp. 580-81.

[52] The Virgin Mary also declares herself willing to beg for this grace,
prostrate at the feet of her Son, in the version contained in MS. *Bib. nat.
fr. 2333 A:*

> Virgo subintulit: pro tantis questibus,
> Pro tot suspiriis et tot gemitibus
> *Dilecti filii prostrata pedibus,*
> Donec indulgeat, insistam precibus.

Alfred Weber, " Zwei ungedruckte Versionen der Theophilussage," *ZRPh,*
I (1877), 529.

He then exalts the patience, charity, and compassion of God towards sinners, and acknowledges the divine right to pardon, as well as the Marial rôle of mediation or intervention under the expressive figure of the " bridge " between God and men:

> Quis non miretur, fratres mei, *ineffabilem patientiam Dei?*
> Quis non stupeat *inenarrabilem conpassionem et caritatem Dei*
> erga nos peccatores? . . . Demus igitur et nos simul cum eo
> gloriam Deo nostro, *qui* sic misericorditer *exaudiuit peniten-*
> *tiam* confugientis ad se *per interuentionem* immaculate semper
> uirginis Marie, que est *inter Deum et homines pons* ueris-
> simus.[53]

As a Mediatrix Mary merely presents petitions to God:

> Ad eum quem genuit, Dominum nostrum, *petitiones offert* et
> accipit peccatorum nostrorum indulgentiam . . . Certe mag-
> nificata sunt *opera tua, Domine,* et non sufficit lingua ad
> gloriam mirabilium tuorum!

When the face of Theophilus becomes transfigured and resplendent after his reception of the Eucharist, " amplius glorificabant *Deum, qui facit mirabilia magna solus.*" Many of the theocentric traits of Paul the Deacon's text are incorporated in later versions, two-thirds of which are derived from his translation.[54]

Sigebert of Gembloux [55] testifies that to Paul the Deacon is also due the Latin translation in the *Vitae Patrum* of the life of Mary of Egypt as told by Sophronius, Patriarch of Jerusalem (633-636).[56] According to this biography, the Abbot Zosimas comes upon her in the desert. The fact that she reveals to him his name

---

[53] The metaphor of the " pons," expressive of mediation, appears early in Greek literature. Salzer, *op. cit.,* pp. 519-20.

[54] Franz Ludorff, " William Forrest's Theophiluslegende," *Anglia,* VI (1884), 66. Grace Frank gives very helpful bibliographical indications in her introduction to Rutebeuf, *Le Miracle de Théophile* (Paris, 1925: " *CFMA,* no. 49 ") pp. v-viii. For a list of many variants in medieval manuscripts and collections see Crane, *RR,* II, 276 ff.

[55] *Liber de scriptoribus ecclesiasticis,* 69 (*PL,* CLX, 562). See also the letter of dedication from Paul the Deacon to Charles the Bald. *Epistolae Karolini aevi,* no. 29 (ed. E. Dümmler, *MGH,* VI, 1 [Berlin, 1902], 194).

[56] Karl Krumbacher, *Geschichte der Byzantinischen Litteratur,* 2d ed. (Munich, 1897), p. 189.

and is elevated from the ground in prayer leads him to believe that she is an illusion of the devil, but finally convinced of her sanctity, Zosimas entreats her to relate her life that the works of God may be manifest:

> Obsecro te per Dominum Jesum Christum, verum Dominum nostrum, qui de virgine nasci dignatus est, . . . omnia, quae circa te sunt, edicito mihi, ut *Dei magnalia facias manifesta.* . . . Dic mihi omnia propter Deum; nec enim pro gloriatione aut ostentatione aliquid dicis, sed ut mihi satisfacias peccatori et indigno. Credo enim Deo, cui vivis, cum quo et conversaris, quoniam ob hujuscemodi rem directus sum in hanc solitudinem, ut ea quae circa te sunt *Deus faciat manifesta.*[57]

She then tells him of her life of sin before she reaches Jerusalem, and how she is unable to enter the church in order to adore the Cross. Seeing an image of the Virgin, she begins to pray:

> Domina virgo, quae Deum genuisti secundum carnem, . . . ob hoc effectus est Deus homo, quem ipsa digna genuisti, ut peccatores vocaret ad poenitentiam, adjuva me . . . et mihi licentiam tribue ecclesiae patefactum ingredi aditum, et non efficiar aliena a visione pretiosissimi ligni, in quo affixus Deus homo, quem concipiens ipsa virgo peperisti, et *proprium sanguinem dedit pro mea liberatione.* Jube, o Domina, et mihi indignae ob divinae crucis salutationem januam patefieri, et te ex te genito Christo dignissimam do *fidejussorem,* . . .[58]

She then enters without hindrance and does not fail to express her gratitude to the Virgin of the image upon her return:

> Tu quidem semper, o benignissima Domina, tuam ostendisti pietatis misericordiam: . . . vidi gloriam quam peccatores merito non videmus, gloriam omnipotentis Dei qui per te suscipit peccatorum poenitentiam. . . . Domina, Regina totius orbis, per quam humano generi salus advenit, noli me derelinquere.

Zosimas listens to the story of her forty-seven years of penance and when she concludes with a request for prayers, he falls upon the

[57] *De Vitis Patrum I: Vita Sanctae Mariae Aegyptiacae,* 11 (*PL,* LXXIII, 679).

[58] *Ibid.,* 16 (col. 682).

ground and, prostrate, blesses not the Virgin, but God who alone performs miracles:

> Benedictus Dominus Deus *qui facit mirabilia magna solus,* gloriosa et vehementer stupenda quibus non est numerus (Job 9 : 10). Benedictus es, Domine Deus, qui ostendisti mihi quanta largiris timentibus te. Vere enim non derelinquis quaerentes te, Domine (Ps. 9 : 11).

After her death, he returns to his monastery, "benedicens et laudans Deum, et hymnum laudis decantans Christo Domino nostro."

Flodoard

Flodoard (894-966), a canon of Reims and later Bishop of Noyon and Tournai, was both historian and poet. His metrical work, *De triumphis Christi et SS. Palaestinae,* contains six Marial legends, five of which are derived from Gregory of Tours.[59] The first forty-two lines which constitute the invocation are theocentric:

> Lux immensa Deus, mundum fulgore serenans,
> Aetheraque aeternae collustrans lucis amoeno,
> Sidereo astriferum pingis qui lumine coelum:
>
> .   .   .   .
>
> Ad verum revocas lumen vitamque perennem,
> Praecipui divina raptum ditione triumphi.[60]

He continues the metaphor, calling Mary the "stellam, *divini luminis* aulam," [61] in the legend concerning the construction of the church. According to her instructions, the columns are raised by three school-boys, whence Flodoard concludes that God rejoices in simplicity:

> .   .   .   . utque probetur
> Simplicitate Deum gaudere, ... [62]

The account of the Jew boy is brief and no mention is made of God. Mary is referred to as the "woman":

[59] Manitius, II, 157, n. 3.
[60] *PL,* CXXXV, 491.
[61] *Ibid.,* ii (col. 493).
[62] *Ibid.* (col. 494). For Gregory of Tours, cf. *supra,* p. 3.

> Illa, infit, *mulier* cathedra quae sedet in aula
> Qua sumpsi panem, puerum sinuamine gestans,
> Palliolo me contexit ne tangeret ignis.[63]

Seven lines suffice to narrate the story of the relief miraculously given to the starving monks in the monastery of Jerusalem.[64]

The story of the reliquary also has its source in Gregory of Tours. A leper has been cured by washing in the waters of the Jordan:

> . . . . morbo
> Leprae exutus aquis Christi baptismate sacri
> (Saepe quibus tali plures a labe levantur), . . .[65]

His case of relics is taken by robbers who then cast it into the fire. Even the cloth covering is untouched by the flames. One must conclude from the source that the relics were of the Virgin.[66]

The rôle of Mary as Mediatrix is more evident in Flodoard's life of Mary of Egypt. Unable to enter the church to adore the cross, she appeals to the Mother of God:

> Nosco quidem digne quia squalida abominer a te,
> Audio sed *Christum nostra ob purganda piacla*
> *Assumpsisse tuo sanctum de corpore corpus*;
> Unde, precor, fer opem nusquam solamen habenti
> Jam ni in te Natoque: tibi peto, praecipe pandi
> Limina sacra mihi, sine regia visere sanctae
> Signa crucis, coeli domina, qua corpore passus.[67]

Her prayer is answered and she stops before the image to acknowledge her gratitude:

> Monstrasti, domina, ecce mihi miseratio quanta
> Sit tua, suscipiens indignae famina servae.
> .   .   .   .
> Gloria summa Deo, *per te qui suscipit omnes*
> *Ad vitae quos vera viam conversio ducit.*[68]

---

[63] *Ibid.*, iii (col. 494). Cf. *supra*, p. 3.

[64] *Ibid.*, iv (cols. 495-96).

[65] *Ibid.*, v (col. 495). Cf. Gregory of Tours, *op. cit.*, § 18 (pp. 499-500).

[66] Gregory of Tours writes: " Hec reliquas beatae Mariae ab Hierusolymis accipiens. . . ." *Ibid.* (p. 499).

[67] *Ibid.*, iii, 4 (col. 545).

[68] *Ibid.*

From the viewpoint of theocentrism it is significant that Flodoard should place miracles ascribed to Mary among the "triumphs of Christ."

Hrotsuitha

The nun of Gandersheim, Roswitha or Hrotsuitha, who was born about 930 [69] wrote a metrical version of the Theophilus legend. As in the account of Paul the Deacon, Mary is appealed to as Mediatrix.

When he realizes the enormity of his sin, Theophilus has one hope:

> Sola mihi veniae potis est medicamina ferre,
> Si pro me proprium dignatur *poscere natus.* (184-85) [70]

Here also, Mary reprimands him severely:

> Quod praesumpsisti tradendus perditioni,
> Blasphemando mei sanctum contemnere natum,
> Qui, deus aeternus, de patre deo generatus
> Retro principii primordia cana sereni,
> Ex me dignatus sumpsit sub tempore *corpus,*
> *Quod dedit* humanae morti nationis *amore.* (229-34)

He overcomes her seeming reluctance by recalling the three examples of the Ninevites, David and Peter:

> . . . . aliis multisque figuris
> Admonitus, similem me sperabam pietatem
> *A Christo* citius *per te conquirere posse.*   (270-72)

The *credo* of Theophilus, poetically expressed, describes the sufferings of Christ for sinners in more detail than the profession of faith as written by Paul the Deacon. It ends:

> Commenda me, virgo, tuo, sanctissima, nato,
> Impetraque tuo veniam famulo sceleroso.   (330-31)

The reconciliation is effected and Theophilus pleads with the Virgin as his only hope "post Dominum" to obtain the charter.

In the *Te Deum* of the Bishop the mercy of God is praised:

[69] Manitius, I, 619.

[70] *Lapsus et conversio Theophili Vicedomini,* in *Hrotsvithae Opera,* ed. Karl Strecker (Leipzig, 1906), p. 72.

Eia, dilecti fratres, intendite cuncti,
Quam pie peccantes dominus tolerat bonus omnes,
Quos scit converti post tristia facta piacli.
Quis non miretur, quis non supplex veneretur
Laudandam mitem dulcem Christi pietatem,
Illum quaerentes semper qua sublevat omnes? (401-406)

In contrast to the divine goodness whose power is to spare and pardon, Mary's rôle is a minor one of intercession:

Qui iam criminibus miserans parcebat et huius
Ipsius illustris precibus sanctaeque parentis,
Per quam naturae periit maledictio nostrae
Et per quam mundo venit benedictio cuncto. (408-11)

The conclusion of this metrical version seems to be original with Hrotsuitha:

Unicus altithroni genitus retro tempora mundi,
Qui miserans hominis descendit ab arce parentis,
Et carnis veram sumpsit de virgine formam,

.   .   .   .

Quod sumus et quod gustamus vel quicquid agamus,
Dextera factoris benedicat cuncta regentis. (448-55)

The nun of Gandersheim follows Paul the Deacon closely in details of narrative.[71] She did not, however, exert a great influence on the Marial legend. According to Wilhelm Meyer, " dem Mittelalter war Hrotsuiths Erzählung nicht bekannt." [72]

John, Disciple of Odo of Cluny—Nalgodus

It was as a companion in the last travels of Odo, that John, his Italian disciple, became acquainted with the intimate life of the Abbot of Cluny.[73] According to John's biography, written about 943,[74] it was Odo's custom to invoke the Virgin under the title of " Mater misericordiae." [75]

[71] Manitius, I, 620.

[72] *Loc. cit.*, p. 58.

[73] Manitius, II, 130.   Cf. E. Sackur, *Die Cluniacenser* (Halle, 1892-94), I, 357 f.; II, 336 ff.

[74] Molinier, *Sources de l'histoire de France* (Paris, 1903), II, 238.

[75] *Vita S. Odonis*, ii, 23 (*PL*, CXXXIII, 72).

This favorite appellation was due to a vision of a dying monk who had once begged the Abbot for admission into the monastery that he might expiate a life of thievery by prayer and penance. The Virgin appears to him and having presented herself as the " Mater misericordiae," reveals to him the hour of his death. Upon Odo's authority, John writes that the monk died at the hour predicted.[76]

Nalgodus, a monk of Cluny, who wrote in the twelfth century, gives the same account in abridged form.[77] In both versions Odo firmly believes in the apparition, especially after hearing the humble confession of the dying monk, who admits stealing a rope from the wine-cellar to use as an instrument of penance. Nalgodus writes:

> Stupefactus vir Domini immisit, funem circumvolutum carne et sanie [sanguine] simul avulsit, *Deumque mirabilem prae-dicans* in latrone, tertia die defuncti fratris exsequias cele-bravit.[78]

The legend appears in many of the later collections.[79] In one variant, erroneously attributed to Saint Anselm, but now ascribed to Maurilius of Rouen,[80] Mary appears to a sick monk, introducing herself under the same title of *Mater misericordiae*.[81] No allusion is made in this version to the monk's former life.

Fulbert of Chartres

Many evidences of devotion to the Virgin Mary are to be found in the life of Fulbert of Chartres (d. 1028). He dedicated to her the Cathedral of Chartres; he established there the Feast of her

---

[76] *Ibid.*

[77] *Sancti Odonis vita,* 44 (*PL,* CXXXIII, 101-102). Nalgodus writes that he attempted to improve upon the biography of John, *ibid.* (cols. 85-86) ; Manitius, II, 134.

[78] *Ibid.* (col. 102).

[79] *Die lat. Vorlagen,* pp. 26-28. Vincent of Beauvais, *Speculum Historiale* (Venice, 1494), xxiv, 61; Adgar, *Marienlegenden,* ed. C. Neuhaus (Heilbronn, 1886), pp. 149 ff.; H. Kjellman, *Deuxième collection anglo-normande,* pp. 19 ff.; MS *Bibl. nat fr. 818* published by Mussafia, *Studien,* V, pp. 31.

[80] Cf. *infra,* pp. 24-25.

[81] For the theocentrism of this title, cf. *infra,* pp. 85, 88, 213-14.

Nativity; he wrote hymns and sermons in her honor.[82] Chroniclers relate as historical fact the miracle of his restoration to health through the milk of the Virgin. William of Malmesbury refers to Fulbert " quem Domini mater Maria olim aegrotum lacte mamillarum suarum visa fuerat sanare." [83]

Among his sermons in which he gives instructions on the Trinity, the Incarnation, penance, and Marial feasts, three treat of her Nativity and it is in these that he inserts the legends of Basil and Theophilus. According to Fulbert, Mary is shown more honor than the other saints because " majorem gratiam apud Dominum creditur invenisse." [84] She is superior to them since she " Salvatorem edidit a quo glorificata in coelo, *nunquam terrigenis patrocinari desistit.*" [85] He introduces his two legendary accounts with a still further explanation of her dignity:

> Tali ergo tantaeque personae, quid tandem ad honoris cumulum potuit accedere majus: eo quod Dei Filium Virgo concepit, Virgo mater edidit, hac nempe dignitate venerabilis facta est ipsis quoque sanctorum ordinibus angelorum.[86]

Moreover, he adds that " hac eadem dignitate facta est etiam

---

[82] Manitius, II, 688; *HLF*, VII, 264 ff. The epitaph on his tomb testifies to his devotion to the Virgin Mary:

> Terrenum Mariae templum, Fulberte, parasti . . .
> Hujus tu primus Natalia festa per orbem
> Vulgasti laudis cantica sacra canens.
> Haec depascentem vultum compescuit ignem,
> Lacte suo sanans perdita membra tibi, . . .

Bouquet, *Recueil des historiens des Gaules et de la France* (Paris, 1738-1904), X, 498, n. f. See Karl Benrath, " Zur Geschichte der Marienverehrung," *Theologische Studien und Kritiken*, LIX (1886), 211-15.

[83] *Gesta Regum Anglorum,* ed. William Stubbs (London, 1887-89: " Rolls Series, no. XC "), II, 341. See also Albéric des Trois-Fontaines under the year 1022, *Chronicon:* " Florebat Fulbertus . . . qui etiam ab eadem Dei Genitricis in infirmitate sua visitatus, esse dicitur, et de ejus lacte sanctissimo recreatus. Hic enim multo amore et felicissimo in honorem B. M. V. Dei Genitricis exarsit," *Recueil*, X, 490, n. c. The account is almost literally the same in Helinand of Froidmont, *Chronicon*, xlvi, an. 1030 (*PL*, CCXII, 928).

[84] *Sermones ad populum*, iv (*PL*, CXLI, 320).

[85] *Ibid.*

[86] *Ibid.* (col. 323).

imperiosa," and as an example of her imperious exercise of authority, he relates the two anecdotes. That of Basil is short:

> Illa igitur olim in auxilium magni Patris Basilii misit sanc-
> tum angelum, et mortuum suscitavit, qui male viventem pes-
> sumdedit persecutorem ejus Julianum apostatam, et haec
> historia notissima est. [87]

In the legend of Theophilus Mary is the Mediatrix who obtains his
reconciliation. After forty days of penance during which he im-
plores her patronage.

> Respexit hunc propitia misericordiae Mater, et per visionem
> illi apparens de impietate coarguit, *ad Christi confessionem
> excitans.*[88]

The charter is regained and burned in the presence of the congre-
gation.   Three days later " in ecclesia piae Matris Domini, *per
quam reconciliatus fuerat,* a laboribus suis beata fine quievit."
Fulbert concludes with an exhortation:

> *Veniant* igitur ad eam *justi* cum Basilio laudantes ac bene-
> dicentes, effectumque celerem suis sanctis desideriis postu-
> lantes sine dubio percepturi. *Veniant peccatores* cum Theo-
> philo tundentes rea pectora cum interno fletu . . . o clemens
> et propitia Domina nostra, quo possimus recuperare et habere
> perpetuam *gratiam filii tui* Jesu Christi Domini nostri, qui

---

[87] *Ibid.* The legend is contained in the *Vita S. Basilii,* falsely attributed
to Amphilochius, Bishop of Iconium (d. ca. 400). See Otto Bardenhewer,
Geschichte der altkirchlichen Literatur (Freiburg, 1912), III, 130, n. 1
and 227. It is believed that the first Latin version is due to Ursus who
lived in the ninth century, although this attribution is questioned. *Vita
Sancti Basilii (PL,* LXXIII, 312-13, n. 3) ; *Acta SS.,* 14 June, p. 417. According to the legend, Saint Basil and the Christians spend three days in
prayer and fasting that the people of Caeserea may be spared, " ac Deum,
ut scelesti Imperatoris consilium dissipet, rogent." After this time he
has a vision: " Videt in somnis Basilius, multitudinem coelestis militiae,
hic illic in monte; mediamque illorum, in sede gloriosa, muliebri habitu
feminam, sic affantem adstantes illos viros magnificos. Vocate mihi Mer-
curium, ibitque ut Julianum interficiat; qui *in filium meum et Dominum
Jesum inique egit." Acta SS., ibid.,* p. 424. See John of Salisbury,
Polycraticus, viii, 21 (*PL,* CXCIX, 798). Various versions are indicated
by Maurice Vloberg, *La légende dorée de Notre-Dame,* pp. 210-11.

[88] Fulbert of Chartres, *ibid.* (*PL,* CXLI, 323).

cum Patre et Spiritu sancto vivit et regnat unus Deus in aeternum.[89]

As Mediatrix, Mary does not displace the Mediator. In one of his sermons on the Trinity, Fulbert, quoting the epistle of Saint John, writes: " Si quis peccaverit, advocatum habemus apud Patrem Jesum justum: ipse est exoratione pro peccatis nostris (I John 2 : 1-2).[90] He exalts Mary as the " summi Auctoris et Creatoris Genitricem," [91] and as he says elsewhere: ". . . quoniam per Virginem venit Dominus omnium potestatum et virtutum et dominationum." [92]

Johannes Monachus

To a monk from a cloister in the south of Italy who translated Greek manuscripts into Latin at the order of the Roman Consul Pantaleon [93] is due one of the earliest Latin versions of the legend concerning the Jew who lends to a Christian. This translator was Johannes Monachus who probably lived between 950 and 1050.[94] According to his version, the Christian merchant Theodorus loses all his goods at sea. Sad at heart he reveals his plan to enter a monastery to an acquaintance who counsels him to borrow from his friends:

> Et Deus omnipotens habet ea restituere tibi que perdidisti et alia pluriora. Tu enim exercitatus es in marinis negotiis. . . . Tu autem spem tuam *in domino nostro Ihesu Christo* pone, et ipse diriget uiam tuam.[95]

His failure to secure the money leads him to approach the Jew Abramius who lives near the four columns erected by Constantine where an image of the Savior is suspended:

[89] *Ibid.* (col. 324). Jacobus a Voragine acknowledges Fulbert to be his source for the legend of Theophilus, *Legenda Aurea,* cxxxi, ed. Graesse (Leipzig, 1855), p. 593.

[90] *Sermo* vii (*PL,* CXLI, 333-34).

[91] *Ibid.* (col. 327).

[92] *Ibid.*

[93] Johannes Monachus, *Liber de miraculis,* ed. Michael Huber (Heidelberg, 1913: " Sammlung mittellateinischer Texte, no. V "), p. 1.

[94] *Ibid.,* p. xxi.

[95] *Ibid.,* no. i, p. 8.

> Aspexit inmaginem domini nostri Ihesu Christi et manus ad celum eleuans rogabat eum supliciter ut se dirigeret in opus suum in quo pergebat.

The Jew refuses unless he can obtain a guarantor;[96] the only mediator whom Theodorus is able to offer, after being rejected by his friends, is the Christ of the image. The Jew is so struck by his faith that he accepts and offers him fifty pounds in gold.

Theodorus is successful in Sidon and Tyr but on his return trip an unfavorable wind again causes him to lose all. Before the image he prays:

> Gratias tibi ago, dominator meus Ihesu Christe, qui saluasti animam meam; et nunc queso, ne derelinquas me usque in finem et ne auertas fatiem tuam a me.

A second time he borrows from the Jew and sails to an unknown country where he successfully trades. Here he makes a profit of fifty pounds of gold and this he places in a casket which he commits to the waves, having perfect trust in his Mediator:

> Dominator domine Ihesu Christe, tu es meus mediator. Tu scis, domine, quia plena fide et absque dubitatione pono loculum istum in mari, spem habendo in te qui es meus mediator, Christe Deus meus.

Through a dream both are made aware of the outcome. When Abramius opens the casket and reads the message of Theodorus, he falls upon his face, exclaiming: " Vnus Deus uerus et magnus, qui est Deus christianorum, *qui facit mirabilia solus.*" To test the faith of the merchant the Jew denies the receipt of the casket. Thereupon, Theodorus goes with him to the four columns and adjures the Christ of the image to bear testimony. A flash of light issues from it, so that Abramius falls to the ground in a faint. Restored to his senses, he asks to be a Christian:

> Magnus est Deus christianorum; *tu es Deus qui facis mirabilia.* Viuit Dominus et benedictus Deus, *qui* michi misero *dignatus est ostendere tanta mirabilia,* quia non introibo in domum meam, nisi prius fatiam me christianum.

---

[96] The text reads: " . . . antiphonitin, id est mediatorem vel fideiussorem legitimum." *Ibid.,* p. 10.

Their wonderment becomes greater when it is discovered that the
lead in the merchant's ship has been transformed into silver.
Many are converted and all Constantinople shares in their joy:

> Et factum est gaudium et leticia magna in tota urbe, dantibus
> autem omnibus laudem et gloriam *Deo qui facit mirabilia
> magna solus* super omnes qui sperant in eo. Quoniam ipsum
> decet omnis gloria et uirtus et potencia et honor et adoratio
> nunc et semper et per infinita secula seculorum.

Many of the theocentric traits, contained in this version, recur
later in variants which present the Virgin Mary as Mediatrix.[97]

The expression, " Deus facit mirabilia solus (Job 9:10; Ps.
71:18), is also found in the legend of the Jew boy as related by
Johannes Monachus. The child tells his rescuers: " Femina
quedam purpurata effundebat super me aquam dicens: Noli
timere." [98] His audience, nevertheless, does not fail to see in his
preservation from death the intervention of the Almighty:

> Omnes qui uiderant et audierant miraculum quod factum
> fuerat, dederunt pariter laudem *Deo qui* ad saluationem nos-
> stram *facit mirabilia,* cui est laus et gloria in secula seculorum.

A second version by the same author is no less theocentric. Here
the boy is baptized by his playmates who then take bread and say
over it " Christe Deus noster, benedic." [99] He comments:

> Hec autem in simplicitate et in innocentia acta sunt a pueris
> in agro. Sed Deus omnipotens qui uult omnes homines saluos
> fieri et ad agnitionem ueritatis uenire, qui dixit: Nisi conuersi
> fueritis et efficiamini sicut paruuli, non intrabitis in regnum
> celorum, puerorum opus per presentiam sancti Spiritus uera-
> citer demonstrauit.[100]

---

[97] The history of the legend has been traced by Erik Boman, *Deux
miracles de Gautier de Coinci* (Paris, 1935), pp. vii-lvii.

[98] *Ibid.*, no. 5, p. 44. Analogous to the story of the Jew Boy is an anecdote
in the *Vita Sanctae Aldegundis*, written by Hucbaldus of St. Amand in the
early part of the tenth century (Manitius, I, 589, 592). In this legend a
nun falls into a fire which is heating a large caldron of water: " At illa,
cum caderet, *sanctae Trinitatis nomen* invocavit." She is found to be
neither scalded nor burned, by the " orationibus et meritis beatae Mariae
suffragantibus." *Vita S. Aldegundis,* 5 (*PL,* CXXXII, 870).

[99] Johannes, *op. cit.,* no. 6, p. 46.

[100] *Ibid.* See Caesarius of Heisterbach: " Et licet haec a pueris in

The father, curious concerning the sweet odor which emanates from the boy's body, discovers the truth and in a fury throws him into the furnace which heats the public baths. There he is found by the bishop, who has been led to investigate " per prouidentiam uero Dei." [101]   His face is radiant with an angelic splendor " sicuti beatus Daniel admirando *Dei uirtutem* ante prescripserat de illis tribus sociis suis, qui in babilonicam fornacem missi fuerant." The woman who extinguished the fire is believed to be the Virgin Mary, although Johannes has already said:

> Quoniam enim descenderat *angelus Domini* in babilonicam fornacem ad protegendum illos tres pueros, *ipse* et cum puero isto descendit et flammam ignis extinxit *una cum gratia Spiritus sancti* qui eum perfuderat.

The writer concludes with a prayer to her as intercessor:

> Cuius intercessionibus omnes in fide roboremur et a flamma eterni incendii per conuersionem bonorum operum liberemur adiuuante Domino Deo Christo nostro qui uiuit et regnat cum Patre et Spiritu sancto in secula seculorum.

Certain details of narrative in the legend of the Merchant and the second version of the Jew Boy are rarely found in later versions. The theocentric phrase of Johannes Monachus: " Deus qui facit mirabilia solus . . ." has already been noted in Paul the Deacon [102] and reappears in the twelfth and thirteenth century collections. [103]

Maurilius of Rouen

The legend, " Mater misericordiae," included in *Oratio XLIX* among the authentic works of Saint Anselm, [104] has been accepted as genuine by some scholars. Only the prayers L, LI, LII are

---

simplicitate acta sunt in agro, tamen *omnipotens deus opus puerorum praesentia sancti spiritus sanctificavit.*" *Libri VIII Miraculorum,* ed. A. Meister (Rome, 1901: " Römische Quartalschrift, Supplementheft, 13 "), no. 18, p. 147.

[101] Johannes Monachus, *op. cit.,* p. 47. Cf. *Libri VIII Mirac.:* " . . . ex providentia divina," *ibid.,* p. 148.

[102] Cf. *supra,* p. 12.

[103] Cf. *infra,* p. 70, n. 38.

[104] *PL,* CLVIII, 946-47.

[105] Mussafia, *Studien,* I, p. 925; Ward, II, 587 (5); Welter, *op. cit.,* p. 90.

Anselm's according to the investigations of A. Wilmart, who presents definite evidence that XLIX was composed by Maurilius:

> Le no. XLIX se présente fréquemment, depuis le xii⁰ siècle, sous le nom de son véritable rédacteur: Maurille, archevêque de Rouen (1055-1067). Jusque dans le manuscrit *622* de Lyon, on remarque encore le souvenir de ce fait littéraire; le titre y est libellé comme suit: Oratio eiusdem—c'est-à-dire saint Anselme—*vel secundum quosdam beati Maurelii Rothomagensis ad beatam Mariam virginem.* A la même époque, l'évêque d'Exeter John Grandison (1327-1369), qui pourrait avoir connu une collection semblable à celle de Lyon, dit encore simplement: *Oracio beati Maurelii Rothomagensis archiepiscopi.*[106]

The legend, very briefly told, is inserted towards the end of the prayer:

> Memini et meminisse delectabile est, qualiter ad commendandum miseris unicum patrocinium tuum, cuidam tuo servo agenti in extremis revelasti memorabile nomen tuum apparens enim ei, cum esset in angustias . . . tu, domina, dixiste: Ego sum misericordiae mater.[107]

This revelation to the dying man, " Ego sum misericordiae mater," is probably based on an incident in the life of Odo of Cluny,[108] to whom a thief monk confided the vision. Later writers interpret the title theocentrically.[109]

Petrus Damiani

Writing more than four centuries after Gregory the Great,[110] Petrus Damiani (d. 1072) also compares the marvels of nature to those wonders which require the supreme intervention of supernatural power, and shows no astonishment as to their occurrence:

---

[106] *Auteurs spirituels et textes dévots du moyen âge latin* (Paris, 1932), pp. 480-81. See, J. N. Dalton, *Ordinale Exoniense* (London, 1909: " H. Bradshaw Society, vol. xxxviii "), II, 527.

[107] *Op. cit.* (col. 946).

[108] Cf. Mussafia, *Studien*, I, 925. Cf. *supra*, pp. 17-18.

[109] Cf. *infra* pp. 85, 88, 213-14.

[110] Cf. *supra*, p. 5. Petrus Damiani was acquainted with the works of Gregory the Great, *Opusc. XIV: De ordine eremitarum* (*PL*, CXLV, 334).

> Quid ergo mirum, si omnipotens Deus in magnis magnus osten-
> ditur, cum etiam in minimis atque extremis quibusque rebus
> tam mirabiliter operetur? . . . Enimvero quis tot virtutis
> divinae magnalia, quae contra communem naturae ordinem
> fiunt, enumerare sufficiat? [111]

All nature is subject to the will of its Creator [112] to Whom Petrus
addresses the eulogy of Esther:

> Domine, rex omnipotens, in ditione tua cuncta sunt posita, et
> non est qui possit tuae resistere voluntati. Tu enim fecisti
> coelum et terram, et quidquid coeli ambitu continetur; Domi-
> nus omnium tu es, nec est qui resistat majestati tuae (Esth.
> 13 : 9-11).[113]

While these citations fail to give the full import of the writer's
conception of the omnipotence of God as he develops it in his
treatise, *De divina omnipotentia,* they serve to show that Petrus
Damiani, in his devotion to the Blessed Virgin, does not minimize
or overlook the importance and function of God.

In his Marial legends Mary is a powerful Mediatrix. In one
which is important in the evolution of the *miracula* inasmuch as it
appears so frequently in later collections, she intervenes in the
strife of the devils and angels over the soul of a certain Bassus who
dies suddenly and unconfessed. While the monks are praying over
his body, he revives and begs that they continue chanting the
psalms, that they may put the devils to flight by their prayers " ad
Deum." [114]   He then recounts that at his death two angels came
to receive his soul, but that the evil spirits contested their rights
on the plea that he had lived according to the flesh. The angels
contended that he died "in obsequio reginae celestis," and the
devils, that " Deus est justus," and therefore they would not be
robbed of the soul. However, when the Blessed Virgin intervened,
she took little account of the justice of God, and stressed His
mercy:

[111] *Opusc. XXXVI: De divina omnipotentia,* 9 (*PL,* CXLV, 613-14).

[112] Petrus writes: ". . . qui naturam condidit, naturalem ordinem ad
suae deditionis arbitrium vertit: quicunque creata quaelibet dominanti
naturae subesse constituit, suae dominationis imperio naturae obsequentis
obedientiam reservavit." *Ibid.* (col. 612).

[113] *Ibid.* (col. 620).

[114] *Opusc. XXXIII: De bono suffragiorum,* 2 (*PL,* CXLV, 563).

Nunquam . . . *piissimus* et *clementissimus* Filius meus, ac
Dominus patietur eum vestris fieri crudelitatibus subditum,
quem sub mei famulatus obsequio cernit in peregrinatione
defunctum.

They reminded her that she was the " mater veritatis, et aeternae
justitiae," and therefore, could not ignore that he died in sin and
unconfessed. To this Mary replied:

> Verum quidem, est quod objicitis; sed quoniam apud miseri-
> cordem Dominum meum ac Filium *misericordia superexaltat
> ex more judicium* (James 2:13) eumque non tam delectat
> poena peccantium, quam remissio peccatorum, me confestim
> intuens ait: Ad corpus homo praesto regredere.

Her power over the infernal spirits is also evident in another
legend in which John the patrician is released from their bonds
in answer to the insistent prayer of a poor woman.[115] Her intercession for the souls of Purgatory is so efficacious that when the
" regina mundi . . . *preces fudit,*" [116] the number of souls liberated
" per interventionem ejus " on the Feast of the Assumption, ex-
ceeds the population of Rome.

In the legends of Petrus Damiani are to be found the earliest
attestation of the practice of the daily recital of the hours. He relates how the monastery of Saint Barnabas of Gamugno, about the
year 1056,[117] is visited by many calamities when this custom is
abandoned. He warns them:

> Christus, . . . est pax nostra, de quo etiam de Virgine recens
> nato, angelitus dictum est: " Gloria in excelsis Deo, et in
> terra pax (Luke 2:14)." Quia ergo matrem verae pacis de
> suo monasterio projecerunt, dignum est ut inquietis calamita-
> tum tribulationumque procellis atque turbinibus agitentur.[118]

They resume this devotion and the writer in figurative language
attributes to God the peace which returns:

[115] *Opusc. XXXIV: Disputatio de variis apparitionibus et miraculis*, 4
(*PL*, CXLV, 587-88).

[116] *Ibid.*, 3 (col. 587).

[117] Pierre Batiffol dates this 1056. Cf. *Histoire du Bréviare romain*
(Paris, 1893), p. 187. 1053 is the date given by Edmund Bishop, *Liturgica
Historica* (Oxford, 1918), p. 226.

[118] *Epist.*, vi, 32 (*PL*, CXLIV, 431).

> Post coruscos atque tonitrua, tanta coeli serenitas rediit, ut ex tunc usque hodie fratres jucundae pacis otio perfruantur, ac de Scyllaea voragine se delatos ad portum, *gubernante Filio Virginis,* gratulentur. Impletum ergo est quod per prophetam dicitur: " Revertimini ad me, et ego revertar ad vos, dicit Dominus (Mal. 3: 7)."

Moreover, in the conclusion of this epistle he refers to God as the " animorum medicus omnipotens Deus." [119]

It is because of his daily recitation of the hours that a clerk, after a life of sin, presumes to call upon Mary on his deathbed:

> O janua coeli, fenestra paradisi, vera Mater Dei et hominis, tu mihi testis es, quia septies in die laudem dixi tibi, et quamvis peccator, quamvis indignus, omnibus tamen canonicis horis tuae laudis obsequium non fraudavi.[120]

His sorrow and self-accusations are rewarded by a visit of the Virgin who announces that his sins have been forgiven " ex largitate *divinae* misericordiae." This devotion is also referred to in the legend of the priest who is deprived of his faculties by the bishop and who is reinstated at the order of Mary because of his daily recital of the *Ave Maria.* Petrus comments:

> Si igitur ille unum duntaxat laudis canendo versiculum, corporei victus alimenta promeruit; quam fideliter aeterna sperabunt, qui beatae reginae mundi quotidiana horarum omnium vota persolvunt? [121]

In two other legends it is apparent that reverence is to be shown to Mary because of her divine Motherhood. The lay-brother Marinus whom she consoles in his death agony calls her " mater imperatoris . . . beata Redemptoris nostri mater," [122] and Petrus here refers to her as the one " cujus virginitas peperit verae pietatis auctorem." One monk honors her joys as Mother of God:

> Gaude, *Dei Genitrix* virgo immaculata; gaude, quae gaudium ab angelo suscepisti; gaude, quae *genuisti aeterni luminis*

---

[119] *Ibid.* (col. 432). See also *Opusc. LIII: De patientia,* 1 (*PL,* CXLV, 230).

[120] *Opusc. X: De horis canonicis,* 10 (*PL,* CXLV, 230).

[121] *Opusc. XXXIII: De bono suffragiorum,* 3 (*ibid.,* col. 564).

[122] *Ibid.* (col. 566).

claritatem; gaude, *mater*; gaude, sancta *Dei Genitrix* virgo. Tu sola *mater* innupta. Te laudat omnis factura. *Genitrix lucis*, intercede pro nobis.[123]

The antiphon became a popular one in later miracle collections.[124]

He more definitely asserts her status in his sermons and hymns. Before telling the anecdote of Theophilus,[125] he describes her exalted position and then asks:

Nunquid quia ita *deificata*, ideo nostrae humanitatis oblita es? Nequaquam, domina . . . *Naturam nostram habes, non aliam* . . . Fecit in te magna *qui potens est.*[126]

In the same sermon he refers to her as " post Deum." [127] Elsewhere, he uses this expression and reminds his brothers to consider themselves indebted to her: " Debitores simus huic beatissimae Dei Genitrici, quantasque illi *post Deum* de nostra redemptione gratias agere debeamus." [128] In the hymns of Damiani she is also " post Deitatem " and a Mediatrix to whom he gives the title of " scala ":

> Te *Deo* factam liquet esse *scalam,*
> Qua tenens summum, petit altus imum,
> Nos ad excelsi remeare coeli
>   Culmina dona.
> Te beatorum chorus angelorum,
> Te sacri vates et apostolorum
> Ordo praelatam sibi cernit unam
>   *Post Deitatem.*[129]

The figure of the ladder, so frequently used by medieval writers,[130]

---

[123] *Opusc. XXXIV: Disputatio de variis apparitionibus,* 4 (*ibid.,* col. 588).

[124] For variants, cf. Crane's notes to Pez, pp. 83-84. It is also found in the *Miracula sanctae Virginis Mariae,* ed. Dexter (Madison, 1927), no. 1, p. 19; *Liber exemplorum ad usum praedicantium,* ed. A. G. Little (Aberdeen, 1908), no. 41, p. 24; Caesarius of Heisterbach, *Libri VIII Mirac.,* iii, no. 21, pp. 150-51.

[125] *Sermo* xliv (*PL,* CXLIV, 740). Cf. Bernard of Clairvaux, *Ad Beatam Virginem Deiparem* (*PL,* CLXXXIV, 1010).

[126] *Ibid.*

[127] *Ibid.*

[128] *Sermo* xlv (*PL,* CXLIV, 743).

[129] *Carmina et preces,* xlvii (*PL,* CXLV, 934).

[130] Salzer, *op. cit.,* pp. 88 and 536-38.

is expressive of Mary's mediate position as a means and not an end—the status which Petrus Damiani seems to assign to her in the eight Marial legends which constitute his contribution to this genre. Benrath indicates his indebtedness to the Greek writers for symbolism and says that with Petrus there was inaugurated as a type of literature, the Marial anecdote, "in welchen Maria, wie schon in der alten Theophilussage, ihren Verehrern *als Helferin* in der höchsten Not erscheint." [131]

Guaiferius Casinensis

In the *Carmina* of Guaiferius, a Benedictine of Monte-Cassino (d. 1089), occurs the legend of the pilgrim of St. James, told on the authority of Hugo of Cluny.[132] Guaiferius, who describes the youth as "simpliciter simplex," makes him an easy prey to the devil who deceives him under the guise of the Apostle, promising eternal life as a reward for death. Quite different is the Saint himself who appears after the pilgrim's death, and in the company of Mary, drives away the devils who have come for the soul:

> . . . . . . in aethere Mater
> Virgineis stipata choris astare . . . [133]

James is the chief protagonist and it is through his intercession that the pilgrim is restored to life. However, both the Virgin and the Apostle are relatively secondary in the poet's mind since he introduces this anecdote which treats of suicide by celebrating the triumph of Christ over death and sin:

> Mortis in immanem te mersit culpa ruinam,
> Christi mors erexit, homo. Mors sola redemit,
> Sola dedit vitam, sola spem, sola salutem.[134]

---

[131] "Zur Geschichte der Marienverehrung," *loc. cit.*, pp. 216-17.

[132] *Carmina*, no. ii (*PL*, CXLVII, 1287). Cf. Manitius, II, 487-88. Raby considers this poem the most important of the *Carmina*, "full of Virgilian reminiscence . . . and remarkable for versification," *A History of Christian-Latin Poetry* (Oxford, 1927), pp. 240-41. For the many variants of the legend, cf. Crane's notes to Pez, p. 85; Ward, II, 606 (14).

[133] *Carmina, ibid.* No mention is made of the Virgin Mary in the account of Hugo of Saint Victor in his *De Sacramentis*, ii, 16 (*PL*, CLXXVI, 583-4). Cf. Guibert of Nogent, *supra*, p. 38.

[134] *Ibid.* (col. 1285).

Only in this version of the legend does one find such a theocentric explanation of the pilgrim's readiness to accept the devil's equivocal statement that death gives life.

Lanfranc

From the words of Lanfranc (d. 1089) one may infer that a large number of Marial miracles circulated as oral traditions and were not recorded:

> Beata Domini Mater et perpetua Virgo Maria, . . . per quam salus mundi apparuit, quo majorem apud Deum prae caeteris gratiam invenisse dignoscitur, eo frequentius ab hominibus, et fiducialius atque familiarius in necessitatibus invocatur: et ipsa celer clementiae suae multis impendere solet beneficium. Unde non nulla illius subventionis exempla inveniuntur scripta, plurima passim jugi sentiuntur effectu; *quae propter multitudinem non sunt commendata memoriae.*[135]

To preserve one which he deems worthy to be known by posterity, Lanfranc[136] tells a miraculous incident in the life of his friend William Crispin:

> Et est res memoriae digna, et beatae Domini Matri congrua, quae humano generi *post Deum* singulariter est amabilis et per saecula cuncta laudabilis.[137]

William, before going out on an expedition against the Franks who were devastating the district of Vexin, stops at the Monastery of Bec to ask for the blessing of Herluinus and the monks. With the words of the Abbot in his ears—" Deo te et sanctissimae Matri ejus commendamus "—,[138] he and his companions set forth but are suddenly surprised by the enemy lying in ambush. Resistance is useless and all flee. As the leader, he is the object of pursuit. About to be overtaken, William has recourse to prayer:

> *Domine Jesu Christe,* . . . *miserere mei,* et per merita Patris Herluini et fratrum ejus, quibus me suppliciter hodie com-

---

[135] *De nobili genere Crispinorum* (*PL* CL, 735).

[136] This was written while Lanfranc was Archbishop of Canterbury (1070-1089).

[137] *Ibid.* (col. 737).

[138] *Ibid.* (col. 739).

> mendavit, *libera me de hoc imminenti periculo mortis.* O
> generosa Virgo, intacta Domini Mater, suscipe indignas tui
> peccatoris preces, et contribulati cordis sacrificium *ante Deum,*
> et ante te ascendat in odorem suavitatis.

Suddenly, a beautiful woman appears at his side, covering him
with her sleeve, and although his enemies almost touch his feet
with their lances as they prod the trees and thickets, he is rendered
invisible. When they abandon the search, his protectress turns to
him and says:

> Nosti nomen meum, quae tibi ministravit in mortis angustia,
> respirendi solatium? Ego sum bona *Dei Mater,* cui te abbas
> Herluinus toto corde commendavit, quando hoc tua intentio
> devote postulavit.

With these words, she disappears.

Lanfranc relates another incident in the life of the grandson,
also named William Crispin. In a surprise attack, the knight's
horse receives a mortal wound but, nevertheless, he spurs him on
in his flight, shouting: " Sancta Maria Becci, adjuva me, sancta
Maria Becci, adjuva me." [139]   With a great leap the horse crosses
a large ravine, falling dead once his master is safe from his pur-
suers. Lanfranc says that William was wont to relate this miracle
" ad honorem Dei et ejus sanctae Genitricis."

Radbod

According to Radbod II, Bishop of Noyon (d. 1098), to relate
the miracles of the saints is to praise God inasmuch as He operates
through the blessed:

> Laudatur siquidem Dominus in sanctis suis, cum *per eos
> operans,* corda illuminat perfidorum, *virtutem* largitur mira-
> culorum, eorum beneficiis infirmi sustentantur, et praevarica-
> tione prima a paradiso expulsi postmodum coelestis regni
> haeredes revocantur.[140]

Adopting his theme from Psalm CL—" Laudate Dominum in
sanctis ejus "—Radbod relates a miracle wrought through the
intercession of Mary:

---

[139] *Ibid.* (col. 742).
[140] *Sermo de Annuntiatione Beatae Mariae Virginis* (*PL,* CL, 1528).

Cum ergo . . . in sanctis suis Dominum suadeat laudari, in ea et per eam eum praecipue docet honorari *per quam ipsorum omnium sanctorum redemptionis summa processit,* sanctissima videlicet Maria genitrice Domini nostri Jesu Christi.[141]

The anecdote concerns a girl who sews on the Feast of the Annunciation and by " divino judicio " is punished, a theme frequently used by later writers.[142] Her outcries at the pain occasioned by a knot of the thread which bores into her tongue attract a large crowd:

> In tanto igitur plebis conventu *misericors ille solus* qui revelat parvulis et abscondit sapientibus, *miserorum miseratus miseriam,* sua ipsius in missione, *ad matris* suae matrem *eos direxit ecclesiam,* ut ejus liberaretur meritis in quam peccaverat, et *ejus* absolveretur *precibus quam* temere *offenderat.*[143]

All pray for the afflicted girl:

> Hi lacrymis profusi, tacitis illi precibus *divinam exorant clementiam,* . . . mater cum filia, sacerdotes cum populo, ejusdem Dei Genitricis compuncte sollicitant suffragia, ut . . . pietatis in eam convertat viscera, *quo ad ejus liberationem et gratiae Deo per eam referantur.*

Finally the Virgin " judicium vertit in misericordiam, *apud eum qui per eam ad ereptionem miserorum in mundum venit.*" At first, the thread is loosed but the pain is still intense. The prayers of all become more fervent and God perfects His work:

> Et ecce iterum populus ad lacrymas devotionis Deo pro percepta jam remissione reddunt gratias, cumpunctione devotiori *Deum postulantes, ut qui benigne coepit, benignius et ipse perficiat. Benignitas* tandem *Salvatoris* nostri preces suscepit humilium *per intercessionem* gloriosae semper Virginis, remissionis *immisit antidotum.*

Radbod concludes his sermon by a reversion to his original theme in which he clearly states that veneration paid to the Virgin Mary does not derogate from the honor due to God:

---

[141] *Ibid.* (cols. 1528-29).
[142] Vincent of Beauvais, *op. cit.,* vii, 89; Guibert of Nogent, cf. *infra,* pp. 37 and 38; for other collections, cf. *infra,* pp. 197-98.
[143] Radbod, *op. cit.* (col. 1531).

Filii matrem venerentur in exsultatione, collaudent filium matris in sancta devotione; ut sicut laus discipuli honor est magistri, *sic et veneratio virginis gloria sit Christi,* et impleatur prophetae David admonitio: " Laudate Dominum in sanctis suis." Nunquid enim et in hoc non condecet laudari Christum in sancta sua Genitrice, cum post multa et innumerabilia *quae per eam operatus est miracula* suae ad honorem solemnitatis puellae quam praetexuimus tam clementer dignatus est subvenire? [144]

His explicit statement that God performs innumerable miracles through Mary is indicative of Radbod's theocentric conception of Marial *miracula.* In his lives of Saints Medard and Godebert it is evident that he conceived all miracles as operations of God through the instrumentality of His creatures.[145]

Sigebert of Gembloux

Sigebert, a Benedictine of Gembloux (d. 1112), records in his chronicle three of the Marial miracles: Theophilus, the Jew Boy, and the " Pierced Christ-image." Brief as these entries are, they present Mary in the rôle of Mediatrix.

The first under the date 537 relates the familiar story of the pact and Theophilus' reconciliation:

Primo piam Dei matrem Mariam sibi reconciliavit; eaque sibi apparente abrenuntians diabolo, Christumque verum Dei filium verumque Deum et hominem ex Maria virigne natum, et omne christianismi propositum profitens, *per eam etiam Christi filii* ejus gratiam recepit.[146]

The second, dated 552, tells how the Jew boy in " aecclesia sanctae matris Christi Jesu corpus et sanguinem Christi perciperet." [147]

---

[144] *Ibid.* (col. 1534).

[145] Radbod writes: " Ducimus ad propositi nostri seriem redire, quaeque post transitum gloriosissimi confessoris ad honorem ejus *Deus operatus sit miracula.*" *Vita S. Medardi,* 5 (*PL, CL,* 1514). In the *Vita S. Godebertae* he proposes to relate " quaeque per eam *Deus operatus sit miracula.*" *Ibid.* (col. 1519).

[146] *Chronica,* reprinted from *MGH, SS.,* VI, 268-374, by Migne (*PL, CLX,* 102).

[147] *Ibid.* (col. 104) ; Wolter, *Der Judenknabe* (Halle, 1879: " Bibliotheca Normannica, II "), p. 42.

For this deed he is cast into the furnace by an enraged father. His protectress is the " mulier, quae in illa aecclesia puerum tenens depicta erat, pallio suo flammas ignis a se eventilasset." Sigebert is directly dependent upon Gregory of Tours for this anecdote.[148]

Under the year 765 the chronicler recounts the story of an image of Christ pierced by Jews:

> . . . faciem conspuentes, eam percutientes, criminose convitantes, manus et pedes ejus clavis configentes, acetum et fel ei porrigentes; tandem lancea latere ejus aperto, exivit de eo sanguis et aqua.[149]

The cures wrought by the blood from the crucifix converted many. A feast was instituted to offer reparation at which the Bishop " predicabat magnalia dei." Compared with the account in Gregory of Tours, this is much more detailed.[150]

Guibert of Nogent

Three of the works of Guibert of Nogent (d. 1124) contain Marial legends: *De laude S. Mariae* which was written after 1108; *De pignoribus sanctorum,* composed after 1112 or 1113; *De vita sua,* also called the *Monodiarum,* written in imitation of the *Confessions* of Augustine about 1114 or 1115.[151]

According to the autobiography, even before his birth Guibert was consecrated to the Virgin Mary,[152] an event which gave him sentiments of great hope:

> Dixi tibi, summa benignitas Deus, quod spem, aut spei quantulaecunque specimen ex tam gaudiosae diei praestolatione mihi nato ac renato, sed et omnium *post Deum* oblato reginae contuleris.[153]

---

[148] Wolter, *op. cit.,* p. 21; Pelizaeus, *op. cit.,* p. 21. Cf. *supra,* pp. 2-3.

[149] *Chronica* (col. 145). Other miracles in Sigebert's Chronicle are treated in the chapter on Local Collections, cf. *infra,* pp. 117 and 121.

[150] The legend, as told by Gregory, Sigebert, Jacobus a Voragine, Herolt, and other writers, has been investigated by Galtier, " Byzantina: L'image blessée par le Juif," *Romania,* XXIX (1900), 517-23.

[151] Molinier, II, 186. The miracles of Laon in the *De vita sua* are treated among the local collections, cf. *infra,* pp. 90, 104, and 129.

[152] *De vita sua,* i, 3 (*PL,* CLVI, 842).

[153] *Ibid.*

After sixty years he rejoices in such "bondage":

> Et, o mundi et coelorum *post unicum tuum* Domina, quam
> bene senserunt, qui me sub illa tibi necessitate voverunt! . . .
> Verum etsi multoties hac me tibi fraude subduxi, ad te tamen,
> et *per te ad Dei Patris*, et *tuum unicum* hujus oblationis
> intuitu securius recucurri.[154]

His intention to leave his monastery for another was changed by
a dream of his mother, who seemed to see her son with the other
monks reduced to a dwarf's size and dressed in tattered garments.
Her sorrow was dispelled when she beheld a woman of beauty and
majesty, the "domina Carnotensis,"[155] who declared that she
would not allow the church which she had founded to be deserted
and thereupon touched Guibert, saying: "Hunc, . . . huc adduci,
et monachum feci, quem nullo modo patiar hinc abduci." At her
words all became of normal stature, and Guibert no longer desired
to go to another monastery.

In the autobiography are found many of his personal experi-
ences of supernatural character. He relates that while the monks
were chanting the Office, a bolt of lighting struck the church and
shattered a large crucifix. Guibert was one of the first to notice
the perturbed look on the face of an image of the Virgin:

> Vidi, Deum testor, post horam qua haec acciderant, beatae
> Dei Genitricis imaginem, quae infra crucifixum stabat vultu
> adeo turbulento et a solita serenitate mutato, ut penitus alte-
> rata videretur.[156]

Others observed the same and it was not until they had confessed
their sins that the face of the image acquired its usual serenity.

Of the six Marial legends in the works of Guibert of Nogent,[157]
three occur in the *De laude S. Mariae*, where he gives a simple
explanation of their occurrence:

---

[154] *Ibid.* (col. 843).

[155] *Ibid.*, 16 (col. 871). Guibert adds: "Quod nec mora conjiciens,
beatam Dei Genitricem intellexit, cujus nomen et pignora ibidem totius
pene Latini orbis veneratione coluntur."

[156] *Ibid.*, 23 (col. 886).

[157] See also the chapter on local miracles, *infra*, pp. 90 ff.

Et corda, iniquitate abundante, torpentia ex iis recalificans, munificentiarum insolitarum impensione recolligit: haec eadem namque signa, quae antiquitus fidei aedificandae valuerant, jam nunc eidem sine operibus vix constanti et moribus erigendis valent.[158]

Moreover, the miracles are performed in favor of three persons who, in Guibert's estimation, are great sinners. Thus, Theodeberta,[159] because of her deep contrition for the murder of her son-in-law receives the protection of Mary in an ordeal by fire.[160] Peter who plows his field on the feast of Saint Mary Magdalen and curses his oxen, is afflicted with the " ignis sacer " and loses his leg. Twice he is visited by the martyr Hippolytus and Mary, " super omnes creaturas *post Filium,* et *per Filium* benedicta." [161] He is completely cured, " et apud Deum, et *Dei opera,* nil existere imperfectionis acclamat." An adultress is converted, when she finds that Mary has refused to punish her in answer to the prayer of the wronged wife:

Unde factum est ut ex eo quo ista castitati se redderet, illa simultatem deponeret, et hoc *totum ad salutem* utriusque inter omnes feminas *benedicta disponeret.*[162]

In the *De vita sua* Guibert relates a miracle which he says is similar to that narrated by Radbod.[163] While acknowledging the resemblance of the two accounts, he considers them distinct events in the history of Noyon. In Guibert's anecdote a young girl has dis-

[158] 9 (*PL*, CLVI, 564). This is also the attitude of the writers of the local collections, cf. *infra*, p. 96.

[159] Herman of Tournai, author of the Laon collections, calls her Soiburga. *De Miraculis S. Mariae Laudunensis*, iii, 27 (*PL*, CLVI, 1008).

[160] *De laude S. Mariae*, 10 (*PL*, CLVI, 564-68).

[161] *Ibid.*, 11 (col. 570). Cf. H. Isnard, " Recueil des miracles de la Vierge du XIII⁰ siècle," *Bulletin de la Société arch. du Vendomois*, XXVI (1887), 206-210. E. Levi, *Il Libro dei cinquanta miracoli della Vergine* (Bologna, 1917), pp. cxii ff.

[162] *Ibid.*, 12 (col. 574). For a conspectus of the history of this legend in both Latin and Old French see *The Exempla, or Stories from the Sermones Vulgares of Jacques de Vitry*, ed. T. F. Crane (London, 1890), p. 224. See also H. Kjellman, *Deuxième collection anglo-normande*, p. lxviii.

[163] *Op. cit.*, 18 (col. 953). For Radbod, cf. *supra*, p. 33.

honored the feast of the martyr Nichasius by sewing, and it is only after fervent praying to the " Regina martyrum " that she is able to loose the thread which has bored into her tongue. The second legend contained in this work concerns the pilgrim of Saint James, whose farm adjoined the land of the lord of the castle of Sambre in Burgundy. The latter became a monk and it is upon his authority that Guibert recounts the history. According to his account the youth has committed fornication, and although he undertakes the pilgrimage in expiation, he indulges in sinful thoughts on the way. Deluded by the devil in the form of the apostle, he mutilates and kills himself. Restored to life he tells his companions that while his fate was being debated before God,[164] Saint James had entreated the Virgin to intercede for him:

> Pro me Benedictam illam precaretur, ipsa ex ore dulcissimo sententiam protulit, homini misero indulgendum fore, quem malignitas diaboli sub sancta specie sic contigit corruisse. Sic me in saeculum haec [hoc] evenit ad mei correctionem, et horum denuntiationem, *Deo jubente rediisse.*

One legend in the *De pignoribus sanctorum* is more Eucharistic than Marial, but is found with certain variations in later collections.[165] An acolyte at Saint Quentin's offers bread on his paten to the image of Christ crucified. The image speaks: " Ego in proximo tibi de meo pane dabo." [166] The boy dies within a few days.

The status of Mary, according to Guibert of Nogent, is clearly set forth in the opening words of his work, *De laude S. Mariae*:

> Feminam illam super omnes creaturas *post Filium,* et *per Filium* benedictam, *omnium creaturarum sub Dei* cultu dignissimam, labiis omnino fidelibus, licet minus idoneis, praedicemus.[167]

---

[164] The Latin reads: " Illic cum quid de me fieret coram *Deo* tractaretur, . . . " *Ibid.*, iii, 19 (col. 956). For variants, see Crane's notes to Pez, p. 85.

[165] Ward, II, 623 (2). Cf. *infra*, p. 43, n. 189.

[166] *Op. cit.*, i, 2 (col. 617).

[167] *Op. cit.*, i (col. 537).

She was created to be a mediatrix:

> Nonne est nostrae consummatio gloriae, si vel possimus inter
> nos et tuum Filium te *mediatricem* habere? Ex debito est,
> Domina, si nostri memineris, *propter hoc* enim *facta*; *propter
> hoc es electa,* ut apud dulcissimum Filium causam nostram
> piissima tuearis.[168]

His personal appeal to her is partly inspired by the precedent of
her mercy shown to Mary of Egypt and Theophilus:

> Graves mei sunt reatus; placa Deum, Domina,
> Si te piam sensit olim meretrix Aegyptia,
> Virque qui te atque tuum Filium negaverat.[169]

He has confidence too in her power of intercession before God:

> Apud Deum sic vox tua constat impetrabilis
> Ut ad aures Regis regum nulla tam sit habilis.[170]

She is a creature but " benedicta inter creaturas ";[171] she is the
mother of the Author of all things (*Auctoris omnium*).[172] Her
status is repeatedly said to be *post Deum*.[173]

Guibert is an important figure in the evolution of the Marial
miracula. The legends of Theodeberta, the adultress, the girl of
Noyon, and the pilgrim of St. James form a part of many of the
medieval collections. His acquaintance with the writing of Radbod
is evidence that the literary tradition is becoming definitely
established.

Hildebert

Hildebert, Bishop of Mans and Archbishop of Tours (d. 1133),
wrote a metrical version of the life of Mary of Egypt. He begins

---

[168] *Ibid.*, 14 (col. 577). Adam of Perseigne expresses the same thought
when he writes that the Virgin Mary will intercede for man in all necessi-
ties: " Rogabis plane, quia qui Filium tuum inter Deum et homines posuit
Mediatorem, te quoque inter reum et judicem posuit *mediatricem. Ad hoc*
nimirum *electa es.*" *Mariale* (*PL*, CCXI, 703).

[169] " Rhythmus ad B. Virginem, et S. Joannem Evangelistam," (*PL*,
CLVI, 577).

[170] *Ibid.* (cols. 577-78).

[171] *De laude S. Mariae* (*ibid.*, col. 552).

[172] *Ibid.* (col. 543).

[173] *Ibid.* (cols. 537, 541, 558, 564, 570).

with a history of Zosimas and the legend might be considered an incident in the life of the hermit.[174]   Hildebert follows the account of Paul the Deacon,[175] in having Zosimas urge the penitent to relate the story of her conversion " quo Christo glorificetur." [176]

As in Paul's version, the Virgin is asked to intercede with her Son that the sinful woman may be allowed to enter the church in order to adore the cross.   Mary of Egypt has full confidence in her power of intercession:

> Hoc per te spero, per te succedere quaero.
> Nam licet iratus cedet, te supplice, Natus;
> Cedet enim, siquidem Pater est et Filius idem.[177]

Her later life in the desert is one of trial and temptation, but she overcomes all by the grace of God.   The inspirations which she has received in the things of the spirit are also attributed to the same divine source:

> *Omnibus est victus Deus,* omnibus omnis amictus,
> Coelum Rex coeli moderatur, adestque fideli.
>
> .   .   .   .
>
> Si divinorum monimenta retracto librorum
> Coelitus ecce datur, *Deus haec docet,* haec operatur.[178]

The two other miracles of which Zosimas is a witness, the dry passage made for him over the Jordan and the digging of the grave by the lion, are works of God for the glorification of Mary of Egypt in which no mention is made of the Virgin whose rôle is of minor importance in Hildebert's version.

Walter of Cluny

Walter of Cluny was born at Compiègne and wrote his *De miraculis S. Mariae Virginis* after 1141, dedicating it to a monk at St. Venantius in Tours.[179]   The first miracle which he relates contains an allusion to the pestilence of 1133, called the " ignis sacer ": [180]

---

[174] *Manitius*, III, 861.
[175] Cf. *supra*, p. 13.
[176] *Vita B. Mariae Aegyptiacae*, 5 (*PL*, CLXXI, 1328).
[177] *Ibid.*, 9 (col. 1332).   [179] Manitius, III, p. 677.
[178] *Ibid.* (col. 1335).   [180] Cf. *infra*, pp. 99-100.

Cum *divina providentia* anno ab Incarnatione Domini 1133 peccatis nostris exigentibus, ad correctionem multorum sacro igne quorumdam corpora depasci *permitteret,* supra dicta ecclesia tanta *divinae largitatis gratia redundabat,* ut quicunque patiens hanc infirmitatem coram beatae Virginis vulta adveniret, statim *superna gratia visitatus* ardoris sui refrigerium sentiret. [181]

Having once said that the Virgin relieves the sufferers by virtue of the divine bounty, Walter does not repeat this theocentric statement. The miracle which occurs in a church at Dormans on the Marne bears a resemblance to one related by Hugo Farsit.[182] A woman whose face has been eaten away by the disease is brought to the church by relatives and friends. The nuns of the adjoining convent keep vigil with them, " psalmis et orationibus cum lacrymis et cordis contritione Dei misericordiam et B. Virginis auxilium invocantes." [183] She is abandoned by her husband and children, and finally, lest the stench of her decaying flesh become unbearable to others, she too leaves the church. That night the Virgin appears to reprimand her for her want of faith and to cure her:

> . . . manu benigna vultum attrectat, et omni effugato dolore pristinae eam sanitati sub momento restituit, . . . benedictaque muliere, visio gloriosa disparuit.

According to Walter, the woman in gratitude " tradidit . . . seipsam in perpetuam ancillam eidem ecclesiae *ad laudem et gloriam nominis Jesu Christi."*

In his version of the adultress protected by Mary, which agrees in details of narrative with that of Guibert of Nogent,[184] the Virgin replies to the wife:

> Verum dicis, mulier, quia mihi *data est* potestas omnium quae in coelo sunt et in terra, et in daemones facio justitiam; sed peccatrix illa quotidie mihi reducit in memoriam gaudium majus quod unquam habui in praesenti saeculo, proferens mihi salutationem angelicam, *quae fuit gaudium restaurationis*

---

[181] *De miraculis S. Marie Virginis (PL,* CLXXIII, 1380).

[182] *De miraculis B. Mariae Virginis in urbe Suessionensi,* 7 (*PL,* CLXXIX, 1781-82). Cf. *infra,* p. 118.

[183] Walter of Cluny, *op. cit.* (col. 1381).

[184] Cf. *supra,* p. 37.

humani generis; et ideo non possum pati ut aliquod infortu-
nium illi contingat.[185]

God's power is of Himself; Mary's, however, has its limitations
prescribed by the word " data " which implies a dependence upon
the One who bestows it.

In the fourth miracle Walter recounts the story of the drowned
sacristan.   Because he has recommended himself to her care,
Mary pleads for his soul before her Son:

> Animam hanc, charissime Fili, sub mea positam custodia
> invaserunt daemones, . . . cumque judicium vestrum quaesis-
> sent, ecce coram vobis assistens *oro* ut revocetur ad corpus
> suum, et deinceps vivat ut monachus nec illusionibus et de-
> ceptionibus daemonum amplius acquiescat, ne deterius in fine
> illi contingat.[186]

The Judge whom Walter describes as " benignissimus " decides the
case in favor of His Mother: " Quomodo non licet, Mater vene-
randa, me tibi aliquid negare, . . . " The resuscitated sacristan
hastens to the church, and invites all to hear his public confession
of guilt, and the miracle: " Convenite huc ad me qui Dominum
timetis, et Matrem misericordiae veneramini." The writer then
exhorts:

> Veniant itaque ad eam poenitentes cum interno gemitu rea
> pectora tundentes, sine dubio, si vere poeniteant, *meritis* hujus
> sanctissimae *Virginis recuperaturi gratiam benignissimi Filii*
> et Domini nostri Jesu Christi qui vivit, . . . [187]

This passage, like a similar one in Fulbert of Chartres,[188] points
to the primary source of grace from which Mary must draw.   She
acts as a means in regaining the favor of her Son.

The work of Walter of Cluny, were it not so brief, might be considered a collection, since its title, *De miraculis S. Mariae Virginis*,
is common to most later ones and indicates its exclusively Marial
character.   Although he treats but four miracles, two of these have
already been noted in Guibert of Nogent and all with the possible

---

[185] *Ibid.* (col. 1382).

[186] *Ibid.*, 4 (col. 1384).   For popularity cf. Mielot, *op. cit.*, pp. xxiii-xxv;
Crane's notes to Pez, pp. 82-83.

[187] *Ibid.* (col. 1386).   [188] Cf. *supra*, p. 20.

exception of " Bread to the Child-Christ " [189] recur again and again. Later versions add few accretions to the narrative. Less is left to the imagination of the writers. Hence the Marial *miracula* may be said to have reached a point of development where there is a standardization of the anecdotes and the genre has become clearly defined.

Honorius Augustodunensis

Honorius Augustodunensis who wrote between 1122 and 1137 [190] inserts in his *Speculum Ecclesiae* five Marial *exempla.* The story of angel music on the Nativity of the Virgin recurs in the works of Etienne de Bourbon [191] and Vincent of Beauvais. [192] The versions of the Jew Boy, Mater misericordiae, Theophilus, and Mary of Egypt present Mary in the rôle of Mediatrix.

The anecdotes are usually followed by an exhortation· Thus, Honorius concludes the story of the Jew boy with the words:

> Hanc reginam angelorum, karissimi, imitamini humilitate et castitate. Hanc pro vestris miseriis *apud Filium suum* devotis precibus *intervenire exorate*, ut, cum venerit in sanctis suis fieri admirabilis, immarcescibilis gloriae in templo ejus coronam percipiatis. [193]

He ends his anecdote of the dying monk who is consoled by the " Mater misercordiae " with a similar appeal: " Ad hanc confugiat omnis miserabilis, ut *per ei reconcilietur* qui in sanctis suis est mirabilis." [194]

---

[189] Walter's version of " Bread to the Child-Christ " differs somewhat from the story of Guibert of Nogent (cf. *supra*, p. 38), and resembles that of Vincent of Beauvais (*Spec. Hist.*, vii, 99). It is not a Marial miracle since the chief protagonist is the " puer quem beata Virgo in manibus tenebat." *Loc. cit.*, 3 (col. 1383.)

[190] *Molinier*, II, 313.

[191] *Anecdotes historiques, légendes et apologues tirés du recueil inédit d'Etienne de Bourbon*, ed. Lecoy de la Marche (Paris, 1877), no. 107, pp. 95-96.

[192] *Spec. Hist.*, vii, 119; see also Kjellman, *op. cit.*, p. xxxii.

[193] *Speculum Ecclesiae* (*PL*, CLXXII, 852). The peroration quoted here is not reprinted by Wolter, *op. cit.*, p. 43.

[194] *Speculum Ecclesiae* (*ibid.*, cols. 1001-1002). The narrative is also in the *Liber sacramentarium*, 45 (*ibid.*, col. 769).

In the version of Theophilus by Honorius the mercy of God is exalted:

Tandem spe animatus *ejus misericordiae* qui omnes homines vult salvos fieri (I Tim. 2 : 4), *inexhausta divinae pietatis viscera* continuis precibus pulsat ejusque piam Genitricem largis fletibus invocat; et *misericors* et *miserator fons pietatis* non sprevit neque despexit deprecationem pauperis (Ps. 21 : 25).[195]

When the Virgin places the charter upon his breast, she exhorts "ut gaudeat de *beneficiis Dei.*" She diverts attention from her own act of mediation to the signal grace of divine forgiveness; likewise, Theophilus expresses his thanksgiving to God, the source of the benefits he has received, rather than to Mary who merely acted as a Mediatrix: "Exultat in *Domino,* ineffabile gratiae ejus et caro exultaverunt in *Deum vivum* (Ps. 83 : 2)." His face becomes illumined and Honorius, in relating his death, fittingly develops the metaphor of light: "et mox *per Dei Genitricem ad videndum verum lumen Christum* in lumino Patre ad superna regna vocatur."

His version of Mary of Egypt is also theocentric. The "divina virtus"[196] prevents her from entering the church, and by the "nutu Dei" she glances at the image of the Mother of God and is moved to pray. In the desert she is found by Zosimas, "Domino ducente." When he brings her the Eucharist, miracles attend his steps: "Senex vero videns gloriosa miracula, solvit illi laudum praeconia *qui facit solus mirabilia.*" In his peroration Honorius directs his listeners to the "Star of the Sea":

Haec, karissimi, maris stella in summo coelo super omnes choros angelorum splendida rutilat, post cujus humilitatem et castitatem omnes navim vitae suae dirigant qui in salo hujus saeculi navigant ut *per eam vitae portum obtineant* quo perhenniter cum omnibus sanctis gaudeant, . . .[197]

Despite her exaltation over the choirs of angels, Mary's nature, according to Honorius, does not transcend that of humanity. Concerning the words of the Psalmist, "Veritas de terra orta est (Ps. 84 : 12)," he writes:

[195] *Speculum Ecclesiae* (cols. 993-94).
[196] *Ibid.* (col. 906).   [197] *Ibid.* (col. 908).

Quae veritas *de terre* orta est, cum de sancta Maria humanitatis sumpsit exordia. *Haec* idcirco *terrae comparatur,* quia
sicut prius Adam de munda terra formatur, ita secundus
Adam Christus de munda virgine procreatur.[198]

The Blessed Virgin is preëminently a Mediatrix in the legends of
Honorius: " per eam " one is reconciled to Him Who is admirable
in His saints; " per Dei Genitricem " one is called to the true
Light, Christ; " per eam " souls may arrive at the Port of Life.
There is a theovergent significance in the words " per eam," since
through her, according to Honorius, one is led to God Himself—
" qui facit solus mirabilia."

William of Malmesbury

To William of Malmesbury (d. 1147) is attributed the authorship of the MS *Salisbury 97,* which is considered by Kjellman to
be the original source of many English collections, including the
MSS Oxford *Balliol 240* and Cambridge, *M. 6. 15.* and, indirectly
through intermediaries, the vernacular miracles by Adgar and the
anonymous author of *Old Royal 20 B XIV.*[199] Mussafia has published no. 37, " Vision of Wettin " and no. 42, " Love through
Black Arts." [200] The first derives from the vision narrated by
Hatto; [201] the second has its prototype in the *Vita S. Basilii* by
Amphilocius.[202]

In the version of William of Malmesbury, the clerk continues to
say his Hours despite his negotiations with the devil. The Virgin
Mary appears to him on his wedding day, while he is in prayer, and
reproves him for his fickleness. With the permission of the Bishop
he puts away his bride and lives an exemplary· life of which William of Malmesbury theocentrically comments:

---

[198] *Ibid.* (col. 849). The significance of the word " terra " as applied to
Mary's status is more apparent in the words of Richard of Saint Lawrence:
" Et beata virgo omni puro homine, qui de terra est, superior, *Deo inferior.*"
Salzer, *op. cit.,* p. 391. See also *ibid.,* pp. 494-95.

[199] *Op. cit.,* pp. xii, xix, xx.

[200] *Studien,* IV, pp. 34-51, 53-80.

[201] Cf. *supra,* pp. 8-9.

[202] *Vitae Patrum I: Vita S. Basilii,* 7 (*PL,* LXXIII, 302-305). Cf.
supra, pp. 10, n. 49 and 20, n. 87.

> Ita clericus deinceps malorum fugax, bonorum ferax evi exegit reliquum ut perservatricis sue gratie specioso *miraculo Deus* eius monstraret innocentiam.[203]

At the death of the clerk a white dove is seen to issue from his mouth and fly toward heaven:

> His operibus, ultra humanam possibilitatem insuper affluentibus, felix virgo humanorum patrona, *divinorum arbitra* comprobatur.[204]

The title " arbitra " as a synonym for Mediatrix is unusual.

In his historical works, also, William relates incidents which were developed in later legendaries. During the siege of Chartres (A. D. 911) by Rollo, as related in the *Gesta Regum*, the citizens, " nec armis nec muris confisi," [205] display a relic of the Virgin's garment:

> Camisiam quoque ejusdem virginis, quam Carolus Calvus cum aliis reliquiis a Constantinopoli advexerat, in modum vexilli super propugnacula, custodum trita pectoribus, ventis exponunt hostes visam ridere, et in eam per inane sagittas dirigere; non impune, nam mox, oculis obnubilatis, nec retro regredi nec ante tendere valuere.[206]

Many are killed but Rollo is saved: " . . . quem suae fidei *Deus* reservabat."

Two miracles are contained in the *Memorials of Saint Dunstan*, both being also narrated by " B," a Saxon priest (ca. 1000), by Osbern (ca. 1090), a precentor of Christ Church, Canterbury, and

---

[203] Mussafia, *Studien*, IV, p. 71.

[204] *Ibid.*, p. 73.

[205] *Gesta Regum Anglorum*, I, ii, 138. For variants, cf. Ward, II, 603 (5) and Mielot, *op. cit.*, p. viii.

[206] The reverence shown to this relic is evidenced by another historical event told by Suger of Louis le Gros. In his siege of Chartres in September, 1119, he had begun to set fire to the city, when " subito tam cleri quam cives, beate Dei genitricis camisiam preferentes, ut pro ejus amore tanquam ecclesie tutor principalis misericorditer parcat devotissime supplicant." The king then gave orders to spare the city through " ecclesie amore et timore." Suger, *Vie de Louis VI le Gros*, ed. Henri Waquet (Paris, 1929: " Les classiques de l'histoire de France au moyen âge, no. 11 "), pp. 198-200.

by Eadmer who wrote between 1109 and 1122.[207] William's *Vita S. Dunstani* was written about 1126.[208] The first concerns Ethelfreda, the widowed friend of Dunstan.[209] Having invited King Athelstan to Glastonbury, she suddenly finds that her supply of mead is insufficient for the royal party, but rejects the offer of his servants to supply any deficiency in the matter of provisions:

> Quod ubi accepit mulier *immodicae in Deo spei* respondit, " Nolit unquam sancta Christi mater, ut propter minus sufficientem hujusmodi potum dominus rex declinet meam domum." [210]

She then prays to the Virgin and obtains the mead in abundance.

The second miracle in the *Vita S. Dunstani* is a vision which was granted to the Saint while he was at Saint Augustine's outside the walls of Canterbury. The Mother of God exhorts her choir of virgins to sing " ad *Christi* laudem " :

> Cantemus *Domino*, sociae, cantemus honorem,
> Dulcis *amor Christi* personet ore pio.[211]

The choir responds:

> Foemina sola fuit patuit qua janua lethi,
> Per quam vita redit, foemina sola fuit.

Commenting upon the " sweetness of the Blessed Mary " in thus appearing to her servant, William of Malmesbury thinks that this apparition outweights all miracles " quae quisquam fecit facturusve sit." Both this vision and the miracle of the mead appear in the

[207] Charles Gross, *The Sources and Literature of English History from the Earliest Times to about 1485*, 2d ed. (London, 1915), pp. 283 ff.

[208] *Ibid.*

[209] For the identification of Ethelfreda, see *Memorials of Saint Dunstan*, ed. Wm. Stubbs (London, 1874), p. lxxvii.

[210] *Ibid.*, p. 266. Cf. the biography by " B," *ibid.*, pp. 17 f.; by Osbern, *ibid.*, p. 86; by Eadmer, *ibid.*, p. 176. For variants, cf. Mielot, *op. cit.*, pp. xii-xiii.

[211] *Ibid.*, ii (p. 317). Cf. biographies by " B," *ibid.*, p. 48; by Osbern, *ibid.*, p. 118; by Eadmer, *ibid.*, p. 208. Crane lists variants in his notes to Pez, p. 93. For the hymn of Sedulius, cf. *PL*, XIX, 753.

Anglo-Norman collection by Adgar [212] and the anonymous author of MS *Old Royal 20 B XIV.*[213]

Pseudo-Anselm

Four Marial legends occur in the spurious works of Anselm [214] and of these all but one concern the Feast of the Immaculate Conception. Of the two versions of the pilgrim of Saint James, one makes no mention of Mary; [215] in the other Giraldus is restored to life at the command of the Virgin, but the anonymous writer describes his companions, " demonstrantes illum in quo *Deus per beatum apostolum Jacobum* tam insolitam rem *operatus est* atque mirabilem." [216]

From the legend of Elsinus who as Abbot of St. Augustine's at Canterbury was sent, shortly after the Norman Conquest, to negotiate with the Danes, derive many variants.[217] There are two versions among the works formerly ascribed to Anselm; both relate that upon the return trip a storm threatens to wreck the ship and the passengers have recourse to prayer:

Animarum solummodo magnis clamoribus salutem *Creatori* suo commendarent, et beatissimam Virginem Mariam Dei genitricem, miserorum refugium, et desperatorum spem devote reclamarent, . . . [218]

Preces cum lacrymis Deo fundunt et se graviter deliquisse miserabiliter gemunt . . . clamabant ad Deum fortius. O *Deus clementissime, Pater misericordiae,* dignare nos respicere mersos pro nostro crimine. Respice, *clementissime,* de sede tuae gloriae, visita nos jam positos in extremo vitae periculo. Assit nunc *tua gratia!* assit *tua benignitas!* assit *maxima boni-*

---

[212] *Marienlegenden*, pp. 122-26 and pp. 206-209.

[213] Kjellman, *op. cit.*, pp. 167-71 and 224-26. See also *ibid.*, pp. lv ff. and lxvi ff.

[214] *Opera spuria, PL,* CLIX. As Mussafia indicates, " Von Ersterem wird behauptet, dass er von seinem Neffen Anselmus in den Jahren 1141-1148 verfasst worden sei." *Studien,* I, p. 930. The question remains undecided.

[215] *PL*, CLIX, 335-38.   [216] *Ibid.* (col. 340).

[217] Ward, II, 614 ff. (36); Crane's notes to Pez, p. 90 and in *RR*, II '1911), pp. 259-60.

tas! assint *bona gratuita dona!*
Succurre nobis miseris, *pietas
ineffabilis,* ne nos sorbeat infernus nunc pro nostris criminibus . . . Qui promisisti miseris
qua hora ingemuerint et corda
poenituerint salvos protinus
fieri, parce nunc confitentibus
. . . Maria, Mater Domini, *ora*
pro nobis miseris, *tuo filio,* o
domina, commenda nostra fla-
mina. Namque mari sunt tradita misera nostra corpore, *tuus
filius* animas in requiem *suscipiat.*[219]

A divine messenger who appears enjoins the celebration of the
Feast of the Immaculate Conception, and when the promise of
Elsinus is given to him, the storm is immediately quelled. Both
versions end with an exhortation to observe this solemnity in honor
of the Virgin Mary; the rewards promised for this observance,
however, are the gifts of Christ Himself:

Et nos ergo, fratres dilectissimi,
si portum salutis volumus ap-
prehendere, Dei genitricis Con-
ceptionem dignis obsequiis et
officiis celebrabimus, ut *ab ejus
filio* digna mercede *remunere-
mur.*[220]

Hujus solemnitatis celebratori-
bus *detur a Filio* ipsius Virginis
Domino nostro Jesu Christo *pax*
et *longo vita,* et post transitum
hujus vitae *aeterna requies con-
cedatur.*[221]

It is the Virgin who appears to the brother of the King of
Hungary, who has left his bride to say his Hours, and promises:

Si sponsam carnalem, cui adhaerere vis, amore mei dimiseris,
me sponsam in coelesti regno habebis; et si Conceptionis meae
festum annuatim vi Idus Decembris solemniter celebraveris,
et celebrandum praedicaveris, mecum *in regno filii mei* laureatus eris.[222]

---

[218] *Sermo de Conceptione Beatae Mariae, ibid.* (col. 319).

[219] *Miraculum de Conceptione Sanctae Mariae, ibid.* (col. 324).

[220] *Ibid.* (col. 320).   [221] *Ibid.* (col. 326).

[222] *Ibid* (col. 320). Cf. Mielot, *op. cit.,* p. xi; *Legenda Aurea,* appendix,
p. 870.

By the words, " mecum . . . laureatus eris," Mary places herself
in the category of those who are to be rewarded, and therefore,
inferior to God. Moreover, she does not speak of the Kingdom of
Heaven as her own, but as her Son's. To the drowned monk whom
she rescues from the demons for the devout recital of the *Ave
Maria*, she also recommends the observance of the feast of her conception and the amendment of his life.[223]

In his explanation of the doctrine celebrated by the Feast, the
anonymous writer emphasizes Mary's superiority over the Saints:

> Pulchre et digne dominationem super caeteros sanctos illa
> debet habere, . . . sicut sine more *summus rerum Dispositor*
> super omnes sanctos et sanctas illam *dignitatem illi contulit,*
> ut Verbum carnem factum Virgo conciperet et pareret, et
> post partum Virgo permaneret.[224]

Elsewhere, her status is asserted more concisely: " . . . supra te est,
solus Deus est; . . . infra te, omnes quod Deus non est." [225]   She
is " prudens ac nobilis *post filium* tuum imperatrix." [226]

Peter the Venerable

The *De Miraculis* was an occupation of the last years of Peter
the Venerable, ninth Abbot of Cluny (d. 1156). He states his
purpose in the prologue to the second book:

> Doleo enim, et . . . torpori multorum irascor; qui cum
> scientia, litteris, atque eloquio abundent, miranda *omnipo-
> tentis Dei opera,* . . . memoriae posterorum mandare scribendo
> pigritantur . . . Cumque dicat Deo divinus psalmus: " Con-
> fiteantur tibi, Domine, omnia opera tua (Ps. 144: 10) "; hoc
> est laudare de omnibus operibus tuis, *quomodo de illis operibus
> Deus laudabitur quae nesciuntur?* . . . et *cum omnia* sive
> bona, sive mala, quae *vel volente vel permittente Deo in mundo
> fiunt,* ipsius glorificationi, et Ecclesiae aedificationi inservire
> debeant, si ea homines latuerunt, quomodo de his aut Deus
> glorificabitur, aut Ecclesia aedificabitur? [227]

If, according to Peter, everything happens by the will and permission of God, the miracles which he relates are strictly " opera Dei."

---

[223] *Ibid.* (col. 321).
[224] *Ibid.* (col. 322).
[225] *Ibid.* (col. 307).
[226] *Ibid.* (col. 306).
[227] *PL*, CLXXXIX, 907-908.

That this applies to Marial *miracula* is evident in his anecdote concerning the candles which remained unconsumed, while burning on the Feast of the Assumption at St. Mary Major's at Rome. He writes:

> Hoc tam nobile et ante nusquam auditum miraculum, ad commendandam mortalibus gloriam Matris Domini, non in quolibet ignoto vel humili loco, non in qualibet, vel quantalibet civitate, sed in ipsa urbe orbis capite, non semel tantum, ut dixi, sed assidue recursu annuo, *divina pietas et potentia operatur.*[228]

He cites the miracles which God performed for the prophet Elias and then concludes:

> Magna fuerunt illa tempore Mosaicae legis, non minora sunt ista, tempore christianae et evangelicae legis. Non defuerunt prophetae panes et carnes ministratae a corvis mane et sero, non defecit eidem pauxillum farinae et olei per tres tantum annos et dimidium, non defecit, nec deficit in magno festo Matris Domini . . . oblata Deo cereorum quantitas, non solum per tres annos et dimidium, sed jam per centum et eo amplius annos, usque ad hanc nostram aetatem, et *quantum* deinceps *Deo placuerit.*[229]

Christ more than the Virgin is the chief protagonist in the miracles. Peter does not relate the story of the celestial celebrations of the Nativity of Mary;[230] he does, however, tell the anecdote of Hugh of Cluny in which a certain brother saw the Child Jesus turn to His Mother and say with exultation:

> Cernis, mater, *noctem* quae imminet *meae Nativitatis* gaudiis illustrandam, in qua et prophetarum oracula et angelorum praeconia renovabuntur, et meo de te exortu omnia simul coelestia atque terrestria laetabuntur? Ubi est nunc hostis damnati perfidia, ubi ejus potestas, qua ante hoc singulare gaudium mundo dominabatur?[231]

At these words the evil spirit begins to roam through the monastery, trying to find an entrance, and not succeeding, is forced to

---

[228] *Ibid.*, ii, 30 (col. 950).

[229] *Ibid.*   [230] Cf. *supra*, p. 43.

[231] *Ibid.*, i, 15 (col. 880). See also Vincent of Beauvais, *op. cit.*, vii, 114; Helinand, *Chronicon*, xlvi, an. 1048 (*PL*, CCXXII, 943-44).

withdraw " a conspectu piisimi Redemptoris et gloriosae Virginis matris." Hugh then exhorts the monks:

> Cauti igitur estote, et immensas gratias *omnipotenti* ac *misericordissimo Salvatori* agite, qui et nequissimum hostem a vobis expulit, et ipse nobiscum festum suum celebraturus remansit.[232]

Again, a dying monk is consoled, not by the apparition of the " Mater misericordiae " [233] but by the vision of the enviable position he is to occupy at the feet of Christ, conceded him by the Virgin.[234] So also, when Gerardus beholds the Host changed to the form of a small child, he sees Mary and an angel standing at the side of the altar. She is merely a secondary figure, for the angel speaks: " Quid, . . . miraris? hic *puer* quem conspicis, *coelum gubernat et terram.*" [235]

The status accorded to the Mother of God by Peter is apparent in the legend of the " Demon-swine," [236] in which he describes the Carthusian Brother as follows:

> Amori divino, et specialiter memoriae Matris Domini, ita se totum devoverat ut a bonis viris ipsum vitamque ejus cognoscentibus, nihil scire judicaretur, nisi Christum Jesum et hunc crucifixum (I Cor. 2:2), sacramque ipsius crucifixi matrem, ac perpetuam Virginem, *humanae salutis singularem post Domini amatricem*, Mariam.[237]

Attacked by the devils in the form of swine, the brother is about to be overcome:

> Sed *Deus* cui bonus vir ille saepe supplicando dicebat: *Ne nos inducas in tentationem, sed libera nos a malo*, tentationem tam duram non est passus ultra procedere, sed multa misericordia, qua semper suis providet, *eduxit eum a tentatione, et liberavit a malo.*

Nevertheless, his deliverance by God is effected through the instrumentality of the Virgin who interferes when the leader of the swine, in the form of a gigantic man, attempts to grasp him:

[232] *Ibid.* (col. 881).
[233] Cf. *supra*, pp. 18 and 25.   [235] *Ibid.*, i, 8 (col. 866).
[234] *Ibid.*, ii, 21 (col. 932).   [236] Cf. *infra*, p. 84.
[237] *Ibid.*, ii, 29 (col. 946) ; see *Spec. Hist.*, vii, 112.

Statim omnipotentis Filii Dei Mater, Mater vere, ut dicimus, misericordiae, in qua ille, sicut dictum est totam spem suam *post Deum* posuerat, visibiliter adfuit, ac virga levi manu praetensa: Quomodo, inquit, huc detestandi venire ausi fuistis? Non est, non est hic vester.

In his *Carmina* in which Peter asks Mary to mediate with her Son the same position, " post Deum," is accorded to her:

> Dominatrix angelorum, spes *post Deum* saeculorum,
>
> .   .   .   .
>
> Ora, Mater, Deum natum, nostrum solvat ut reatum,
> Et post concessam veniam, det gratiam et gloriam.[238]

Radewin

To Radewin (ca. 1177) who wrote a continuation of the *Gesta Friderici* of Otto of Freisingen between the years 1160 and 1170, is also attributed a long poem treating the legend of Theophilus.[239] After a prologue in honor of the Virgin, the German writer relates the compact with the devil. Poetically, he attributes the first movements of grace to the " manus omnipotentis ":

> tandem *diuina* sanans egros *medicina,*
> *gratia clementis medici, manus omnipotentis,*
> que numquam more nostro de perditione
> gaudet iniquorum nec mortem fecit eorum,
> hec inspiratrix et ad omne bonum *mediatrix,*
> nolens gestorum benefacta perire suorum
> egrum, torpentem, miserum miserata iacentem
> preuenit, adtollit, quae duruerant cito mollit.
>
> (253-60)[240]

The remorse of Theophilus is mingled with sentiments of fear before God's justice:

> ante dei potero consistere quomodo uultum,
> cum nihil occultum, cum nil remanebit inultum?
> quid faciam, iudex cum uenerit ille timendus,
> ad cuius nutum tremit orbis discutiendus?   (316-19)

---

[238] *Ibid.* (cols. 1018-19).

[239] For identity of the historian and poet see Wilhelm Meyer, *loc. cit.,* p. 64; Manitius, III, 391.

[240] Meyer, *loc. cit.,* p. 102.

He realizes that he has offended both the Son and the Mother:

> sicut enim matri dolor est iniuria nati,
> sic dolet ille uicem matris, uenerans genitricem. (339-40)

Nevertheless, he thinks:

> quam patiens, quam longanimis manus omnipotentis, . . .
> (359)

He determines to have recourse to Mary and by "hac media" obtain forgiveness from her Son. She appears after his forty days of penance and to her words of severity he replies:

> . . . est dominus meus, omnipotens deus, omnicreator,
> arbiter austerus rerumque saga moderator.
> attamen optimus est et creditur indubitate,
> quod sit iusticia bonus et iustus bonitate.
> ut sapiens, immo sapientia summa probatur,
> sic patiens, immo patientia uera putatur.   (415-20)

Encouraged by the example of other penitents who have been pardoned, he is insistent:

> sic ego, sancta parens, animatus spe generali
> credo tuis meritis me posse reconciliari.   (445-46)

Furthermore, he begs Mary to act in a mediating capacity for the "Good Shepherd":

> ille bonus pastor, qui passus propter ouile,
> errantem reuehat *per te,* precor, inmemor irae! (488-89)

His forgiveness and the restoration of the compact having been obtained through the mediation of the Virgin, he makes a public confession, after which the bishop invites all to join in the thanksgiving:

> *Auctorem uitae,* fratres, *laudare* uenite.
> *que fecit dominus miranda,* uenite uidere.
>
> .   .   .   .
>
> nos igitur, fratres, condignas omnipotenti
> reddamus grates natoque suaeque parenti.   (576-97)

In the epilogue Radewin's appeal to Mary Mediatrix becomes personal:

tu mediatrix, auxiliatrix, optima tota.
cum famulus tuus iste Theophilus, iste beatus,
perpetua nece, uirgo, tua prece sit reparatus.
me quoque, crimina pessima plurima quem male fedant,
fac, genitrix pia, ne cruciamina flammea ledant,
et dum Tartarei deseuiet ira camini,
tu miseri miserere tui uatis Radewini.   (645-51)

Herbert of Torres

Herbert, Archbishop of Torres, wrote his *De Miraculis* in 1178.[241]
He begins his work with a Marial anecdote which he heard in a
personal interview [242] with Rainaldus, a Cistercian monk of Clairvaux. Knowing the latter's reputation for saintliness, Herbert
entreats him, " ut *ad honorem Dei* unam aliquam ex suis consola-
tionibus mihi manifestaret." [243]   The old monk then tells him
that as he sat, one day, admiring the young religious reaping, " quia
videlicet tot sapientes, tot nobiles et delicati ibidem viri, *propter
amorem Christi* laboribus atque aerumnis seipsos exponerent," [244]
the Virgin Mary, accompanied by Elizabeth and Mary Magdalen
came " ad visitandos messores suos." [245]   Shortly before his death
Rainaldus is consoled by a vision of the Mother of God who holds
in her hand beautiful ornaments which she promises to give him
when he " comes to her." However, his assurance of eternal happi-
ness, according to Herbert, depends upon God: " Ornamenta quae
tibi sunt coelitus praeparata nunquam alterius erunt, sed *miserante
Deo* salva tibi et integra permanebunt." [246]
The Virgin is not so attentive to another Monk of Clairvaux who

[241] Molinier, II, 251; Welter, *op. cit.*, p. 43.

[242] This anecdote is also related by Conrad of Everbach (cf. *infra*, p. 57)
who uses the identical words of Herbert of Torres at this point: " Quad-
raginta diebus ante obitum suum, . . . ego sciens eum virum justum et
sanctum a Domino saepius visitatum, in ea confidentia qua illum diligebam
et me ab illo diligi sentiebam, ausus sum sciscitari et petere aliquid ab
eo." Herbert of Torres, i, 1 (*PL*, CLXXXV, 1275); Conrad of Everbach,
Exordium magnum Ordinis Cisterciensis, iii, 11 (*PL*, CLXXXV, 1063).

[243] Herbert of Torres, *ibid.*; Conrad of Everbach, *ibid.*

[244] *Ibid.* (col. 1274); *ibid.* (col. 1062).

[245] *Ibid.*; *ibid.* (col. 1063). See also Ward, II, 629 ff.; Vincent of Beauvais, *Spec. Hist.*, vii, 107; Helinand, *Chronicon*, xlix (*PL*, CCXII, 1077).

[246] *Ibid.* (col. 1276).

is not satisfied with the common food and medicine of the Community. Refusing to him the syrup which she offers to the other religious, she says:

> Vade, itaque, vade, et cura teipsum sicut volueris, quoniam *de his qui curam suam super Dominum jactant,* cura est nobis.[247]

Herbert presents Mary in the rôle of Mediatrix in the anecdote of the child who became epileptic when the Mother declared that she would never allow him to become a clerk. Contrite, she turns to God in distress:

> Heu, heu, *Domine Deus,* quam male locuta sum! Ego, ego sum illa flebilis et misera, quae tuam indignationem promerui;
> . . . Vertatur, obsecro, manus tuo super caput ingratae et perfidae parentis, tantummodo ut vivat filius meus, et tuto perennites obsequio mancipetur.[248]

Believing that God has punished her, she hopes to find in Mary, a Mediatrix: " Piisima Dei Genitrix, tibi commendo, et tibi reddo unicum meum, ut tibi vivat, et tibi serviat quandiu vixerit, in ministerio clericali." As she finishes her prayer, " beatissimae Virginis *interventione* sanatus est puer." [249]

Other accounts depict Mary offering comfort to religious in the hour of death.[250] Christ also appears as Consoler.[251] Indeed, the visions in which Christ is the central figure [252] bear a much larger proportion in Herbert's collection than the Marial legends.

Conrad of Everbach

The first four " distinctions " of the *Exordium magnum Ordinis Cisterciensis* were written by a monk of Clairvaux after 1193;

---

[247] *Ibid.,* 14 (col. 1366); *ibid.,* 19 (col. 1076). Here Conrad's wording is slightly different but the same in thought. See Caesarius of Heisterbach, *Dial. Mirac.,* vii, 47 and the *Lib. VIII Mirac.,* iii, no. 69, pp. 193-94. *Spec. Hist.,* vii, 108.

[248] Herbert of Torres, *ibid.,* iii. 11 (col. 1363).

[249] *Ibid.* For the term " intervention " as used in local collections, cf. *infra,* pp. 120-21.

[250] *Ibid.,* i, 34 (col. 1306); ii, 44 (col. 1354); iii, 9 (col. 1360). See Conrad of Everbach, *op. cit.,* iii, 21 (col. 1080).

[251] *Ibid.,* i, 18 (col. 1293); 24 (col. 1299); ii, 5 (col. 1316); 33 (col. 1344); iii, 7 (col. 1358); 15 (col. 1366); 17 (col. 1368).

[252] Welter notes as many as fourteen Eucharistic miracles. *Op. cit.,* p. 91, n. 42.

the fifth and sixth are attributed to Conrad of Everbach who probably wrote them before 1221 when he was elected abbot of Clairvaux.[253]　The verbal resemblance of the anecdote of the monks at
their field-work to the story in the *De Miraculis* of Herbert of
Torres has been noted.[254]　In the legend of the " Virgin's Syrup,"
however, Conrad deviates from Herbert's version, viewing the ex-
traordinary occurrence as an act of God's mercy to correct the
imperfect monk:

> *Clemens* autem *Dominus,* qui misericorditer solet errantes cor-
> rigere, ipsum voluit ad viam veritatis reducere, et ut sciret et
> intelligeret quam salubriter monet nos, omnem sollicitudinem
> nostram projicere in ipsum, quoniam ipsi cura est de nobis
> (I Peter 5: 7), tali modo *visitationem suam* simpliciter delin-
> quenti *praerogare dignatus est.*[255]

The medium through which God effected the " visitation " is Mary
and her reproof has such a salutary effect that " *cooperante gratia
Dei* in brevi decorem et fortitudinem, cum salute corporis et ani-
mae, pariter induit.''

Mercy is again stressed as an attribute of God in the legend of
the woman revived for confession.　After living a life which to all
appearances was most exemplary, she dies unconfessed.　Suddenly,
by the " misericordissima Dei omnipotentis virtute," [256] she revives.
She quiets the fears of the mourners, reassuring them that " miserante Deo '' she is truly alive.　After making her confession, she
tells them that " per interventionem pissimae Dei Genitricis et
Virginis Mariae '' she had been freed from the devils who were
about to carry her soul to hell for concealing a sin in confession:

> Ipsa mater misericordiae accedens ad benedictum fructum
> uteri sui Dominum nostrum Jesum Christum, *adoravit* et ait:
> Obsecro pietatem tuam, Domine, Fili, ne tradas bestiis animam
> illam, quae suam transgressionem coram imagine mea toties
> deploravit.　Cui respondit Dominus: Nosti, dilecta mater,
> quod sine confessione salvari non potest?　At illa: Domine,
> *omnia tibi possibilia sunt.*

[253] Molinier, II, 246; Welter, *op. cit.*, p. 44.

[254] Cf. *supra*, p. 55.

[255] *Exordium Magnum,* iii, 19 (*PL*, CLXXXV, 1077).　Cf. variants,
supra, p. 56, n. 247.

[256] *Ibid.*, v, 5 (col. 1129).　See also variants in *Spec. Hist.*, vii, 117.

" Domino imperante," her soul was restored to her body, and now
that her sin has been forgiven, she says in farewell:

> Tempus est ut abeam, minime jam reditura, sed *in aeternum
> misericordias Domini canitura*, qui me licet indignam, tre-
> mendo judicio suo, eadem misericordia praeveniente et subse-
> quente, tam dignanter subduxit.

Mary's act of adoration before her Son in the above anecdote is
indicative of her position as creature. This is also her status in
the version of the persecuted monk, who continually prays for the
gifts of patience and charity.[257]   God is not unmindful of him:

> . . . sed qui consolatur humiles, tribulatorum susceptor Domi-
> nus exaudivit vocem ejus, impletumque est in eo quod
> sapientissimus Salomon ait: Cum placuerint Domino viae
> hominis, etiam inimicos ejus convertet ad pacem (Prov. 16: 7).

Furthermore, he is favored by an apparition of the Virgin who
appears while the monks are chanting the *Gloria Patri.* As they
bow in adoration, she too, " vere humilis ancilla Domini inclinis
permansit." She comforts him with the promise that his adver-
sary will be overcome by his patience and at his request identifies
herself as " Maria Mater Dei." He expresses his astonishment at
her humble inclination:

> Si ergo tu es illa, per quam salus humano generi venit, quam
> reveretur et laudat universitas creaturae; cur, quaeso et tu
> tanquam una de caeteris, ipsis etiam potestatibus angelicis
> honorandum caput tuum inclinas? [258]

Mary replies:

> Scire debes quia quotiescunque gloria sanctae Trinitati cum
> metu et reverentia exhibetur in terris, toties omnes virtutes
> caelorum commoventur, et ad laudem sui Creatoris excitantur.

After she vanishes, a spirit of peace and charity fills the hearts of
all and Conrad concludes:

---

[257] The text reads: " quatinus divina gratia . . . se in charitate confirma-
ret." *Ibid.*, v, 15 (col. 1161).

[258] *Ibid.* (col. 1163). Cf. Vincent of Beauvais, *op. cit.*, vii, 109; for
other versions, cf. *infra*, p. 82.

Oremus ergo Dominum, fratres, ut *per sancti Spiritus sui
dulcedinem*, exstinguat in nobis discordiae amaritudinem, . . .
quatenus omnes unanimes idipsum in invicem sentientes, tanquam *filii Dei*, cum simus filii pacis, habitemus in domo
Domini omnibus diebus vitae nostrae.[259]

Helinand of Froidmont

Helinand, a monk in the Abbey of Froidmont, enters several
miracles, not of local character,[260] in his Chronicle which he wrote
between 1211 and 1223.[261] His legends of the vision of Saint
Dunstan [262] and the monks at fieldwork [263] differ but slightly from
the accounts as they have already been considered. One anecdote,
also related in the *Gesta Francorum*,[264] recounts the vision of a
priest who has been praying for the famine-stricken army of Cru-
saders. Accompanied by the Virgin Mary and Saint Peter, Christ
appears, " cruce super caput Domini resplendente." [265] When he
threatens to punish the Christians still more because of their sins
of fornication, " mater misericordiae, et beatus Petrus ceciderunt *ad
pedes ejus*, supplicantes, ne pro paucorum culpis cunctis irascere-
tur." Christ acquiesces to the petition of the two suppliants.

Under the year 1161 Helinand records the vision of Gunthelm,
who is dissuaded from making a pilgrimage to Jerusalem by a Cistercian monk who proposes that he " crucem religionis acciperet,
et ad coelestem Jerusalem properaret." [266] Tempted by the devil,
he decides to return to his former plan but that night an evil spirit
so harasses him that he is taken half-dead to the infirmary. There
Saint Benedict appears to him and orders that he follow him. He
does so in spirit and attempts to mount a series of steps despite the
efforts of demons to prevent him. At the top he sees a tiny chapel

---

[259] *Ibid.* (col. 1164).   [260] Cf. *infra*, pp. 91, 110 and 116.

[261] For date see J. Neale Carman, *The Relationship of the Perlesvaus and
the Queste del Sainte Graal* in *Bulletin of the University of Kansas, Humanistic Studies*, V (1936), 12.

[262] *Chronicon*, xlvi, an. 966 (*PL*, CCXII, 905-906). Cf. *supra*, p. 47.

[263] *Ibid.*, xlix, an. 1184 (col. 1077). Cf. *supra*, pp. 55 and 57.

[264] Cf. *infra*, p. 94, n. 31.

[265] *Ibid.*, xlvii, an. 1098 (col. 991).

[266] *Ibid.*, 48 (col. 1060). See also Vincent of Beauvais, *op. cit.*, xxxix,
6-10; Mussafia, *Studien*, II, p. 50 (21).

suspended in mid-air and begins to marvel at its size. Thereupon Benedict says:

> Noli mirari forinsecam capellae angustiam; quia nescis, quam lata et ampla, quam alta et pretiosa sit intus. Mortalis homo non debet mirari opera Dei, *qui scit solus rationem operum suorum.*

Within is the "Mother of Mercy." At her desire, the novice enters and the following conversation takes place:

> "Vis morari in domo mea mecum, ad serviendum mihi, sicut promisisti?" Ait: "Etiam, domina."—"Ergo, inquit, jura mihi super illud altare, et vove, *quod mihi servies semper, et opera Domini facies et custodies.*"

The rest of the vision concerns his visitation of Paradise and Hell.

Helinand does not introduce Marial *exempla* in his sermons; he does, however, allude to the legends of Theophilus, Mary of Egypt, and Basil in the consideration of Mary's mercy toward sinners and her justice:

> At a mollitie gratiae dicta est Maria mulier, quae *prae omnibus mortalibus Deum timuit, pro Deo doluit, Deum dilexit:* ... Est enim mater misericordiae, et ideo cito mollitur lacrymis poenitentium, cito flectitur ad preces humilium, cito convertitur ad rogandum pro eis judicem filium ... Mollit enim peccatorem ut poeniteat, flectit judicem ut parcat, punit contumacem ut blasphemare desistet ... Malleus pietatis fuit, quando Aegyptiacam convertit, et Theophilum: malleus justitiae, quando contrivit Apostatam Julianum.[267]

In reference to her rôle of Mediatrix he uses a curious figure:

> Per collum quippe caput unitur corpori, et idem collum et tale pulchre Mariam significat, quae *post Christum* qui est caput ejusdem corporis, quod est Ecclesia, eminentissimum membrum est, et mediatrix nostra, per quam meruimus auctorem vitae suscipere: *per quam Christus factus est mediator Dei et hominum.*[268]

The title Mediatrix is a favorite one with Helinand.[269]

---

[267] *Sermo xx, In Assumptione B. Mariae* (*PL*, CCXII, 648).

[268] *Sermo xix, In Assumptione B. Mariae* (col. 640).

[269] *Ibid.* (col. 640); *Sermo* xx (col. 652); *Sermo* xxi (col. 652); *Sermo* xxii (col. 662); *ibid.* (col. 667). For the popularity of the title of Mediatrix among the Latin writers, see Salzer, *op. cit.*, pp. 580-81.

Conclusion

A comparison of the position of the Blessed Virgin in those legends which appear in Latin writings between the sixth and eleventh centuries with that which she occupies during the twelfth and thirteenth, reveals no essential difference in her status as a creature. Her position—*post Deum*—assigned to her once by the ninth century writer, Paul the Deacon, is conceded to her six times in one work of Guibert of Nogent, and again by Hrotsuitha, Lanfranc, Peter the Venerable, the Pseudo-Anselm, and Helinand. Honorius Augustodunensis goes further than his contemporaries who place her in the category of creatures (*benedicta inter creaturas*) by designating her with the expressive symbol " terra." If in the ninth-century version of Theophilus she declares herself willing to plead his cause, prostrate at the feet of Christ, in the thirteenth century *Exordium Magnum* she adores her Son before presenting her appeal for a sinful woman and in another legend bows in the deep respect of a creature at the words of the prayer, *Gloria Patri*.

Gregory the Great and Petrus Damiani consider even the simple wonders of nature to be miracles which have ceased to excite astonishment because of their frequency. It is obvious that Peter the Venerable has the same point of view when he gives utterance to the philosophy of the Middle Ages in the prologue of his work— that all happens by the permission and the will of God. Radbod relates miracles in order to praise God in His works; Peter the Venerable laments that there are so few who will make His works (i. e. miracles) known that He may be praised. The theocentric expression, *Deus facit mirabilia magna solus,* used by Paul the Deacon and Johannes Monachus, recurs in the work of Honorius Augustodunensis. *Domine, omnia tibi possibilia sunt* is the plea of the Virgin Mary as she stands, a suppliant, before Christ in a legend of the *Exordium Magnum*.

One may, therefore, conclude that the Mary legends prior to the twelfth century do not differ in theocentrism and Marial status from those which appear in the twelfth and thirteenth. While they as yet constitute a very small part in the mass of anecdotes of which Christ and the Saints are the subjects, the basic concept of Mary as Mediatrix which underlies them, is the same as in the more numerous legends of the twelfth and thirteenth centuries.

CHAPTER II

LATIN COLLECTIONS OF THE TWELFTH AND THIRTEENTH CENTURIES

The twelfth and thirteenth centuries are a period of richest development for the Marial legend. Of the many collections written at this time, one of the most important is the *Liber de miraculis Sanctae Dei Genitricis Mariae*, wrongly attributed to Potho or Botho of Priefling,[1] which Mussafia used as a starting point for his investigations. It contains a group of seventeen legends, designated HM (Hildefonsus-Murieldis), which goes back to the eleventh century, but is not now extant as a separate whole; it likewise includes two of the four legends in the second oldest collection of the same century, dealing with the four elements, and nine of the eighteen in the third oldest group, designated TS (Toledo-Saturday). Very early, also, is MS *Phillipps 25142*, if conjectures as to its date are correct—the first half of the twelfth century.[2]

The *Dialogus Miraculorum* of Caesarius of Heisterbach[3] was a very popular work, judging from the many copies and translations indicated in the inventory of Schönbach.[4] Finished in 1222, it is a dialogue between Caesarius and a novice whom he instructs by means of *exempla*. *Distinctio VII* is exclusively Marial, as is also the third book of Caesarius' *Libri VIII miraculorum*, which its editor, A. Meister, maintains was completed between 1225 and 1237.[5]

---

[1] Bernhard Pez who published this collection in 1731 ascribes it to Potho, an attribution which is rejected by Mussafia, *Studien*, I, p. 937; III, pp. 54-55. See also the documented article of J. A. Endres, "Boto von Prüfening und seine schriftstellerische Thätigkeit," *Neues Archiv*, XXX (1905), 605-646. The reprint of Pez by Thomas F. Crane has been used in this dissertation.

[2] *Miracula Sanctae Virginis Mariae*, ed. Elise Dexter, pp. 7-9.

[3] Ed. J. Strange (Cologne, 1851).

[4] "Studien zur Erzählungsliteratur des Mittelalters," *Sitzungsberichte der kais. Akad. der Wissenschaften in Wien* (phil.-hist. Cl.), CXLIV (1902), Abh. ix, 4 ff.

[5] *Libri VIII Miraculorum*, pp. xxxvi ff. See also Schönbach, *loc. cit.*,

The legends also appear as *exempla* in the sermons of an Augustinian, Jacques de Vitry (ca. 1180-1240). As a preacher of the crusade against the Albigensians, he became acquainted with the Dominican, Etienne de Bourbon (d. 1261), who frequently borrows from Jacques in his treatise, commonly known as the *Liber de septem donis*, and which was composed between 1250 and 1261.[6]

Three other Dominicans continue the Marial tradition. Vincent of Beauvais (d. 1264), according to his own indication, drew from an older collection, " ex Mariali magno," those miracles which he inserted in his *Speculum Historiale*.[7] The first redaction of this work, which forms a part of the encyclopedic *Speculum maius*, probably appeared in 1244, and the second in 1250. The legends are also included in the *Bonum universale de apibus* by Thomas of Cantimpré (d. 1280), who composed his moral treatise between the years 1270 and 1272.[8] Under the Feasts of the Blessed Virgin the more familiar miracles are related by Jacobus a Voragine (d. 1298), who compiled the *Legenda Aurea* in the interval from 1244 to 1264.[9] To these may be added a short collection attributed with question to Peter Celestine (d. 1296).[10]

Of the collections of *exempla* arranged in alphabetical order, two[11] will be considered in this study: the *Liber exemplorum ad*

pp. 45-46; A. Poncelet, " Note sur les Libri VIII Miraculorum de Césaire d'Heisterbach," *Anal. Boll.*, XXI (1902), pp. 46-47.

[6] Lecoy de la Marche, *Anecdotes historiques, légendes et apologues tirés du recueil inédit d'Etienne de Bourbon*, p. xx.

[7] About 1333 the *Speculum Historiale* was translated into French by Jean de Vignay at the request of Jeanne de Bourgogne. Guy E. Snavely, " Jehan de Vignay and His Influence on Early English Literature," *RR*, II (1911), 323-330.

[8] Cologne, ca. 1473. See also for date, E. Berger, *Thomas Cantipratensis Bonum universale de apibus quid illustrandis saeculi decimi tertii moribus conferat* (Paris, 1895), pp. 15-16.

[9] For date, see P. E. Baumgartner, " Eine Quellenstudie zur Franziskuslegende des Jakobus de Voragine," *Archivum franciscanum historicum*, II (1909), 17-31. The translation of Jean de Vignay appeared in 1334. Guy Snavely, *loc. cit.*, p. 327.

[10] *Opusculum VI, De Miraculis B. M. V.*, in the *Maxima Bibliotheca Veterum Patrum*, XXV (Lyons, 1677), 813-17. Cf. J. Celidonio, *La non-autenticità degle Opuscula Coelestina* (Sulmona, 1896).

[11] The *Alphabetum Narrationum*, once attributed to Etienne de Besançon

usum praedicantium, composed by a Friar Minor of Warwickshire between 1275 and 1279; [12] the *Speculum Laicorum*, possibly by John of Hoveden (d. 1272), but surely by a preacher of a mendicant order, writing within the period 1279 and 1292.[13] In addition, the miracles of the Virgin Mary contained in the thirteenth century MSS *Cornell B. 14*,[14] *Vendôme Cod. Lat. 185*,[15] *Copenhagen Thott 128*[16] and divers others of the British Museum [17] which have been published, will be treated. While these in no way exhaust the list of works given above, nevertheless, they form with them a representative number upon which one may reasonably base conclusions as to the status of the Blessed Virgin in the Latin *miracula* of the twelfth and thirteenth century collections.

Theocentrism of the Miracula

While it is to be supposed that the authors of the *Miracula Sanctae Virginis*, true to their theme, focus attention upon the Virgin, the problem of determining to what extent Mary " over-

(d. 1294), is now ascribed to Arnold of Liège. For authorship, see J. A. Herbert, *Catalogue of Romances* (London, 1910), III, 423 ff. Since it is of the fourteenth century it will not be treated here.

[12] It is published from MS *Durham V. W. 19* by A. G. Little. For date, cf. p. ix.

[13] Ed. J. T. Welter (Paris, 1914), pp. v-ix.

[14] T. F. Crane, " Miracles of the Virgin," *RR*, II (1911), 235-279.

[15] H. Isnard, " Recueil des miracles de la Vierge du XIIIᵉ siècle," *Bulletin de la Société archéologique scientifique et littéraire du Vendomois*, XXVI (1887), 23-63, 104-49, 182-227, 282-311. Excerpts ed. Charles Bouchet, *ibid.*, IX (1870), 187-99. Since the codex comes from the Abbey of Vaux-Cernay, the author was, no doubt, a Cistercian monk. Isnard dates the manuscript before 1230; however, Watenphul places it about 1250. *Die Geschichte der Marienlegende von Beatrix der Küsterin* (Göttingen, 1904), p. 38, n. 3.

[16] R. Becker, *Gonzalo de Berceos Milagros und ihre Grundlagen mit einem Anhange: Mitteilungen aus der Lat. Hs. Kopenhagen, Thott 128*, pp. 59-94.

[17] MSS *Cotton Cleopatra C. x.*, and *Arundel 346*, published in part by C. Neuhaus, *Die lateinischen Vorlagen zu den alt-französischen Adgar'schen Marienlegenden*; Oxford MS *Balliol 240*, in part by Kjellman, *Deuxième collection anglo-normande*. Thomas Wright published legends from various manuscripts, *A Selection of Latin Stories from Manuscripts of the Thirteenth and Fourteenth Centuries* (London, 1842).

shadowed the Trinity " [18] necessitates an investigation of the status
of the Divinity in the legends. The following prologue is found
in several of the earlier collections:

> Ad omnipotentis Dei laudem cum saepe recitantur miracula
> Sanctorum, quae *per eos egit divina potentia*, multo magis
> Sanctae Dei Genitricis Mariae debent referri praeconia, quae
> & sunt omni melle dulciora. Ergo ad roborandas in ejus
> amorem mentes fidelium, & exercitanda corda pigritantium,
> ea, quae fideliter narrari audivimus, *largiente Domino* recitare
> studeamus. [19]

The words " per eos egit divina potentia " are weighty in connotation. They ascribe to God the power by which the miracle is
performed and at the same time include the instrumentality of
the Saints. Moreover, these words introduce miracle collections
which are exclusively Marial. The prologue also states that the
miracula are related for a theocentric end—the praise of the
omnipotent God.

A close analysis of the Pez legend, concerning the Jew who
lends to a Christian, discloses as its central theme, a desire on the
part of the Christian to prove to the Jew the divinity of Christ
rather than to exalt the Virgin. In their conversation before the
bargain is made, the Jew frankly states his unbelief:

> Jesum, . . . Christum Dominum esse non credo, sed quia eum
> hominem justum & Prophetam fuisse non dubito, hunc si
> mihi pro vade dederis, indubitanter accipio. [20]

Standing before an image of the Mother of God, " Filium suum
in gremio tenenti," the Christian offers Christ, not as a just man
but as God in surety, [21] and confidently petitions Him to return
the money in case of mishap:

[18] H. Adams, *Mont-Saint-Michel and Chartres*, p. 90.

[19] Pez, p. 3. Among other collections considered in this study, the prologue is found in *Die lat. Vorlagen*, p. 29; Dexter, p. 15; R. Becker, p. 59.
Only those variants which are equivalent to passages quoted in wording or
in thought and which may be found in published works are cited in
footnotes.

[20] Pez, no. xxxiii, p. 42; Becker, no. 27, p. 85.

[21] Rigord writes that the Jews were wont to receive objects of cult as a
forfeit for non-payment of debts: ". . . vasa ecclesiastica Deo dicta,

Domine Jesu Christe, quem pro pecunia ista vadem dedi, pro me quoque huic Judaeo fide jussorem tradidi, te suppliciter exoro, ut, si casu praepeditus fuero, & pecuniam istam die statuto reddere huic ipso nequivero, tibique illam tradidero, *tu eam pro me redde,* quomodo, vel quo ordine placuerit.

As a successful merchant in Alexandria, the Christian is so immersed in business affairs that he becomes aware of the date too late to make his payment by natural means. In his dilemma he places the money in a casket and commits it to the waves in the care of Him, "qui mare et aridam fecit." [22] The author adds: "Mirum dictu, sed *Domino* nihil difficile." [23]

The Jew alone is able to secure it from the sea but refuses to acknowledge its receipt after the Christian returns. Before the image "nostri Salvatoris," the latter adjures Christ as the Son of God and man to bear witness to the truth:

Domine Jesu Christe, servum tuum exaudi, & sicut *Dei, & hominis verus es Filius,* testimonium exhibe veritati, utrum huic Judaeo reddiderim, quidquid mihi praestitit.

The image speaks and the Jew with his household accepts Christianity.

In the version by Caesarius of Heisterbach and in Oxford **MS** *Balliol 240,* Abraham the Jew is willing to accept the Virgin as surety " quia sciebat sanctam Mariam *post deum* esse primam spem christianorum." [24] When the Jew denies having received the

---

scilicet cruces aureas et argenteas, habentes imaginem crucifixi domini Jesu Christi, et calices, que pro instanti necessitate ecclesiarum, nomine vadii, fuerant eis supposita in vituperium et opprobrium christiane religionis tam viliter tractabant . . ." *Gesta Philippi Augusti,* ed. H. F. Delaborde (Paris, 1885), I, § 13, 25; *ibid.,* § 14, 27.

[22] Pez, p. 43; Becker, no. 27, p. 85. Crane's summary of this legend in his notes to Pez (p. 93) is misleading. As he indicates, it is taken from Ward, *Catalogue of Romances,* II, 638 (10). The Pez legend, unlike the version in MS *Royal 6 B. xiv,* described by Ward, does not state that the Virgin alone is given as surety nor that a prayer is said to her as the casket is committed to the waves.

[23] Pez, p. 43; Becker, p. 86. See also Vincent of Beauvais, *op. cit.,* vii, 82: "Mari et *ei qui mare fecit* gubernandam commisit. Mirum dictu: sed nihil deo impossibile factu."

[24] *Libri VIII Mirac.,* iii, no. 70, p. 194; Kjellman, *op. cit.,* p. 204.

money, " *qui* olim sub Balaam *asinam fecit loqui,* tunc *dedit* ser-
monem imagini." The Jews present recognize the divine manifestation and are converted. Caesarius' conclusion is theocentric:
" Unde in multis modis divinis laudibus benedicitur *deus, qui
facit mirabilia solus.*"

Caesarius elsewhere refers to the miracle of Balaam's ass. When
a mother's child is carried off by wolves, she seizes the image of
the Savior from a statue of the Virgin, and declares that it will
not be returned until she recovers her daughter:

> Mira humilitas reginae coeli. Quasi timeret carere filio suo,
> si mulier non rehaberet filiam suam, lupo protinus imperavit,
> et ille puellam dimisit.[25]

In the dialogue which follows, Apollonius the novice says that he
is more astonished at this than at Balaam's ass which had life in
it, while there is no breath of life in wood, or stone, or metal.
To this the monk replies:

> *Divinus spiritus* in omni creatura per essentiam, et per poten-
> tiam, cui nihil impossibile est, nihil miraculosum, *qui* ad
> honorem sanctorum suorum *haec et* his *similia* quotidie
> *operatur.*[26]

Parallels between the miracles of God performed in the Old
Testament and the manifestations of divine power in favor of
Mary's clients are frequently made. Thus, when the monks seek
the body of the drowned sacristan, they find it incorrupt after
nineteen days with the water arching over like a vault:

> Siquidem *virtus illa divina,* quae aquas rubri maris divisas
> quasi murum circa Israeliticum populum stare fecerat, hujus
> quoque virtutis aquas in specie fornacis arcuatas supra corpus
> miro modo suspenderat.[27]

The style of Jacobus a Voragine is too concise to permit such
digressions; however, in treating of the Assumption of the Virgin
Mary, he waxes eloquent in rhetorical questions:

> Si elegit *divina voluntas* inter ignium flammas puerorum ves-
> timenta servare illaesa, cur abnuat in matre propria, quod

---

[25] *Dial. Mirac.,* vii, 45, p. 63.   [26] *Ibid.,* p. 64.
[27] Pez, no. xl, p. 73. For similar parallels, see *ibid.,* p. 26; *ibid.,* p. 29.

elegit in veste aliena? Jonam servare in ventre ceti incorruptum *voluit sola misericordia*, Mariam incorruptam non servabit gratia? Servatus est Daniel in desperatissima fame leonum, non servanda est Maria tantis donata etiam meritis dignitatum?[28]

An express attribution of a prodigy to God is to be found in his version of the "Ave Maria Lily." A soldier, rich and noble, renounces the world and becomes a Cistercian. The *Ave Maria* is the only prayer he can master. After his death there comes from his grave a lily with the words *Ave Maria* in letters of gold on each petal: "Intellexerunt ergo, quanta devotione illa duo verba dixerat, quem *dominus* tanti honore prodigii illustravit."[29] This conclusion is not given by Thomas of Cantimpré who prefers to rhapsodize on the beauty of the words "benedictus fructus ventris tui."[30] Caesarius also relates a variant in which a Polish convert, unable to conform to the custom of the people who, upon entering the church, recite the *Miserere mei Deus* or the *Pater noster*, easily masters the *Ave Maria*. Later these words are found upon the leaves of a tree which has its roots in the heart of the man. Caesarius concludes:

> Pius *dominus* tam dulci miraculo *ostendere dignatus est,* quantum ei placeat in servis suis et ancillis memoria dilectae matris. Quid enim dixerim eandem arbusculam nisi salutationem angelicam? Quid radicem cordi infixam nisi matris eius memoriam? Puto de fructu benedicto figurare arboris, id est de filio virginis. . . . Ecce fratres, quod olim per Isaiam (Is. 11:1) de Yesse mistice prophetatum est, in isto quodammodo ad litteram completum est.[31]

Vincent of Beauvais frequently gives direct expression to the part which God has in the performance of the miracle or in the answer to a prayer. He tells of the seamstress at Noyon who dishonored the Feast of the Annunciation. She suffers great pain

[28] *Legenda Aurea*, p. 527.

[29] *Ibid.*, p. 221. This version is literally the same in the MS *Cornell B. 14*: "Intellexerunt ergo cum quanta devotione illa duo verba dixerit quem dominus tanti horis (honore) prodigii illustravit." Crane, *RR*, II, no. xxv, 269. For variants, cf. *ibid.*, p. 270.

[30] *Op. cit.*, ii, 29, no pagination.

[31] *Lib. VIII Mirac.*, iii, no. 3, p. 130.

when the thread sticks to her lips and tongue but is finally cured in the cathedral dedicated to the Mother of God through the " gratia divina." [32] When the Chaste Empress, after many tribulations, is marooned upon a rock, sailors " *a deo* missi " [33] rescue her. When her identity is discovered by the emperor, he looks upon her as " *a deo* resuscitatam." In another legend a knight buys a girl from her parents for his evil purposes, but upon hearing that her name is Mary and that she wishes to vow her chastity to Christ, " spiritus domini descendit in mentem militis " [34] and he spares her virginity. An evil spirit enters the service of a rich man and wins his confidence. He then attempts to drown his master by capsizing his boat, but " *dei protegente gratia* conatus eius ad nihilum redactus est." [35] Nor is he successful in a hunting expedition: " *Dei repulsus auxilio* in nullo prevaluit ei nocere." The devil is finally forced to admit his evil intentions to a saintly Bishop who finds that the rich man received this grace because of a daily prayer, *O intemerata*.[36] In another account a certain Jocius was wont to say five psalms whose initial letters formed the word *Maria*. At his death five roses are found growing out of his face, one from his mouth having on it the word *Maria*. Among those who viewed this phenomenon were three Bishops " quorum unus fuit Attrebatensis episcopus qui prius fuerat abbas Cisterciensis et multi alii clerici et laici qui viderunt *magnalia dei*." [37]

[32] *Op. cit.*, vii, 89.   [33] *Ibid.*, 92.

[34] *Ibid.*, 102. See the variant of Caesarius of Heisterbach where the young man dies and is secretly buried: " Sed *dominus noluit* hoc *occultari*, quod precibus suae matris preciosae *operabatur* in illo." The body is honorably interred. *Lib. VIII Mirac.*, iii, no. 41, p. 170.

[35] *Spec. Hist.*, vii, 101.

[36] The *O intemcrata* was a very popular prayer in the Middle Ages. Dom Wilmart presents conclusive proof that the prayer appeared toward the end of the twelfth century as it may be found in four manuscripts of that period and therefore, its attribution to St. Anselm (*Oratio* liii, *PL* CLVIII, 959) is false. See *Auteurs spirituels et textes dévots du moyen âge*, pp. 481 ff. For its appearance in the *Livre d'heures*, see V. Leroquais, *Livres d'heures manuscrits de la Bibliothèque nationale* (Paris, 1927), I, xxv; II, 434 ff.; Paul Lacombe, *Livres d'heures imprimés au XVe et au XVIe siècle conservés dans les bibliothèques publiques de Paris* (Paris, 1907), p. xx.

[37] *Spec., Hist.*, vii, 116.

Finally Vincent of Beauvais gives unmistakable expression to his theocentric attitude in the legend of Theophilus. After the latter's reconciliation he is permitted by the Bishop to receive Holy Communion. His face becomes resplendent and the worshippers seeing the transformation " magis glorificabant *deum qui facit mirabilia solus.*" [38]

From such expressions of Vincent and other writers one may conclude that the medieval concept of a miracle does not exclude God as the source of power. In the Marial collections miracles are invariably performed at the prayer of the Virgin Mary who intercedes for a client. Therefore, she is given the title of Mediatrix in this study.

Mary as Mediatrix

The rôle of Mary as Mediatrix in the Marial legends assumes three aspects which are in themselves theocentric: God performs the miracle because of her importunities or in her honor; the divine power uses her as an instrument or agent; [39] Mary is a suppliant, dependent upon the good will of God for those favors which she petitions for her clients.

The author of MS *Cotton Cleopatra C. x.*, asserts that Christ will perform miracles if for no other reason than His sonship and love for souls:

> *Faciet* nobis pro eius amore *filius ejus* dominus noster Jesus Christus. qui sicut multi dicunt *pro nulla alia causa est ipse filius eius et illa mater eius.* nisi ut misericordiam faciant miseris et peccatoribus.[40]

That God should honor His Mother by manifesting His power in

---

[38] *Ibid.*, xxi, 70. The same words are found in MS *Copenhagen Thott 128*; cf. Becker, no. 28, p. 94. See also *Die lat. Vorlagen*, p. 20.

[39] There still remains the sovereign causality of God. Upon this point of theocentrism A. Michel writes: " La possibilité du miracle implique . . . l'intervention de la causalité souveraine de Dieu. La réalisation des faits miraculeux montre que l'intervention de la causalité suprême, n'est pas exclusive de la collaboration des créatures. . . . Dieu peut agir seul; en fait, il se sert fréquemment d'instruments choisis parmi les créatures. Il faut examiner le cas des anges, de l'humanité de Jésus-Christ, des hommes, des créatures corporelles." *Dict. de Théologie catholique*, X, 2, 1833.

[40] *Die lat. Vorlagen*, p. 55. See also Dexter, no. xxvii, p. 43.

a miraculous way in behalf of her servants is a frequent theme in the legends of Caesarius of Heisterbach. A Polish duchess is stricken with leprosy:

> Christus, qui multum est misericors, *ostendere volens, quantum matrem, de qua carnem assumpserat, diligeret,* leprosam ducissam quadam nocte in somnis his verbis allocutus est dicens: Si oratorium beatae virginis Mariae aedificaveris et sancto apostolo Bartholomeo, a lepra tua mundaberis.[41]

The oratory is built, the cure is immediate, and the glory of the miracle redounds to God:

> Et ecce! mirum in modum, mox ut deus ibidem laudari coepit, laudantis virtus infirmam sanavit, et factum est gaudium magnum in terra illa, *omnibus deum glorificantibus, qui tanta eis ostendere dignatus est mirabilia.*

To save her virginity, a girl leaps from a church tower in Hildesheim:

> *Christus* vero, qui est amator castitatis, tam *propter honorem matris suae,* in cuius honore ecclesia illa dedicata fuerat, quam propter zelum virginitatis servandae *angelum suum misit,* qui virginem sine omni laesione per aera ad terras destinavit.[42]

In another anecdote of Caesarius God grants the grace of repentance to a youth who would not deny His Mother: ". . . propter honorem matris, quam non negaverat." [43] In the story of Walter of Birbech, the knight resolves to lead a saintly life, when he discovers that the Blessed Virgin has upheld his honor in a tournament. His death is followed by miracles: " Ut autem *ostenderet Dominus* quanti apud ipsum esset meriti matris suae dilectus, signis post mortem illum glorificavit." [44]

In MS *Phillipps 25142* it is related that a Jew insults an image of Mary " ob Christi ex Maria nati dehonorationem." [45] A Christian " qui habuit zelum dei " discovers the picture and restores it to a place of honor. A miraculous oil is exuded: " *Hoc* ideo *omnipotens deus ostendit,* ut nobis intimaret, cuius uenerationis

---

[41] *Lib. VIII Mirac.,* iii, no. 6, p. 134.
[42] *Ibid.,* no. 7, p. 135.
[43] *Dial. Mirac.,* ii, 12, p. 80.   [44] *Ibid.,* vii, 37, p. 56.
[45] Dexter, no. xxx, p. 45. Cf. *supra,* p. 7.

6

digna sit gloriosa Christi." The same account in Oxford MS
Balliol 240 concludes by attributing the miracle directly to God:
" Per omnia benedictus *Deus, qui facit mirabilia.*" [46]

God works a similar miracle to honor Mary in the legend of
Sardenay.[47] According to MS *Cornell B. 14,* a pious woman
founds an oratory near Damascus where she offers hospitality to
the poor and to pilgrims in honor of the Virgin. A monk who
has promised to bring her a picture of the Mother of God from
Jerusalem is reminded of it by a voice from Heaven. When
neither a lion nor robbers can harm him on his journey, he decides
that the image has divine virtue,[48] and he will retain it for himself. During a storm at sea an angelic voice commands him to
hold the image up to Heaven.[49] This he does and the storm
ceases. Arrived at the oratory, he continues to oppose the will of
God (" dei voluntatem "), until it becomes quite impossible for
him to quit the place without leaving the picture. It emits a
liquor which has curative qualities, but the cures, according to
this version, are attributed to the power of God:

> Cum autem predicta ycona in magna reverentia haberetur a
> populo cepit liquorem quemdam emittere et sudare, quem cum
> sindone munda predicta domina colligebat et infirmantibus
> ministrabat, quos *dei virtute sanabat.*[50]

---

[46] Kjellman, *Deuxième collection anglo-normande,* p. 229.

[47] For the historical element, see G. Raynaud, " Le miracle de Sardenai,"
Romania, XI (1882), 517-37; *ibid.,* XIV (1885), 82-93.

[48] The passage reads: " Tunc regressus Ierosolimam emit yconam, cum
qua civitatem egressus ferocissimo obviavit leoni a quo *per misericordiam
dei* nil mali passus, inde procedens incidit in latrones, a quibus *dei virtute*
nec se movere nec loqui valentibus illesus evasit." Crane, *RR,* II, no. xxi,
264. Matthew Paris uses similar theocentric expressions in his *Chronica
majora,* ed. Henry R. Luard (London, 1874: " Rolls Series, no. LVII "),
II, 485-86.

[49] For the words " ad celum " Matthew Paris substitutes " ad Deum."
Ibid., p. 486.

[50] Matthew Paris writes that the monk remained at the oratory " propter
virtutes *quas Deum fecisse* cognoverat per imaginem Suae sanctae Gene-
tricis. Coepit iconia deinceps valde ab omnibus venerari, et coeperunt
omnes in ea *Dei magnalia* admirari." *Ibid.* He adds that a soldier, hearing of the image " pro qua *Deus* tanta *operabatur miracula,*" came to
Damascus and was cured. *Ibid.,* p. 487.

The second aspect of Marial mediation—God uses the Blessed Virgin as an instrument or agent—is apparent in the words of the prologue in Oxford MS *Balliol 240* in reference to the "multe ac maxime *virtutes, quas per* beatissimam *Mariam* misericorditer *ostendit Omnipotens.*"[51] The author of the *Liber exemplorum ad usum praedicantium* very definitely makes her the agent through whom God deigns to operate the miracle:

> Invenimus in quodam libello scripta quedam miracula gloriose Dei genetricis Marie, quedam dico, quia multi libri de miraculis scribendi essent si omnia scriberentur, quia *per eam Christus Deus* noster benedictus fructus ventris illius in hoc mundo *operari dignatus est.*[52]

It is to be noted that his statement is very comprehensive, inasmuch as he assigns this rôle to her in the "multi libri de miraculis" which were written.

In the legend of John of Damascus as told by Vincent of Beauvais it is evident that Mary acts by the power of God. Because of a letter forged in the handwriting of the saint, the emperor has ordered that his hand be cut off. While John is lamenting before the image of the Virgin that he can no longer write hymns in her honor nor offer "*deo patri* sacratissimum corpus & sanguinem filii tui multociens in honore tuo ad omnium peccatorum salutem,"[53] she appears and addresses him with motherly words:

> Quid agis, inquit, puer meus fidelissime? . . . Confortare fili *in domino*: manum tuam tibi *restaurare potest qui totum hominem plasmauit ex nihilo.*[54]

With deft fingers she restores the hand. In thanksgiving a high Mass is sung and the monks unite with John "ad *magnalia dei* glorificandum."

Etienne de Bourbon relates an anecdote which he maintains occurred during the schism when Anacletus (Petrus Leonis 1130-

---

[51] Kjellman, *op. cit.*, p. 4. [52] Little, *op. cit.*, p. 23.

[53] *Spec. Hist.*, xvii, 105.

[54] *Ibid.* MS *Cornell B. 14* reads: "Quid agis, fili, Iohannes? . . . Fili mi, citius tibi manum *restaurare poterit qui totum corpus fecit ex nichilo.*" Crane, *RR*, II, no. xxiii, 267.

1138) presumed to claim the papal throne. Anacletus has just
taken his seat when a beautiful woman accompanied by an old
man, carrying a pastoral staff, enters. Striking him with the
staff, she says:

> Cur sedere presumpsisti in sede quam filius meus concessit
> Petro apostolo et successoribus electis canonice? [55]

Anacletus dies and Etienne adds: " Et sic pater quod preces
servorum suorum *exaudit Deus per eam.*"

A distinction between Mary the agent of God's will and the
" virtus Dei " by which her action is possible, is made in the
legend of " Childbirth in the Sea." A woman on a pilgrimage to
Mont-Saint-Michel is overtaken by the tide. In her plight the
author sees the will of God to glorify Himself and to honor His
Mother:

> Quod forte non casu, sed magis *divina* gestum constat *volun-*
> *tate*, quatenus ex hoc *Christi bonitas*, maxime etiam Genitricis
> ejus misericordia omnibus claresceret. Igitur absente humano
> auxilio recurrit *ad divinum.*[56]

As the other pilgrims look upon the scene, imploring the " adjutorium Christi," the Virgin appears and while she keeps off the
waves with her sleeve, the woman gives birth to a child. Despite
the active part which Mary takes in the miracle, the writer theocentrically attributes it to God: " O mira *virtus Dei!*" Similarly,
in the siege of Chartres the Virgin's garment is displayed as a
banner, but it is by the divine power that the army of Rollo is
stricken with blindness: " Nec defuit virtus divina." [57]

The power of God is not obscured nor excluded in those legends
in which Mary obtains a favor by her supplications. When the
noblewoman of Glastonbury is miraculously supplied with mead
in order to entertain King Athelstan, the author of Oxford MS
Balliol 240 concludes his account with the words: " Hoc, *precibus*
sanctae Marie, *Omnipotens* ad laudem nominis sui *fecit*, qui cuncta
gubernat secula." [58] During the twelfth century plague, known as

---

[55] *Op. cit.*, no. 138, p. 119.
[56] Pez, no. xxii, pp. 25-26; Becker, no. 20, p. 74; *Die lat. Vorlagen*, p. 22.
[57] *Die lat. Vorlagen*, p. 26.
[58] Kjellman, *op. cit.*, p. 224.

the *Mal des ardents*,[59] the populace turns to Mary " per cujus misericordissima, & gloriosa patrocinia *Filius suus, Dominus noster Jesus Christus*, infirmorum languoribus *praestat remedia*." [60] The words are literally the same in MS *Phillipps 25142*.[61]

In the story of Châteauroux as narrated by Etienne de Bourbon, the Coterelli, sent by Richard, enter the city of Déols, destroying and burning all things before them. The villagers flee to the church and before a stone image of the Virgin and Child, " orabant [Deum] ut eos beate Marie *precibus* liberaret." [62] One of the soldiers, blaspheming, throws a stone and breaks the arm of the Infant, whereupon the statue bleeds.[63] The miscreant falls dead and his companion dies the next day. Etienne de Bourbon bases his account upon Rigord, placing the event in 1187.[64] Both Vincent of Beauvais and Etienne refer to the miracles and cures wrought by virtue of the blood from the arm of the Christ Child but the latter does not mention that the figure of Mary rent its clothes " propter ignominiam et iniuriam quae illata fuerat sibi et paruulo suo." [65]

Vincent of Beauvais in one legend presents the Virgin as a gracious messenger, announcing that God has heard the prayer of

[59] Cf. *infra*, pp. 99-100.

[60] Pez, no. xviii, p. 21; *Die lat. Vorlagen*, p. 53.

[61] Dexter, no. xxv, p. 40.

[62] *Op. cit.*, no. 130, p. 111.

[63] Vincent of Beauvais says that he saw the blood and mutilated statue: " Ego qui scripsi sanguinem illud vidi oculis meis et imaginem nudatam ac vestimentum reuulsum." *Spec. Hist.*, vii, 110.

[64] Rigord adds that the other Cotarelli who witnessed the scene praised God " qui nullum scelus impunitum relinquit," and the monks, seeing the miracles " *Domino* operante," removed the image to a place of honor, " ubi ad honorem Domini nostri Jesu Christi et beate virginis Marie multa fiunt miracula usque ad hodiernum diem." *Gesta Philippi Augusti*, I, §52, 79-80. Other chroniclers who relate this event are: Gervase of Canterbury, *Opera historica*, ed. William Stubbs (London, 1879: " Rolls Series, no. LXXIII "), I, 370; Gerald of Barry, *Giraldi Cambrensis opera*, edd. J. S. Brewer, Dimock, and Warner (London, 1861: " Rolls Series, no. XXI "), II, xxxii, 104-105.

[65] *Spec. Hist.*, vii, 110. Concerning this incident Gervase of Canterbury writes: " Ipsa vero imago Mariae, *ac si suo compateretur filio*, conjectis manibus ad humeros proprios vestimentum lapideum abrupit, et corpus proprium fere usque ad mamillas detexit." *Op. cit.*, I, 370.

a suppliant. A poor man severely injures his foot on a rock and in his pain calls upon the devil. Suddenly he is stricken with a loathesome disease. He becomes bed-ridden and from his window is forced to beg alms from passers-by. Despite his infirmity he is completely resigned, and endeavors "in doloribus suis *deo* gratias agere . . . humiliter *deo supplicare.*" [66] He is in prayer on Easter Sunday, imploring the "salvatoris clementiam," when a beautiful woman appears and says: "Noveris preces tuas esse *exauditas a domino.*" She then commands him to go before her image in the church dedicated to her honor and there he will experience the "virtutem *diuini . . . auxili.*" With alacrity he obeys and is cured by the "*dei auxilio* et eius matris pie *suffragio.*" Two words, *auxilium* and *suffragium*, mark the difference between the divine assistance which effects the miracle and the intercessory power of the Blessed Virgin which is secondary.

The implications are the same in the legend of the "Son Restored to Life." The wife of a French knight has long prayed to the Virgin for a child:

> Obtine *precibus* tuis *apud Filium tuum Jesum Christum Dominum nostrum,* qui nihil negans tibi, te semper honorat, quatenus munus foecunditatis mihi sterili sua gratia *largiatur, qui* olim annosam & sterilem *Saram* inopinato *germine foecundavit.*[67]

The woman's prayer is answered; however, the child suddenly dies of a fever and the grief-stricken mother has recourse to Mary:

> Ad te iterum confugio, rursus ante oculos tuos lacrymas fundo, iterumque pietatis tuae januam importunis, & necessariis precibus pulso meum solum *post Dominum* refugium.

The cold, rigid limbs of the infant become warm with life and the fame of the miracle is spread abroad: "Mirantur omnes, & gaudent, *auctorem vitae* praedicant."

Mary's zeal for the early Church is the subject of the legend "Lydda," [68] which is particularly interesting since it shows the

---

[66] *Op. cit.,* vii, 98.

[67] Pez, no. xxiv, p. 29; Becker, no. 22, p. 27.

[68] Pez, no. xx, p. 23, has *Lidda.* In *Cotton Cleopatra, C. x.* it is *Libia, Die lat. Vorlagen,* p. 56. According to Ward, it is a mistake for *Lydda, op. cit.,* II, 611 (26). G. F. Warner indicates in the Introduction to the

medieval belief that Marial intercession was prevalent in Apostolic times. The Apostles bought a synagogue near Diospolis and converted it into a church dedicated to the honor of the Virgin Mary. The Jews, envious that " Dei templum fecissent, & Christum in ea praedicarent," [69] complain to the Emperor who commands that it be closed for forty days until " *Dominus ostenderet,* cujus esse deberet." The Apostles have recourse to Mary who was then living on Mount Sion:

> O tu Beata Virgo, *obsecra Christum Filium Dei,* quem tu benignissima Mater secundum carnem genuisti, ut secundum suam magnam misericordiam hanc domum, quam suo nomini, & in tuo honore dedicare curavimus, ad praedicandum verbum ipsius nobis *concedere dignetur.*

The above prayer, indicative of the belief in the Apostles' acceptance of Mary as an intercessor and Mediatrix,[70] received an answer which reads like an apocryphal sequel to the story of Pentecost in the *Acts of the Apostles* (I : 14) : " Ite, & nolite turbari, quia ego vobiscum sum in ipsa Ecclesia in adjutorium." At the end of forty days, the Jews are terror-stricken to see a picture of Mary on the wall; nor did they later dare to touch it, when Julian, the persecutor of the Church, ordered its removal.

It is needless to multiply examples where Mary's rôle is one of intercession, and therefore, secondary in relation to God. When she acts as the divine instrument, the dependence of her prodigious charity upon Him is quite obvious and leads to the glorification of the source of all gifts—God Himself. In the legend of " Sudden Death," the monks praise God through Whom the Blessed Virgin saved their brother from the clutches of the devil:

Miracles de Nostre-Dame of Jean Mielot, no. 27, p. xix, that the source is a legend related by John of Damascus in his *Epistola ad Theophilum Imperatorem* (*PG*, XCV, 350).

[69] Pez, *ibid.*

[70] The tradition that Mary was accepted by the Apostles as a Mediatrix is to be found in the legends of Jacobus a Voragine who portrays the Apostle John as consoling himself in view of Mary's approaching death with the words: "In te, celeberrima virgo quasi ipsum dominum et magistrum nostrum adspicientes consolabamur, hoc solum refrigerium habemus, quod *te mediatricem apud Deum* nos habere speramus." *Legenda Aurea,* cxiv, p. 519.

> Qui gaudentes nimium *laudant Dei filium,*
> *per quem* mater talia fecerat miracula.   (179-80)[71]

The words *per quem* indicate that she derives from God the power
to perform the miracle. The lines which follow prove that the
author's concept was theocentric:

> . . . serviamus virgini, que Dominum genuit,
> per quam *ipse Dominus* in nostris temporibus
> *fecit hec miracula* adhuc tam recentia.   (198-200)

In the legend of the "Devil in Beast-shapes" Mary herself explicitly declares that she would be utterly helpless to aid her
servants, were it not for Him to Whom she owes her being:

> Ad haec illa se Mariam matrem *Domini Salvatoris* nominat,
> *a quo* facta est, dum non erat, sicut & cuncta fuerant, *per
> quem* ipsa suos servos sic *adjuvare poterat.*[72]

As long as the medieval writer sees in her a creature possessed
of no power save such as God bestows upon her, there is no danger
of mariolatry.

Mary the Creature

In the legend of the "Devil in Beast-Shapes" as narrated in
Oxford MS *Balliol 240,* Mary presents herself both as Mother of
the King and as a creature: "Maria sum," ait, "regis regum
mater & filia, quae genui eum qui me fecit & omnia."[73] Jacobus
a Voragine speaks of her body "cum beatissima anima quam de
nihilo creavit Deus,"[74] and Caesarius of Heisterbach makes her
no less a creature. He relates that a young noble, having dissi-
pated all his wealth, is willing to make a compact with the devil
in order to regain it. He denies Christ but cannot be made to
deny the Virgin. The evil spirit mocks him: "Quare? . . .
Fecistis quod maius est, facite nunc quod minus est. Maior est
creator, quam *creatura.*"[75] The youth refuses and entering a
church, before an image of the Mother and Child, he begins to
lament his sin:

---

[71] *Studien,* V, p. 69.

[72] Pez, no. xxiii, p. 28; *Die lat. Vorlagen,* p. 62; Becker, no. 21, p. 76.

[73] Kjellman, no. xlii, p. 189.

[74] *Legenda Aurea,* clxxxix, p. 872.   [75] *Dial. Mirac.,* ii, 12, p. 80.

Tantam ei *Dominus* propter honorem matris, quam non negaverat, *contritionem donare dignatus est,* ut pro fletu rugiret,
et pro planctu nimiis clamoribus ecclesiam repleret.

A knight, who is now in possession of his property, by the " nutu
divino " also enters the church. He witnesses a strange scene.
The image speaks: " Dulcissime fili, miserere huic homini." The
Infant turns away His face. Again the Mother importunes her
Son Who turns His back and says: " Homo iste negavit me, quid
ei faciam?' Hereupon Mary rises, places the Child upon the altar
and prostrates herself: " . . . eiusque pedibus se prona prostravit."
At His feet she pleads:

> Rogo, fili ut propter me dimittas ei peccatum hoc. Mox infans
> matrem elevans, respondit illi: Mater, nunquam tibi aliquid
> negare potui, ecce propter te totum dimitto.

In the versions of Peter Celestine [76] and the author of MS *Vendôme*
185 [77] her method of persuasion is the same.

She assumes the attitude of suppliant in another legend of
Caesarius, who relates that while the sequence, " Ave praeclara,
audi nos," was being chanted,

> Imago beatae virginis Mariae accepto filio, quem habebat in
> gremio suo, ipsum deposuit in altari et ipsa *genibus flexis ad*
> *genicula sua convoluta* pro eiisdem oravit.[78]

While the nuns of the convent of Schönau are singing the same
sequence and come to the words "Audi nos, nam te filius nihil
negans honorat," Elizabeth sees " Dominam nostram *flexis genibus*
pro eodem conventu preces fundentem." [79]

Thomas of Cantimpré once depicts her " ad pedes filii," [80] while
Vincent of Beauvais describes her in adoration before the Host,
as the priest administers Communion to a poor widow: " *Toto*
corpore in terram prostrata adorauit eum cum suis virginibus." [81]

---

[76] *Op. cit.,* 19, p. 816.   [77] Isnard, *loc. cit.,* p. 288.

[78] *Libri VIII Mirac.,* iii, no. 46, p. 174.

[79] *Dial. Mirac.,* vii, 30, p. 39. Cf. Anton E. Schönbach, " Studien zur
Erzählungsliteratur des Mittelalters," *Sitzungsberichte der kais. Akad.*
der Wissenschaften in Wien (phil-hist. Cl.), CLIX (1908), Abh. iv, 6.

[80] *Op. cit.,* i, 1.

[81] *Op. cit.,* vii, 96; *Libri VIII Mirac.,* iii, no. 56, p. 181.

The version of this legend in MS *Vendôme 185* is identical.[82] In another anecdote of the Vendôme collection it is related that Mary prostrates herself before Christ the Judge to plead for the soul of an Abbot who has been devout to her but whose salvation is imperiled because of the excessive care he has taken of his health and bodily comfort.[83]

In the *Liber Exemplorum* an Italian monk, Bartholomew, has a vision in which the "Queen" becomes the humble suppliant. He beholds the "reginam misericordie coram Filio suo, *manibus extensis, genibus provolutam,* que sic provolvebatur suppliciter orans pro quodam peccatore per totam patriam famoso utique male fame." [84] Bartholomew immediately goes to the home of the notorious sinner and to his astonishment he scarcely broaches the subject of repentance, when the man interrupts him to say that he is willing to do all to save his soul and "Deo placare." The writer comments on the Virgin's gesture of petition:

> In hunc etiam ecce modum regina misericordie benignitatem suam in tantum monstrare dignatur, ut pro gratia impetranda, per quam iste salvaretur, *non solum simpliciter rogasset, immo etiam cum manibus extensis genua illa benedicta,* quibus Filium suum parvulum baiulabat, eidem Filio suo humiliter et dulciter flectere curaret.

Jacobus a Voragine twice presents Mary kneeling. A Dominican monk sees a vision of the "beatam virginem flexis genibus et junctis manibus " [85] pleading for the human race:

> Tunc filius victus precibus ait: ad votum tuum adhuc hanc cum iis misericordiam faciam, quod praedicatores meos iis mittam, qui eos moneant et informent, et si se non correxerint, amplius iis non parcam.

In the second vision, that of a Franciscan, Christ is about to hurl three lances at the world: " Cui velociter mater occurrens, quid nam vellet facere, inquisivit." [86] Again she throws herself at His feet and again the divine wrath is averted by the vision of the two Orders which are to combat pride, avarice, and lust.

---

[82] Isnard, *loc. cit.*, pp. 104-106.
[83] *Ibid.*, p. 56.
[84] Little, no. 45, p. 28.
[85] *Op. cit.*, 113, p. 469.
[86] *Ibid.*, p. 470.

Mary's dependence upon the will of God is indicative of her subordinate position. Moreover, she can do nothing unless it be in accordance with the divine wish. This is illustrated in one of the legends of Thomas of Cantimpré. A Cistercian long devoted to God yields to temptation but is immediately moved to deep sorrow for his sin. In tears he has recourse to the Blessed Virgin and as he prays, he sees the " gloriosam virginem et in brachiis eius quasi lactentem puerum paruulum super omnem pulchritudinem speciosum." [87] His supplications become more ardent, but the little Child turns away His face, whereupon the Mother transfers Him to the other arm and with a look of kindness pleads for the suppliant. Again He averts His face and again the Mother changes Him in her arms until He smiles and the sinner is assured of pardon. In this legend Mary is dependent upon the will of even the Child-Christ.

Caesarius of Heisterbach attempts to give an explanation for Christ's apparent unwillingness which later changes to consent. In the legend in which the youth denies Christ but not Mary,[88] the little Lord is obdurate, until the Virgin prostrates herself; then He forgives, and even arranges in a providential way for the return of the knight's property. Caesarius remarks that this delay is purposeful: " Ut iuveni ostenderet, quantum in se peccasset, et ut per dolorem cordis amplius in se peccatum ipsum puniret." [89]

Christ is never pictured in any attitude which is beneath the divine dignity. He remains the Redeemer and the Savior. Mary is reduced to the status of the suppliant. She appears as a mere intercessor in a legend of Caesarius of Heisterbach. Here the Virgin intercedes for a woman who has prayed for her husband's conversion for fifteen years. From Christ's answer to Mary's petition one may conclude that the woman's request will be granted only through the merits of His sufferings:

> Non aestimes pro magno, quod tibi et mihi mulier impedit; omnis enim et eius sollicitudo non possit minimo *dolori meo* respondere, *quem pro ea sustinui.* Et *vertens se ostendit se deorsum laceratum et quasi spinis cruciatum.*[90]

---

[87] *Op. cit.*, ii, 29.
[88] Cf. *supra*, pp. 78-79.   [89] *Dial. Mirac.*, ii, 12, p. 81.
[90] *Libri VIII Mirac.*, iii, no. 81, pp. 204-205.

Then Christ turns to Mary and utters the *fiat* by which the woman's petition is granted: " Fiat ei sicut vis, quare nihil tibi negare."

Moreover, the Blessed Virgin places herself in the relation of a creature to God by her profound inclination at the words of the prayer, *Gloria Patri*. A monk remains with head erect as his brothers sing this response in choir. Glancing up he sees Mary bowing her head in deep reverence. She introduces herself as the Mother of Him " ante quem contremiscunt daemones et cui omnia subduntur." [91] The monk expresses his astonishment that she, the Queen of Heaven, and " mater totius sanctitatis," should bend in respect. She replies:

> Non audisti scripturam dicentem, quanto maior est humiliatio in omnibus, et subiunxit hoc ei dicens: Cum me tantam reginam inclinare inspicis, cur tu fili inclinare dedignaris . . .

In the version of the " Persecuted Monk " [92] contained in MS *Vendôme 185*, the Virgin appears and " cum fratres ad gloriam inclinarent ipsa profunde inclinauit donec perdicerent *gloria patri & filio & spiritui sancto*." [93] In her answer to the monk's query concerning her inclination she places herself, as a creature, among those who thus praise their Creator:

> Scire debes quia quocienscunque gloria sancte trinitati cum metu & reuerentia exibetur in terris; tociens omnes uirtutes celorum commouentur, & *ad laudem sui creatoris* excitantur.

However much the writer of legends exalts Mary as the Mother of God, he attributes to her a becoming humility. The devil, in the guise of the Blessed Virgin, appears to a recluse in one legend and says to her:

> Ne paveas nec formides, ego sum mater Christi, propter te veni, ut videas me. Accede ergo dilecta mea et in signum amoris deosculare pedem meum. [94]

She immediately becomes suspicious:

---

[91] *Ibid.*, no. 55, p. 180.   [92] Cf. *supra*, p. 58.
[93] Isnard, *loc. cit.*, p. 112.   Cf. *ibid.*, p. 46.
[94] *Libri VIII Mirac.*, iii, no. 9, p. 137.

> Quid est hoc, quod loqueris, domina mea dulcissima? Tu vero, *cum sis humilima et mater humilitatis,* quomodo me invitas ad osculandum pedem tuum.

The recluse makes the sign of the Cross and the evil spirit vanishes.

The author of MS *Phillipps 25142* recalls Mary's self-imposed title—*ancilla Domini*:

> . . . *gloriaris pro ancilla* matre? Scio inquit, scio quia regina est, sed *humilitas sue mentis perhorret esse decus honoris.* Iccirco placet, iccirco benedicta est, super omnes mulieres.[95]

According to Jacobus a Voragine, she is able to appease the wrath of God because of her humility: " Talis ancilla dei fuit beata virgo, que deum contra genus humanum iratum *sua humilitate* placauit." [96]

She perfectly fulfills the rôle of Mediatrix as Mother of God and as creature—" Mediatrix Dei ad homines." [97] Jacobus a Voragine compares her to a ship in the midst of the sea, a symbol of the " mediatrix inter Deum et ipsos peccatores "; [98] to the dawn, " sicut aurora est medium inter diem et noctem "; [99] to the moon, " sicut luna lucet in nocte et est *vicina terre* et habet virtutem efficacem super mare." [100] He specifically places her in a plane below the Trinity and above other creatures in comparing her to the sun:

> Nam sicut sol habet tres planetas superiores et tres inferiores et ipse est in medio constitutus : sic et ipsa habet *supra se* tres in trinitate personas; et *sub se* tres status saluandorum, scilicet, virgines; continentes; et coniungatos et *ipsa est in medio* constituta *reconcilians* tres status supradictos saluandorum *ipsi beatissime trinitati.*[101]

In reference to Mary the expression *post Deum* or *post Dominum* is used in the legends with a frequency which almost renders it trite. In the Pez collection, she is " *post Dominum* omnium coeles-

---

[95] Dexter, no. xxxii, pp. 49-50.
[96] *Mariale, sermo vi* (Venice, 1497), p. 4.
[97] *Die lat. Vorlagen*, p. 18; Becker, no. 28, p. 92.
[98] Jacobus a Voragine, *Mariale*: *Sermones quadragesmales*, viii, p. 6.
[99] *Ibid.*   [100] *Ibid.*   [101] *Ibid.*

tium virtutum Domina," [102] and in respect to the power of healing the ills of soul or body, " Mater utique Sancti Sanctorum hac potentia *post Dominum* privilegio speciali prae omnibus sublimatur." [103]   The expression is also used in the legend of the Abbess, who has recourse to the mercy of the Virgin, " totius *creaturae* Dei potentissimae atque dignissimae Mariae." [104]   In her prayer she appeals to Mary as the " singulare *post Dominum* & unicum refugium miserorum."   When the Blessed Virgin appears, it is not to forgive her sin, but to announce to the religious that she has obtained pardon from her Son and may shield her from infamy :

> Audivi, ait, orationem tuam, vidi lacrymas, & *me a benignissimo Filio meo*, qui est poenitentiae susceptor, noveris peccati *veniam* tibi, & ab infamia & confusione, quam times, plenissimam *liberationem impetrasse*.

In the legend of the " Jew Lends to a Christian," as related by Caesarius of Heisterbach, the Jew is willing to accept Mary as surety " quia sciebat sanctam Mariam *post deum* esse primam spem christianorum." [105]   Vincent of Beauvais narrates that a Carthusian is troubled by devils in the form of swine, and is rescued by the Virgin " in quam ille spem suam totam *post Deum* posuerat." [106]   In MSS *Cornell B. 14* [107] and *Royal 6 B XIV*,[108] Stephen, in returning from a pilgrimage at Jerusalem, is threatened with shipwreck.   In this plight he prays: " O domina, O celi regina, O *post Deum* tota spes mea, . . ."   During the siege of Chartres, recounted in MS *Cornell B. 14*, the Bishop " fugit ad auxilium dei et gloriose matris eius " in whom " *post deum* totam spem suam posuerat." [109]   In the *incipit* of *Cotton Cleopatra C. x.* Mary is assigned the position of " *post filium suum* Dominum nostrum Jesum Christum." [110]   Again in the version of the drowned monk, she is appealed to as the " singulare *post deum*

[102] No. xxxiv, p. 45.

[103] Pez, no. xxxvi, p. 51.

[104] *Ibid.*, p. 53; Becker, no. 23, p. 79.

[105] *Libri VIII Mirac.*, iii, no. 70, p. 194.

[106] *Op. cit.*, vii, 112. Cf. *supra*, p. 52.

[107] Crane, *RR*, II, no. 1, 240.

[108] Mussafia, *Studien*, V, p. 25.

[109] Crane, *RR*, II, no. v, 244.

[110] *Die lat. Vorlagen*, p. 9.

refugium." [111] In this same manuscript [112] and in *Copenhagen Thott 128*,[113] Theophilus says: "Tu es *post deum* mea proteccio meumque patrocinium." Finally, in Oxford MS *Balliol 240* the Blessed Virgin is described as "sola . . . *post filium* pia, sola propicia." [114]

Mary is then secondary to God and a creature, but "vere gloriosior, et pulchior, et dignior . . . omnibus *creaturis.*" [115] According to several medieval writers, she realizes the highest ideal which the Creator might have of a creature, since they describe her as "Domina nostra Dei Genitrix semper Virgo Maria *ultra* omnem Angelicam & humanam naturam pia." [116]

The Attribute of Mercy

In consideration of the large part which Mary as Mediatrix takes in obtaining miraculous manifestations of God's power for the sinful or unfortunate, it might seem that the attribute of mercy, peculiar to God, is comparatively dimmed. However, the title *Mater misericordiae*, frequently used in the Marial legends, was considered a tribute to the divine mercy. Oxford MS *Balliol 240* concludes the miracle of Saint Bon by making the Son synonymous with mercy and Mary the Mother: " Quia revera mater est misericordiae, *filiusque* ejus *ipsa misericordia.*" [117] God is mercy, the writers of MSS *Phillipps 25142* and *Cotton Cleopatra C. x.* reason, and therefore Mary is the Mother of Mercy, existing in order that " *Christus* sit misericordia." [118] Both writers add: " Non debemus desperare ne nos adiuuet in necessitatibus nostris, quae *ipsam misericordiam* nostram *genuit.*" From the words which follow this passage, it is evident that the exercise of mercy on the part of the Mother is only possible because Christ has it within His power to do what is asked:

[111] *Ibid.*, p. 59; Neuhaus, *Die Quellen*, p. 22.

[112] *Die lat. Vorlagen*, p. 18.

[113] Becker, no. 28, p. 92.

[114] Kjellman, *op. cit.*, p. 189.

[115] Peter Celestine, *op. cit.*, 4, p. 813.

[116] Pez, no. xxii, p. 26; Becker, no. 20, p. 74; *Die lat. Vorlagen*, p. 22.

[117] Kjellman, *op. cit.*, no. xxxvi, p. 160.

[118] Dexter, no. xxvii, p. 43; *Die lat. Vorlagen*, p. 55.

> Si ex toto corde matrem misericordie diligimus, quod quicquid
> ab ea racionabiliter postulabimus, *faciet* nobis pro eius amore
> *filius eius dominus noster iesus Christus.*

A very popular legend is that of the monk whose ulcered mouth
and throat are healed by the milk of the Virgin Mary. The writer
marvels less at the wonder of the cure than at the condescension
and mercy of the " Mater Altissimi." [119]   His astonishment ceases
when he considers the abasement of the Son of God, His sufferings
and His love for sinners:

> Sed si ad memoriam deducimus, quomodo altissimus *Dei*
> Filius virgineum descendere dignatus est in uterum, & postea
> nasci, circumcidi, tentari, a Pharisaeorum insidiis persequi,
> ac demum pro peccatoribus crucifigi, deinde sepeliri, resurgere
> a mortuis, . . . omne discedit ambiguum, cum *pro peccatori-*
> *bus tanta fecisse recolimus Dominum.* . . . Quid ergo mirum
> si gloriosa Maria, Mater omnis pietatis & misericordiae per
> similitudinem lactis ex ubere suo, ita misericordiam devoto
> famulo impendit, cujus sacro lacte tenera ipsius *fontis miseri-*
> *cordiae, Jesu Christi* scilicet *Domini* nostri, nutritur infantia,
> *qui* etiam postea *dignatus est pro peccatoribus misericorditer*
> *crucis ferre supplicia?* [120]

However much the mercy of the Mother may be exalted in the
cure of a cancerous mouth and throat, the writer does not forget
that this attribute in God Himself, as displayed in the price paid
for man's salvation, is infinitely greater. He reiterates this idea
in the legend which follows—an anecdote taken from the Epistles
of Dionysius the Areopagite.[121]   While Carpus is praying, asking
God to punish certain heretics in the Church, Christ appears to
him, surrounded by a multitude of angels. Extending His hand
over the wretches who seem to lie in a deep cavern, and support-
ing them by the ministry of angels, He says:

> Carpe manu in istos misericorditer constituta & non per miseri-
> cordiam retracta, percute adversum me. Nam *paratus sum*
> *pro hominibus resalvandis iterum pati,* & complaceo super
> his magis, quam super aliis, qui non peccaverunt.[122]

---

[119] Pez, no. xxx, p. 37.   [120] *Ibid.* For Adgar, cf. *infra*, p. 147.
[121] *Epist.* viii (*PG*, III, 1097-1100).
[122] Pez, *ibid.*, p. 38. Little, *op. cit.*, no. 29, pp. 17-18.

The author ponders over these astounding words and questions rhetorically: what man can then doubt that the Mother of Mercy,

> misericordiam in similitudinem lactis praebere suis, cum *ipsa Misericordia, benignus* scilicet *Jesus Dominus noster* qui sedet ad dexteram Patris, qui mortem vicit, nec jam amplius mori posse probatur, *mori velle se asseret pro perfidis?*

In Oxford MS *Balliol 240* an explanation of the symbolism of the milk is offered:

> Credamus illud esse pietatis lac & misericordie, quibus pre omnibus sanctis novit affluere. Nec talia visa posse nisi per corporeas ymagines videri, nec nisi corporeis verbis enunciari, que *omnia fiunt per Jhesum Christum ad salutem animarum.*[123]

The words "omnia fiunt per Jhesum Christum" indicate the theocentrism of the legend and therefore, intrinsically, the miracle glorifies the power as well as the mercy of God.

In the version of "Incest between Mother and Son" as told by Vincent of Beauvais, the portrait of the mercy of Christ is as vivid as the compassion of the Virgin. In this legend a Roman matron strangles a child which she has born to her own son. She performs many acts of charity in expiation for her sins but does not confess until she is denounced to the Emperor by the devil, disguised as a clerk. The Pope,[124] seeing her tears of contrition, and "confisus de *dei misericordia*,"[125] recalls to her mind the mercy of Christ toward Peter, who was not only forgiven but attained the highest dignity; toward Mary Magdalen, who from a life of shame became a saint. "Maior est dei pietas" than her iniquity. The Pope counsels her to invoke the Virgin Mary and enjoins as a penance only the *Pater Noster*. When the woman approaches the tribunal, the devil is confounded, for he sees not the sinner but Mary. Those who attend the trial make the sign of the Cross and the evil spirit, "uirtutem signi saluatoris non sustinens," vanishes.

The hope which first stirs in the heart of Theophilus is a gift

---

[123] Kjellman, *op. cit.*, no. xxxix, p. 176.

[124] The Pope is here called "Lucianus, vel Lucius," probably intended for St. Lucius, Pope in 252-253. Cf. Ward, II, 627.

[125] *Spec. Hist.*, vii, 95.

7

of God's mercy. Vincent of Beauvais writes: "*Creator omnium & redemptor* qui non uult mortem peccatoris . . . qui non despexit creaturam suam sed dedit ei penitentiam." [126]   MSS *Harley 3020* [127] and *Copenhagen Thott 128* [128] add: "*Pius et misericors deus,* qui propriam non despicit creaturam, sed ad se suppliciter, sue recuperacionis spe eius animam recreavit." Theophilus does not ask the Virgin to pardon him, but to "impetrare . . . apud dominum nostrum ihesum christum." [129]   Mary, in Vincent's version, upon demanding a profession of faith, reminds him that God is merciful: "Confitere, homo, Christum, quem ego peperi & tu abnegasti: *misericors enim est* & suscipiat lacrimas penitencie tue." [130]   And to encourage him the more, she speaks the momentous words which explain the major rôle of the sinner in the Marial legend: "Ideo enim ex me carnem sumere dignatus est *ut peccatores saluaret.*" Mary fulfills her office of Mediatrix and in three days she appears to the repentant sinner with the message: "Homo dei ecce ad peticionem meam *suscepit deus lacrimas tuas.*"

In the story of the Abbess told in MS *Copenhagen Thott 128,* Mary is said to commend souls to the mercy of her Son: "Nescit ergo miseros deficere pietas sua, que nos omnes *misericordie dulcissimi filii sui commendet,* domini nostri Ihesu christi." [131]   In the conclusion to the legend of Mary of Egypt in Oxford MS *Balliol 240,* sinners are directed to the consideration of this attribute of God, although Mary is the Mother of Mercy:

> *Ille est ipsa misericordia,* illa est mater misericordie. *Consideret* ergo *omnis peccator Dei pietatem,* imiteturque proposse earum conversionem & penitenciam, quatinus in futuro mereatur intrare regnum celorum.[132]

Mary does not assume the rôle of Christ the Redeemer. In the legends only the Deity forgives sins. She frequently intervenes in the conversion of a sinner, "ne dilecti filii mei sanguis inutiliter

---

[126] *Ibid.,* xxi, 70.
[127] *Die lat. Vorlagen,* p. 15.
[128] Becker, no. 28, p. 89.
[129] *Ibid.,* p. 91.
[130] *Spec. Hist.,* xxi, 70. See also *Die lat. Vorlagen,* p. 17; Becker, p. 91.
[131] Becker, no. 23, p. 81.
[132] Kjellman, *op. cit.,* no. 12, p. 49.

sit effusus." [133] Works of mercy, according to Etienne de Bourbon, are an attraction to bring others to God.[134] Applying this to the Virgin, he writes:

> Maximum enim *attractivum* pietatis et per pietatis graciam *ad Deum, fontem pietatis,* est Maria, mater gracie, mater pietatis et misericordie.[135]

The author of the *Speculum Laicorum* gives a description of God's mercy which offers a striking contrast to the charitable offices rendered by the Virgin to humanity:

> *Deus* quadrupliciter nobis ostendit misericordiam 1 in honorificencia creacionis . . . 2 in magnificencia redempcionis . . . 3 in sollicitudine conservacionis . . . 4 in dulcedine post longam expectacionem nostre redempcionis.[136]

In comparison with the fourfold characterization of this attribute of God, the mercy of the Virgin shrinks to that of a finite creature. Furthermore, the writers of the *miracula* do not hesitate to show her dependence upon the divine will in obtaining answers to prayer for those who appeal for her intercession. Her pity would be of no avail, if God did not answer her requests. One may, therefore, conclude that this subordinate character of the mercy of Mary does not obscure nor dim the mercy of God.

---

[133] Thomas of Cantimpré, *op. cit.*, ii, 9.
[134] *Op. cit.*, p. 121.
[135] *Ibid.*, p. 93.   [136] Pp. 73-74.

CHAPTER III

THE LOCAL COLLECTIONS

The *Miracula ecclesiae Constantiensis* [1] is the earliest local collection. It was written at the order of Bishop Geoffrey of Montbrai (d. 1093) by the canon John who lived during his episcopate.[2] Consisting of thirty-two miracles, it forms a part of the *Livre Noir* in which was recorded the history of the bishops of Coutances, a diocese of great antiquity, dating from the year 430 with its first Bishop Ereptiolus.[3] The cathedral begun by Bishop Robert about 1030 was completed by Geoffrey in 1056.[4] Miracles wrought at the sanctuary of Notre-Dame in the south transept soon drew pilgrims in large numbers. At Geoffrey's request a relative of one of the dignitaries of the church had attempted to record the miraculous events but his pompous style proved displeasing and the work remained unfinished. John the canon, who was also an eye-witness of the many prodigies, took up the task, completing the collection between the years 1106 and 1135.[5]

The destruction of the church at Laon by fire in 1112 occasioned a tour of France by members of the chapter with a reliquary of the Blessed Virgin for the purpose of collecting funds. The miracles wrought during this journey are recorded by Herman of Tournai in the *Miracula S. Mariae Laudunensis*.[6] The second

---

[1] The collection has been published by E. A. Pigeon, *Histoire de la Cathédrale de Coutances* (Coutances, 1876), pp. 367-83.

[2] Léopold Delisle, "Notice sur un Traité inédit du douzième siècle intitulé: Miracula ecclesiae Constantiensis," *Bibl. de l'Ecole des Chartes*, IX (1848), 344.

[3] Pigeon, *op. cit.*, pp. 2 and 386.

[4] *Ibid.*, p. 46.   [5] *Ibid.*, p. 113, n. 1.

[6] *PL*, CLVI, 961-72. G. Waitz identifies Herman of Tournai with the monk of Laon. See "Hermann von Tournai und die Geschichtschreibung der Stadt," *Forschungen zur deutschen Geschichte*, XXI (1881), 431-48; W. Wattenbach, *Deutschlands Geschichtsquellen im Mittelalter bis zur Mitte des dreizehnten Jahrhunderts* (Berlin, 1907), I, 328; Manitius, *Geschichte der lateinischen Literatur*, III, 532. According to J. S. P. Tatlock, Herman of Laon was probably not the same as Herman of Tournai. "The English Journey of the Laon Canons," *Speculum*, VIII (1933), 454.

book of this collection is based upon the testimony of those who accompanied the shrine to England. According to Faral, the whole cannot be anterior to 1135.[7] Tatlock would place the date after 1145.[8] Guibert of Nogent,[9] Helinand of Froidmont,[10] and Vincent of Beauvais[11] have also treated the miracles of Laon.

To Hugo Farsit is due the *Miracula B. Mariae Virginis in urbe Suessionensi.*[12] A canon regular of Saint-Jean des Vignes at Soissons, he was an ocular witness of the miraculous cures obtained through the intercession of the Virgin during the years 1128 and 1132 when those stricken with the *mal des ardents* found relief. His collection was composed after 1143.[13]

The miracles performed during the construction of the church of Saint-Pierre-sur-Dive have been recorded by Abbot Haimo in a letter to the religious of Tutbury in England. The original was thought to be irretrievably lost when a copy made in 1671 by Dom Antoine Beaugendre was discovered by Léopold Delisle. The date of the original, according to Delisle, was 1145.[14]

It was also at this time that pilgrims were first seen drawing carts to Chartres;[15] however, it was not until 1210 that the miracles performed during this period of penitential labor and prayer were consigned to writing. Antoine Thomas edited the *Miracula B. Marie Virginis in Carnotensi ecclesia* from the Vatican MS *Reginenses 339.*[16] A vernacular rendition was made in the thirteenth century by Jean le Marchant.[17]

[7] *La légende arthurienne* (Paris, 1929), I, 229.

[8] *Loc. cit.,* p. 454.

[9] *De vita sua,* iii, 12 and 13 (*PL*, CLVI, 937-42).

[10] *Chronicon,* xlviii, an. 1113 (*PL*, CCXII, 1011-17).

[11] *Speculum Historiale,* xxvi, 12-18.

[12] *PL*, CLXXIX, 1778-1800. See also Vincent of Beauvais, *op. cit.,* xxvii, 2-4.

[13] This date is based upon the statement of Hugo in the third miracle: "Nam Mathildis abbatissa quae tunc ei loco praeerat, . . ." The abbess died December 13, 1143. *PL*, CLXXIX, 1779. See also *HLF*, XII, 294.

[14] "Lettre de l'Abbé Haimon sur la construction de l'Eglise de Saint-Pierre-sur-Dive, en 1145," *Bibl. de l'Ecole des Chartes*, XXI (1859), 115.

[15] Robert of Torigny writes: "Hoc eodem anno ceperunt homines prius apud carnotum carros . . . trahere." Cf. *Chronica* (*PL*, CLX, 461-62).

[16] "Miracles de Notre-Dame de Chartres," *Bibl. de l'Ecole des Chartes*, XLII (1881), 505-550. For treatment, cf. *infra*, pp. 186 ff.

[17] *Le livre des miracles de Notre-Dame de Chartres, écrit en vers, au*

The *Miracula Sancte Marie de Rupe Amatoris* is the largest collection, consisting of three books containing one hundred twenty-six miracles. The date 1172 has been assigned to it by Edmond Albe,[18] who edited the compilation from MSS *12593, 16565,* and *17491* of the Bibliothèque nationale.[19] The erroneous attribution to Hugo Farsit is no longer tenable;[20] nevertheless, from the stories it is ascertained that the author was a native of Rocamadour, a religious versed in the Scripture and the writings of antiquity, and one who scrupulously based his accounts upon the depositions of a notary.[21] The collection presents information of significance for the history of Quercy.

The *Miracula S. Mariae San-Deodatensis*[22] in metrical form was the work of a clerk attached to the Church of Notre-Dame de Saint-Dié, founded in the middle of the seventh century by the anchorite Saint-Dié or Dieudonné at the command of Christ Himself.[23] The collection consists of 352 verses and was completed in the year 1274.[24] The clerk relates only those miracles of which he was an eye-witness or concerning which he had received reliable testimony. The collection of Saint-Dié, together with those of Coutances, Laon, Soissons, Saint-Pierre-sur-Dive, and Rocamadour, forms the basis of the arguments presented in this chapter.

Optimism in the Local Collections

According to the eleventh century chronicler Radulphus Glaber, the world at the time of the millennium was steeped in wickedness:

> Anno post Dominum terris de Virgine natum
> Milleno, gravibus homines erroribus acti,

> .   .   .   .

XIIIe siècle, ed. Georges Gratet-Duplessis (Chartres, 1855). Cf. *infra*, pp. 186 ff.

[18] *Miracles de Notre-Dame de Roc-Amadour au XIIe siècle* (Paris, 1907), pp. 12 ff. See also *Spec. Hist.*, xxix, 4-5.

[19] *Ibid.*, pp. 6 ff.

[20] *Ibid.*, pp. 42 ff.

[21] *Ibid.*, pp. 44 ff. See Prologue II, pp. 166-67.

[22] L'Hote, *Notre-Dame de Saint-Dié* (Saint-Dié, 1894), pp. 29-62. Concerning the correct title of the church, cf. *ibid.*, pp. 81 ff.

[23] *Ibid.*, pp. 9 ff.   [24] *Ibid.*, p. 31.

Fraus, raptus, quodcumque nefas dominantur in orbe;
Nullus honor sanctis, nulla est reverentia sacris.
Hinc gladius pestisque fames populantur ubique,
Nec tamen impietas hominum correcta pepercit.
Ac nisi magna Dei pietas protenderet iram,
Infernus hos terricrepo consumeret ore.[25]

As he says elsewhere, perilous times were at hand for charity had grown cold and iniquity abounded.[26] Among the calamities which divine wrath let loose upon a sinful world—according to the chroniclers—none took such a toll as the recurring famines.[27] Of all the annalists Radulphus Glaber gives the most vivid account of conditions in 1031, when men became veritable cannibals, fighting over human flesh and even devouring corpses taken from graves.[28] He ends his appalling description with a comment from which one may make deductions as to the difference of spirit in which the scourges of God were received in later centuries:

> Illud preterea stupore nimio permirabillimum, quoniam in tam clandestina divine ultionis calamitate *rarissime repperiebantur* qui pro talibus *contrito corde et humiliato corpore*, ut expediebat, *levarent corda cum manibus ad Dominum* sibique subveniendum interpellarent.[29]

Evidently the people did not improve, for the chronicler continues in the same strain when years of plenty returned:

> Sed heu! pro dolor! humana denique stirps, *immemor beneficiorum Dei* ab initio, prona ad malum, veluti canis ad vomitum, vel sus lota in ceni volutabrum, irritum in multis facere proprie sponsionis pactum.[30]

---

[25] *Historiarum Libri V*, ed. Maurice Prou (Paris, 1886: "Collection de textes pour servir à l'étude et à l'enseignement de l'histoire"), iii, 9, § 40, pp. 89-90.

[26] *Ibid.*, ii, 6, § 12, p. 39.

[27] During the reigns of Hugh Capet and Robert the Pious there were famines in 987, 989, 1001, from 1003 to 1008, from 1010 to 1014, from 1027 to 1029, and from 1031 to 1032. In the eleventh century, within seventy-three years there were forty-three such periods. Cf. F. Funck-Brentano, *Le moyen âge* (Paris, 1922), pp. 72-73.

[28] *Op. cit.*, iv, 4, §§ 9-10, pp. 99-100.

[29] *Ibid.*, § 13, pp. 102-103.   [30] *Ibid.*, 5, § 17, p. 105.

The pessimism of Radulphus Glaber is not so pronounced in later annals. Not that other centuries were without their periods of suffering. One may surmise, after a perusal of the frequent entries listing floods, famine, earthquakes, fires, cyclones, pestilence, and wars, that the distress of the people was quite as keen. However, their attitude is different.[31] Ordericus Vitalis, describing the plague of 1109, writes:

> Ultio divina hominum scelera pluribus flagellis puniit, et mortales, solito terrore cum pietate terruit, ut peccatores ad poenitentiam invitaret et *poenitentibus veniam et salutem clementer exhiberet.* In Gallia, maxime in Aurelianensi et Carnotensi provincia, clades ignifera multos invasit, debilitavit, et quosdam occidit.[32]

And in the year 1134 when a flood and torrid heat caused many deaths, the same writer says:

> Vehemens aestus, per xv dies mundum terruit et terrigenas *ad omnipotentis Domini clementiam* per jejunium et orationes suppliciter confugere . . . compulit.[33]

Ordericus refuses to scrutinize the designs of God:

> Rerum eventus ut vidi vel [audivi] posteris benigniter denoto, et *omnipotentem Deum in cunctis operibus suis,* quae vere justa sunt, *glorifico.*[34]

---

[31] A theocentric attitude becomes marked towards the end of the eleventh century. Ordericus Vitalis describes the famine of 1098 as so great "ut equos et asinos, et si quid aliud immundum erat, devorarent." Nevertheless, he adds: "In tanta egestate fideles invocabant Dominum, et ipse exaudivit eos." Our Lord appears as a priest, praying for his people: "Redemptorem mundi agnovit, et devote pronus *adoravit.* Tunc beata Maria, misericordiae mater, sanctusque Petrus, . . . ceciderunt *ad pedes* Domini Salvatoris." They plead and the "Sanctus Sanctorum" acquiesces with the proviso that penance be performed and promising "quod infra quinque dies opportunum illis *auxilium Deus provideret.*" *Historiae ecclesiasticae Libri XII,* ed. Augustus Le Prevost (Paris, 1838-55: "Société de l'histoire de France), III, ix, 546-47. See also Helinand, *Chronicon,* xlvii, an 1098 (*PL*, CCXII, 991-92); *Anonymi Gesta Francorum et aliorum Hierosolymitanorum,* ed. Beatrice A. Lees (Oxford, 1924), ii, 24, pp. 55-56.

[32] *Ibid.,* IV, xi, 296.

[33] *Ibid.,* V, xiii, 38.   [34] *Ibid.*

The year 1196 witnessed devastations by flood waters.[35] Judging from the penitential works recorded by Rigord, there was the same theocentric reaction on the part of the people:

> Videntes autem clerus et populus *Domini* comminantis prodigia in celo sursum, et signa in terra deorsum, timentes denuo cataclysmum, *plebs fidelis Deo devota* cum gemitibus et lacrymosis suspiriis, et jugi jejuniorum et precum instantia, *clamaverunt ad Dominum,* processiones nudis pedibus facientes, ut correctis parceret et ab eis iracundie sue flagella clementer averteret, et ipsos per penitentiam et congruam satisfactionem misericorditer exaudire dignaretur.[36]

Monks from the monastery of Saint Denis carry with them the relics of the passion with which they bless the waters, saying: " Per hec signa sue sancte passionis *reducat Dominus aquas istas* ad locum suum." [37] A similar procession in which clergy and laity take part is recorded for the year 1206.[38] According to an anonymous canon of the Monastery of Saint Genevieve,

> *Gloriosus Deus in Sanctis suis,* qui in abundantia delictorum gratiae suae ostendit superabundantiam, et in flagellis populi sui *non tantum suam, sed etiam Sanctorum suorum manifestavit gloriam.*[39]

Turning from the chronicles to those collections of *miracula* which relate occurrences in local districts of France, one finds in that of Rocamadour, a digression on the uncertainty of life and the feelings of humility this inspired in the people:

> Flagellis quotidie tundimur, tribulationibus premimur, nos cinis et pulvis, putredo et vermis, dedignantes quod homines sumus, super nos extollimur.[40]

---

[35] A famine occurred in the same year. One account of an anonymous chronicler bears comparison for minuteness of detail with that of Radulphus Glaber (cf. *supra*, p. 93). To add to the horror of famine: " Lupi circa Alpes in itineribus et in villis in unum congregati, absque ullo timore homines devorabant . . . nam usque hodie fame moriuntur millia millium." Cf. " Ex annalibus Aquicinctensis Monasterii," *Recueil*, XVIII, 549.

[36] *Gesta Philippi Augusti*, § 109, p. 134.

[37] *Ibid.*

[38] *Ibid.*, § 148, pp. 164-65.   [39] *Recueil*, XVIII, 797.

[40] *Miracles de Notre-Dame de Roc-Amadour*, i, no. 30, p. 124.

Tribulations have become a sign of the favor of God: " Quippe anima que Domino non corripitur flagello, incurabilis est." [41] While Haimo in the letter describing the miracles of Saint-Pierre-sur-Dive may bemoan the wickedness of men, unlike Radulphus Glaber he is optimistic and his joy derives from the visible manifestation of God's mercy through the miracles. Moreover the letter is similar in tone to the accounts of Hugo Farsit and Herman of Tournai.[42] Haimo writes to the religious of Tutbury in England:

> Congratulamini, fratres, congratulamini et exultate in Domino, quia visitavit nos Oriens ex alto, visitavit plane non meritis nostris, sed ex abundantia gratiae et solitae miserationis effudit in nos viscera misericordiae suae, nec continuit in ira sua dona benignitatis suae. O quam magna multitudo dulcedinis ejus temporibus nostris ostensa est mundo, peccatis languido, criminibus saucio, enormitate scelerum desperato, mundo plane qui jam fere sine Deo erat, quia per culpam a Deo alienus erat.[43]

He continues to exalt the mercy of God:

> Respexit de coelo *pius Dominus* super filios hominum, quia non erat qui intelligeret et requireret Deum, et cum omnes fere declinassent ab eo et abominabiles facti essent in iniquitatibus suis, . . . retraxit ad se detrectantes, aberrantesque revocavit.

For the medieval man has, indeed, turned to his Creator. His voluntary self-abasement excites the wonderment of Haimo who marvels to see the powerful, the wealthy, the noble, even women and children bend their necks to the yoke of the carts loaded with the stones, wood, lime, wine, corn, and oil necessary for the con-

---

[41] *Ibid.*, iii, no. 24, p. 316.

[42] Cf. *infra*, pp. 99-100. In an introduction to one of the ancedotes of Gilon of Chartres it is said that God rekindled the hearts of men by virtue of miracles: " *Omnipotentis Dei misericordia inenarrabilis . . .* considerans fragilitatem gentium nostri temporis adeo frigescere in caritate sanctissime fidei catholice, . . . frigida hominum corda *per gratiam sancti spiritus et virtutem miraculorum* ad ardorem dilectionis ipsius *dignata est revocare.*" A. Thomas, *loc. cit.*, no. xxvi, pp. 546-47. This passage is not translated by Jean le Marchant.

[43] " Lettre de l'Abbé Haimon," *loc. cit.*, p. 120.

struction of the church and for the workmen. Nothing is an obstacle before them. Hatreds cease and the silence of labor is broken only by humble admission of faults, confession of sin, hymns and canticles:

> Videas sacerdotes Christi plaustris singulis praesidentes, ad poenitentiam, ad confessionem, ad lamenta, ad melioris vitae propositum universos hortari, ipsos humi prostratos ac toto corpore incumbentes terram diutius osculari, senes cum junioribus et pueris tantillae aetatis matrem Domini conclamare, atque ad ipsam praecipue singultus suspiriaque ab intimis praecordiis cum voce confessionis et laudis dirigere.

It is to be noted that the writer immediately adds in reference to the Virgin: " Ejus enim *post benignum filium* maxime hoc opus esse dignoscitur; ipsa se in hoc opere *post ipsum* praecipue commendavit." [44]

According to the abbot, the people are literally " extorting " an answer to their prayer, the accomplishment of which demands a miracle. In this the multitude act as one. If cures are delayed,

> Videas universos vestes abjicere, nudos simul viros cum mulieribus a lumbis et supra, confusione omni abjecta, solo incumbere, puerulos et infantes idem devotius agere et ab ecclesiae atriis solo stratos non jam genibus et manibus, sed potius tractu corporis totius primum ad altare majus dein ad altaria singula repere, matrem misericordiae, novo quodam obsecrantium genere, inclamare atque ibi statim ab ea petitionum suarum pia desideria *extorquere* certe; quid enim, non dicam non obtineat, immo *quid non extorqueat* iste orantium modus, iste gementium, suspirantium, plorantium atque ideo ascendens usque ad benignas aures matris summae pietatis affectus? Quem certe non moveat, immo cujus cor lapideum intuentis non emolliat illa innocentium pia humilitas nudata latera per terram trahentium? [45]

Even children have recourse to what Haimo terms extortion. When one of five boys remains uncured, the fortunate four begin an irresistible siege to obtain the cure of the suffering one. While they strip and, prostrate, pray for their companion, the on-lookers join with tears and cries. They are not above scolding her " ac si quis servum vel ancillam increpet ":

[44] *Ibid.*, p. 121.   [45] *Ibid.*, 3, pp. 122-23.

Cur . . . domina, servorum tuorum preces attendere dedignaris?
Quid est quod afflictis coram te, quid tribulatis carne et spiritu,
ut moris esse solet, nequaquam compateris? Ecce in conspectu
tuo nudi sumus, suspiramus, ploramus, caedimur, flagellamur
et despicis! . . . Cur innocentium tuorum devotam non respicis
servitutem? Et ubi est illa misericordia tua, illa pietas, illa
mansuetudo, illa clementia? Aegros nobis jam quatuor
sospites reddidisti: quintum, cum id posses facillime, cur,
domina, distulisti?[46]

If their sins have made them unworthy to be cured, the boys
promise amendment:

Si propter peccata nostra, ecce emendationem de praeteritis
pollicemur et jam deinceps nunquam poma, nunquam spicas
de agris furto ablaturos voto nos coram te obligamus.

But the Queen is vulnerable: "Non potuit ultra misericordiae
mater circa afflictos pia viscera continere . . . Vim quidem, ut ita
dixerim, hoc afferre erat, ita agere, *extorquere*."

In the collection of Rocamadour the author early raises the
question: why is the Virgin so capricious? She cures whom she
wills. She is harsh toward one and sweet towards another. He
answers:

Dura, dico, quantum ad desidiosos, que semper mitis mites
convertit ad oculos inconversos peccatores. Devotos aspicit,
humiles recipit, *quia Filii sui gracia* humilibus dat graciam.[47]

One of the distinctive characteristics of the local collections is
the "animorum unitas"[48] of which Haimo speaks. Herman the
monk in his opening paragraph of the *Miracula Sanctae Marie
Laudunensis* presents the doctrine of the Mystical Body as the
keynote of the miracles which he relates:

Quoniam juxta Beatum Paulum apostolum tota sancta Ecclesia unum Christi corpus est [Coloss. 1:24], et hujus corporis
membra sunt diversae Ecclesiae, vel singuli fideles, dumque

---

[46] *Ibid*, 18, pp. 138-39.

[47] *Miracles de Notre-Dame de Roc-Amadour*, pp. 63-64. The editor sug-
gests the following word-order for the passage: "convertit ad inconversos
peccatores oculos" or "oculos ad inconversos peccatores."

[48] *Op. cit.*, p. 121.

patitur unum membrum, compatiuntur omnia membra, [I Cor. 12 : 26], et dum glorificatur unum membrum congaudent omnia membra [I Cor. 12 : 26] tribulationem et dolorem, quem invenit Ecclesia nostra in diebus nostris [Ps. 114 : 3], et consolationem, quam per Dominam nostram sanctam Dei Genitricem post tribulationis luctum recepit, vestrae scribendo notificamus dilectioni, quatenus et vos congaudentes nobis, Deo, et piae Matri ejus gratias agatis.[49]

In Laon the bond of union was brought about by a conflagration which burned the church and many of the homes of the people. It was looked upon as a punishment of God,[50] but the same optimism, noted in the Saint-Pierre-sur-Dive collection, predominated :

> " Deus repulisti nos, et destruxisti nos, iratus es, et misertus es nostri [Ps. 59 : 3] "; et alibi : " Cum iratus fueris, misericordiae recordaberis [Hab. 3 : 4] "; Ecclesiam nostram, quam dure flagellari permiserat, precibus suae piissimae Matris placatus, non distulit misericorditer refovere.[51]

At Soissons the pestilence known as the *ignis sacer* or *mal des ardents,* most virulent in the year 1128, brought the people to a realization of their inability to cope with the plague; nevertheless, their impotence inspired sentiments of confidence in God's mercy. Hugo Farsit introduces his *Miracula B. Mariae Virginis in urbe Suessionensi* with the statement :

> Anno igitur ab Incarnatione Domini 1128, quo judicio Dei et quibus de causis intelligat qui valet, concessa est potestas adversae virtuti plaga invisibili percutere homines diversae aetatis et sexus in pago Suessionensi, ita ut semel succensa corpora eorum cum intolerabili cruciatu arderent usque ad exclusionem animae, *nisi sola Dei medicina occurreret.*[52]

---

[49] *PL*, CLVI, 963. Cf. *infra*, p. 112.

[50] Guibert of Nogent, after relating the murder of Gerard of Crécy and Gaudry, Bishop of Laon, writes : " Nam in tota Francia qualia apud Laudunenses nusquam scelera contigerunt." When the wall of the church, at the spot where Gerard was killed, was shattered by a thunderbolt, he comments : " Et, mirum *Dei judicium*! " See *De vita sua*, iii, xi and xii (*PL*, CLVI, 936-37).

[51] *Op. cit.*, col. 968. See also *Miracles de Notre-Dame de Roc-Amadour*, ii, no. 15, pp. 200-201.

[52] *PL*, CLXXIX, 1777.

Vividly he describes the horrors of the disease,[53] but he, too, is optimistic: " Quanto autem major miseris, tanto gratiosior misericordia." [54]

However, Soissons was not the only town in France which felt the plague. According to the chronicler, Anselm of Gembloux, in the year 1129 " plaga ignis divini Carnotum, Parisius, Suessionem, Cameracum, Atrebatum, et alia multa loca mirabiliter pervadit." [55] None were immune:

> Juvenes etenim, senes cum junioribus, virgines etiam tenerae, in pedibus, in manibus, in mamillis, et, quod gravius est, in genis exaruntur, et celeriter extinguntur.

As late as 1294 one reads among the enactments of the Cathedral of Paris that the church was filled with sufferers, " expectantes *consolationem* Patris et Filii ac Spiritus Sancti Paracliti, *intercedente* glorississima virgine Maria, matre ejusdem Salvatoris." [56]

Besides the humble there is another privileged class who may hope with confidence for a cure, especially when it requires a miracle —the poor. The collection of Chartres states that God manifested His power,

> non tantum in prelatis ecclesie, ut in beato Thoma Cantuariensi archiepiscopo et aliis multis, non tantum in rege Anglie Henrico et filiis ejus et aliis principibus quam plurimum, non tantum in mediocribus personis, ut in sancto Willelmo de Ponte Isare et aliis, . . . sed etiam in omnibus ultime estimationis, scilicet *in pauperibus terrarum cultoribus,* ubi manerat in eternum sermo ille: " Quia quos dedisti michi non perdam ex eis quemquam." [57]

---

[53] Similar in nature to erysipelas, the pestilence ravaged the north of France. The disease in its most malignant form produced a decay of the flesh which disfigured the victims and often proved fatal: ". . . carnem ab ossibus separans et consumens, . . ." *Ibid.* (cols. 1777-78). See Helinand of Froidmont, *op. cit.* (cols. 1010 and 1029). Also A. Luchaire, *La Société française au temps de Philippe-Auguste* (Paris, 1909), pp. 6-7.

[54] *PL*, CLXXIX, 1778.

[55] *Chronicon-Continuatio* (*PL*, CLX, 251).

[56] *Collection des Cartulaires de France,* ed. M. Guérard (Paris, 1850), IV, ix, 43, p. 466.

[57] Antoine Thomas, *loc. cit.*, xxvi, p. 547. This passage is not translated by Jean le Marchant. The Chartres collection as a whole will be

In his *Dialogus Miraculorum* Caesarius of Heisterbach refers to the cures at Rocamadour and other local shrines in favor of the indigent. At Montpellier so many cures are wrought that the doctors in envy of her popularity, turn away the sick-poor who flock to them for attention: " Ite ad ecclesiam sanctae Mariae, deferte ei lumen, et recipietis sanitatem." [58] Although this is said in irony, the poor, thus repulsed, flee to her and are cured.

The wretched condition of the serf is described in the *Livre des Manières* written by Etienne of Fougères about 1170.[59] The *Bible Guiot* startles with its opening line: " Dou siecle pouant et horrible." [60] Other moralists of the time are as depressing. Not so the writers of the local collections of miracles, for there is a strain of optimism in their belief that God in His mercy " respexit de coelo super filios hominum." [61] There is even joy and exultation as the *Te Deum* is chanted in thanksgiving. Herman of Tournai, in relating a triple miracle in the Laon collection, seems to concentrate less on the wonders wrought than on the thanksgiving which rises in a crescendo of emotion. The worshipers in the church are startled when a woman who has been so crippled and paralyzed as to be unable to walk, suddenly enters and excitedly demands that they show her the shrine of Laon. Bishop Ivo sees that a miracle has taken place and he himself begins the *Te Deum*. While the clergy are singing, another cripple who is well-known to the Bishop and to others, is cured. Again the hymn is sung and before it is finished " *divinae pietati placuit* tertium superaddere miraculum." [62] This time a soldier enters to announce his miraculous release from captivity. The Bishop orders that all the churches of the city celebrate " Deo laudes . . . ipse tertio incipiens *Te Deum* laudamus." [63]

---

treated under this author in the chapter on the vernacular, cf. *infra*, pp. 186 ff.

[58] *Dial. Mirac.*, vii, 24, p. 34.

[59] Estienne de Fougères, *Livre des manières*, ed. Joseph Kremer (Marburg, 1887: " Ausgaben und Abhandlungen, no. 39 "), p. 131.

[60] *Les Œuvres de Guiot de Provins*, ed. John Orr (Manchester, 1915), p. 10. According to this editor, the work was finished between 1204 and 1209, probably 1206. Cf. *ibid.*, p. xx.

[61] Cf. *supra*, p. 96.   [62] *Op. cit.*, i, 13 (col. 972).

[63] *Ibid.* See also Helinand, *op. cit.* (cols. 1011-12) ; Vincent of Beauvais, *op. cit.*, xxvi, 14.

If ever the Virgin were given a homage due to God alone, it would have been when the people were in a state of exultation. On the contrary, it was then that their praise of the Almighty knew no bounds,—a clear indication that they recognized the source of Mary's power as God Himself. When the worshippers were at the highest pitch of jubilation, Hugo Farsit writes:

> Haec sunt festa solemnia qualia mandasti populo tuo exhiberi tibi, hi dies celebres in quibus *veri adoratores adorant Patrem in spiritu et veritate*.[64]

Theocentrism of the Local Collections

Geoffrey of Montbrai was the first Bishop of Coutances to order that the miracles which had occurred in his church should be consigned to writing " ad laudem Domini, et honorem gloriosae Dominae suae Dei genitricis, et aedificationem successorum." [65] The intention of the canon John who undertook the task is theocentric:

> Narrabimus laudes Domini et *virtutes ejus et mirabilia ejus, quae fecit,* filiis qui nascentur et exurgent, et narrabunt filiis suis.[66]

That God performs the miracles is reiterated towards the end of his work:

> Sunt quidem ut innumerabilia nobiliora miracula quae *dominus* gratia gloriosae Matris suae in hac sancta Constantiensi ecclesia, . . . *operari dignatus est*.[67]

Moreover, they are to the " laudem suae majestatis." Many more have occurred but John does not trust to his memory, and hence will omit them rather than offend " ipsum Creatorem nostrum, qui vero est via, veritas et vita." [68]

In the Rocamadour collection it is stated that a notary has been receiving the depositions [69] of those miraculously cured and it is from his notes that the writer draws most of the material which he relates " ad laudem et gloriam nominis Domini et ejus generose

[64] *Op. cit.,* 15 (col. 1789).

[65] Pigeon, *op. cit.,* p. 367.

[66] *Ibid.,* p. 368.

[67] *Ibid.,* xxvi, p. 381.

[68] *Ibid.*

[69] *Op. cit.,* Prologue II, p. 167.

matris." [70]   To insure to posterity the knowledge of these facts he
feels himself obliged to commit them to writing:

> *Unde Deus laudetur et ardentius ametur,* gloriosa nichilominus
> ejus Genitrix Domina et prepotens Regina nostra honoretur, et
> proximus edificetur.[71]

Moreover, he is imbued with a sense of his own nothingness and
buoyed up with a confidence in the power of God who can do all
things:

> Cum sine ipso nichil et cum ipso et in ipso possimus plurimum,
> quare non adheremus turri fortitudinis, sapientie fonti,
> omnium bonorum plenitudini?

Hugo Farsit, more specifically, designates God as the author of
those miracles which are to the honor of the Mother:

> Ad laudem et honorem beatae et gloriosae semperque virginis
> Mariae, Genitricis Dei et Domini nostri Jesu Christi, tempori-
> bus nostris *virtutem mirabilium suorum dignatus est ostendere
> Deus* populo suo.[72]

In his optimistic expression of God's purpose he adopts the tone
of the Psalms: " . . . ut credentibus det haereditatem gentium, et
diligentibus se bona quae promisit Israeli." Those who are en-
lightened by the Holy Spirit and possess a deep faith, will enjoy the
consolations of God and experience the power of the invisible kingdom.   Fear is to give way to a love of the divine mercy.   The evils
of the pestilence do but glorify His strength:

> Haec est enim *fortitudo Dei magna per quam mala coerceat,* et
> diligentibus se *bona invisibilia et divitias gloriae suae largiatur:*
> haec est, inquam, fortitudo Dei magna et potentia regni ejus
> maxima, virtus invisibilis, virtus arcana in refrenandis malis,
> quae velut morbus exuberarent in regno ejus, nisi repressa, et
> virtus gratiae et misericordiae e regione sua opera ineffabiliter
> exercens, per quam excluso timore congaudet electis supera-
> bundanti amore praebente fiduciam.[73]

In the collection of Saint-Pierre-sur-Dive the author depicts God
as being touched, so to speak, by the rigor of austerities and

---

[70] *Ibid.*, p. 165.   [72] *Op. cit.* (col. 1777).
[71] *Ibid.*, Prologue III, p. 265. [73] *Ibid.* (col. 1778).

penances which frequently took the form of bloody flagellations, joyfully and voluntarily imposed.[74] For Hugo Farsit, the sufferings of the pilgrim's journey, undertaken barefoot and in severe weather, were so patiently borne as to be a pleasing "sacrificium Deo."[75] The hardships of the travellers of Laon are often lessened by an intervention of God which the people deem miraculous. Once as they attempted to reach a castle, impregnable because of its location, the approach became doubly dangerous as night had fallen and a downpour of rain made them despair of safety:

> "Clamaverunt ergo ad Dominum cum tribularentur, et de necessitatibus eorum eduxit eos [Ps. 106: 28]." Subito enim, *Deo miserante,* tanta transierunt facilitate ut nullum omnino in transeundo impedimentum haberent.[76]

The inhabitants of the castle were so amazed that they offered hospitality "dicentes quod revera *misericordia Domini fuisset cum eis.*" In sailing from Wissant to Dover another peril threatened the band. As pirates drew near, the priest Boso mounted to the highest point of the stern and elevating the reliquary[77] "ex auctoritate Dei matrique sanctae Marie fortiter adjuvando"[78] he forbade their approach:

[74] Cf. *supra*, pp. 96-97.   [75] *Op. cit.*, 6 (col. 1780).

[76] Herman of Tournai, *op. cit.*, i, 12 (col. 971).

[77] Guibert of Nogent gives the legendary history of a collection of relics left at Laon by a Briton King. Because of his desire for the truth a voice from Heaven commanded him to go to Jerusalem. On his way he found hospitality in Laon. He arrived at his destination just after the first Pentecost and was baptized by the Apostle Peter. Before leaving, he begged for portions of the cords which fastened Christ to the cross, of the scourges, of the wood of the cross, and of that garment in which the Mother of God gave birth to the Lord. Upon his return an illness overtook him at Laon and he left the precious treasure, in obedience to a vision, there. Cf. *De vita sua*, ii, 1 (cols. 893 ff.). Guibert describes the actual reliquary "in quo de camisia matris Virginis et de spongia ori Salvatoris illata, et de cruce ipsius, si de capillis ejusdem Dominae nostrae nescio, continetur." *Ibid.*, iii, 12 (col. 938). See Vincent of Beauvais, *Spec. Hist.*, xxvi, 15.

[78] Herman of Tournai, *op. cit.*, ii, 4 (col. 976). See also Vincent of Beauvais, *op. cit.*, xxvi, 16; Guibert of Nogent, *De vita sua*, iii, 13 (col. 940). Tatlock rejects this miracle as a possible fabrication, *Speculum*, VIII, 456.

Et, o mira *divinae virtutis potentia!* mox ut verba complens signum crucis de eodem phylacterio contra hostes fecit, dicto citius, vento vehementi et contrario, navis eorum impulsa retro propellitur, malus navis eorum frangitur.

The writer continues:

Jesu pie, Jesu bone, quae nobis tunc adfuit laetitia et exsultatio, quando concidisti saccum perturbationis nostrae, et circumdedisti nos *laetitia misericordiae tuae!* [Ps. 29: 12] Quantas tibi protinus, Matrique tuae Dominae nostrae laudes erepti de morte persolvimus!

The wind which was so unfavorable to their enemies quickly brought them to port as they joyfully sang the canticle of Moses to celebrate their deliverance.

The collection of Saint-Dié begins " In nomine Domini." [79] According to the writer, the church of Saint-Dié in the Vosges in the diocese of Toul is " again " the scene of " *divinorum operum* circa notos et ignotos, advenas et domesticos." [80] He proposes to relate these:

Ad honorem Domini, Genitique Patris
Et ad laudem Virginis, ejus piae Matris. [81]

Though his own talent may prove insufficient for the task, he finds consolation in the words of the Scripture, promising aid from the Lord:

Vera dicis, aio sed me consolatur
Quod Deus discipulis dixisse probatur;
Aperi os tuum et adimplebo illud. [82]

In all the collections, except in that of Rocamadour, it sometimes happens that a miracle is attributed to God alone, no mention being made of Mary's intercession. This is particularly the case in the work of John of Coutances where the church is referred to as the " Sancti Spiritus inhabitationem," [83] and the pilgrim, having spent much time in prayer—no reference being made to the Virgin—is cured by the grace of God. Rigindua, " cujus pedes igne putrido consumebantur," [84] goes to Coutances,

[79] L'Hote, *op. cit.,* p. 29.
[80] *Ibid.,* p. 30.
[81] *Ibid.,* p. 31.
[82] *Ibid.,* p. 32.
[83] Pigeon, *op. cit.,* no. vi, p. 370.
[84] *Ibid.,* no. xv, p. 376.

> Ubi *gratia Dei,* non solum putridus extinctus est ignis, verum etiam incolumis inobsequio et purgatione ejusdem ecclesiae, multis diebus, *in castitate Deo serviens,* his in Jerusalem perrexit, quod valde laboriosum erat, et minus usitatum tunc temporis.

Two other victims of the pestilence are cured by the "gratia Dei." [85]   Another woman, Orielda by name, so misshapen that her body is in the form of a ball, is ordered in a dream to go to the church. She is brought there by friends and placed before the crucifix. After two days of prayer, " *Gratia Dei,* restaurata est." [86] A certain Vitalis whose life is despaired of, is brought into the church before the altar, " *misericordia Dei praeeunte,* redintegratus est." [87]   One poor cripple who has lived on the alms of Bishop Geoffrey for eight years and is known to all, is cured in his own home. He awakens one night dimly aware of a heavenly visitation:

> Nocte quadam quiescenti in statu suo, *coelestis* illapsa est *medicina.* Prius quidem in seipso contremuit et deinde *Deum invocans,* ejusque pedes suos de grabato statim prosilivit.[88]

One of the canons of the church visits him to offer charitable assistance, and he happily replies that he is able to stand: " *Deique misericordia,* super pedes suos incolumem stare." No mention of Mary is made in his thanksgiving": Et Deo preces et grates ageret." In relating a miracle of a candle which descends from the vault of the cathedral to burn before the altar, the writer uses the expression, " nutu divino." [89]   In reference to a similar prodigy, he writes: " *Ad gloriam Domini* translatum est in alteram partem." [90]   The collection contains a Eucharistic miracle attributed to the " divine potentiae." [91]

Also theocentric are accounts by other authors, although they are not to be found in such number. Herman of Tournai recounts that a child, overcome in a thermal bath, drowns. His body is brought by relatives to the reliquary. The monks use very

[85] *Ibid.,* no. xvi, p. 376.
[86] *Ibid.,* no. xxiv, p. 380.
[87] *Ibid.,* no. vi, p. 371.
[88] *Ibid.,* no. xi, p. 374.

[89] *Ibid.,* no. i, p. 368.
[90] *Ibid.,* no. iii, p. 369.
[91] *Ibid.,* no. xx, p. 378.

practical means to restore him to life and then have recourse to prayer:

> Nec mora, ecce puer, *Deo miserante,* non solum spiritu recepto, sed etiam integra sanitate subsecuta, laetus cum parentibus suis domum rediit.[92]

As a loaded cart is being drawn to the Church of Saint-Pierre-sur-Dive, a number of miracles are wrought. Along the way many volunteer to assist, " quia Dominus erat cum eis." [93] One child who has no hand, tries to help and in stooping to the ground," statim de materia ipsa in manu accepit, acceptamque videntibus cunctis in manu jam restituta portavit." The pilgrims are received with great veneration at their destination, not only in reverence for their pious labor " *pro Deo* assumpti," but also, " propter magnalia quae *Dominus* circa eos *dignatus est ostendere.*

Hugo Farsit tells of a mad man Guarinus, so strong that even an iron collar and chains are scarcely sufficient to restrain him. He recovers sanity " per gratiam Dei," [94] and having been once powerful, rich, and well-known, " Deus celebrius glorificatur." Cured, his first act is one of thanksgiving. He raises his eyes to heaven and glorifies God, " viventem in saecula saeculorum, *qui potens est* superbos humiliare, et arrogantes a suo fastu deducere, et eosdem statuere contra faciem suam."

The poet of Saint-Dié relates a miracle from which he draws further reasons for adoring God:

> Hinc volo mysterium breviter tractare,
> Unde decet quemlibet *Deum adorare.*[95]

A cripple prays at the sanctuary and then rises without the aid of his crutches, returning to his home cured. A child deprived of the use of his limbs is brought to the same place of pilgrimage. The poet's expression of thanksgiving is an indication of the source of supernatural power effecting the prodigy:

> Post preces exiguas extitit sanatus.
> Ad propria remeat pedibus elatus,
> Sanus et incolumis: *Deus sit laudatus.*[96]

---

[92] *Op. cit.,* ii, 22 (col. 986).
[93] *Op. cit.,* no. xv, p. 135.
[94] *Op. cit.,* 17 (col. 1789).
[95] *Op. cit.,* no. xxix, p. 60.
[96] *Ibid.,* no. xv, p. 49.

No mention is made of Mary in the following miracle in which three lines suffice for the entire narrative:

> Tali muliercula laborabat morbo,
> Quae curru deducitur; templum subintrando
> Salus sibi redditur: *sit laus Jesu Christo.*[97]

In the *miracula* of Rocamadour, one usually finds the intercession of the Virgin either expressed or implied. Since its theocentrism might be questioned, the rôle of the Deity and the attributes of God as presented in this collection deserve investigation. All three Persons of the Trinity are invoked. The Father is more frequently referred to as the Creator: "Domine, qui omnia fecisti ex nichilo,"[98] or the "factor omnium."[99] When threatened with shipwreck, mariners invoke His power: "Consoletur igitur eos et relevet *potentia Patris* qua peccata puniuntur, ut *fortitudine* vigeat contra fluctum immanitatem."[100] They then appeal to the Holy Spirit: "Consoletur etiam et assit benignitas Spiritus Sancti ne, quod absit, subintret et desperatio!" The author, himself, prays for light from the Paraclete at the beginning of the collection;[101] and again, in the second book where he suddenly seems overwhelmed by his inability to describe the glory of the Virgin Mary, and receives encouragement from the thought that she may obtain this gift for him from the Holy Ghost:

> Aperiet os nostrum, reserabit sacrarium Spiritus sancti, ut, tanto *edocti doctore,* quod nostrum non capit ingenium infundatur nostre menti rore gratiaque *Flaminis almi.*[102]

As for the Son, he is the "Rex regum."[103] He is the Lord "cui virtus est et imperium cum Patre et Spiritu Sancto per immortalia secula seculorum."[104] He is one with the Father and the Holy Ghost: "[Christo] qui cum Patre et Spiritu Sancto *una est divinitas essentia et potestas, decus et imperium,* per immortalia secula seculorum."[105] A knight invokes him: "Domine, . . . *qui*

---

[97] *Ibid.*, no. xxviii, pp. 59-60.

[98] *Op. cit.*, i, no. 14, pp. 100-101.

[99] *Ibid.*, Prologue III, p. 265.

[100] *Ibid.*, iii, no. 1, p. 271.

[101] *Ibid.*, Prologue I, p. 61.

[102] *Ibid.*, ii, no. 10, p. 192.

[103] *Ibid.*, no. 38, p. 249. See also Herman of Tournai, *op. cit.*, ii, 22 (col. 988).

[104] *Ibid.*, no. 15, p. 206.

[105] *Ibid.*, no. 49, p. 264.

sanas languentes et devios *revocas* quia tu es via et veritas." [106] He became Incarnate, " nostram miserans miseriam." [107] In becoming man He so lowered Himself as to be,

> Passibilis secundum carnem, qua eliam [etiam] paulominus minoratus est ab angelis [Ps. 8:6, Hebr. 2:7], humano velatus amictu qui ex divinitate fuerat incorporeus, incircon-scriptus, invasibilis, impassibilis, *verus Deus, verus homo,* nos illuminaturus sua presentia in hec mundi descendit infima.[108]

Certain mariners of Boulogne, seeing death imminent, invoke Him as the " Agnum sine macula per secula regnantem et mortis solventem vincula." [109]   From the prayer of the Italian knight Anselm, it is evident that to the Redeemer are ascribed the attributes of the Deity:

> *Redemptor omnium,* ne spreveris me facturam manuum tuarum, set [*sic*] fac mecum signum in bono [Ps. 75:17] juxta misericordie tue multitudinem. Scio et confitero quia *juste judicando* nec falli potes, quia *sapiens* es, nec corrumpi quia *justus* es, nec vinci quia *omnipotens,* nec declinari quia *ubique presens.*[110]

The suppliant is not overawed by the majesty of God. He turns to Him as his sole refuge:

> *Quod ergo solum restat de me fugio ad te,* fugio iram, fugio ad misericordiam; non peto ut mecum judiceris set ut mei miserearis; nolo parva querere quia magnum non decet parva dare; nequaquam, Domine, magna postulans, de meritis meis confido, set *tuam magnificentiam honoro.*

From these and similar statements it is quite clear that the three Persons of the Trinity are not in the background in the collection of Rocamadour; further evidence is offered in the consideration of Mary Mediatrix.

The grace of contrition and penance as a direct gift of God is a theocentric trait not to be overlooked. It is the miracle of grace which excites the admiration of Hugo Farsit. Witnessing the devotion of the people at Soissons, he writes:

[106] *Ibid.,* i, no. 14, p. 101.
[107] *Ibid.,* ii, no. 28, p. 232.
[108] *Ibid.,* no. 13, p. 197.
[109] *Ibid.,* no. 37, p. 247.
[110] *Ibid.,* no. 42, p. 255.

> Corporalia qui volunt admirentur, ut vere justum est, mira-
> cula; *nos vero gratiam tuam magis admiramur, Domine, in*
> *peccatoribus* tuo pavore conterritis, et ad devotam poeniten-
> tiam conversis, et de monumento quasi suscitatis, et ob memo-
> riam gratiae non ingratis lacrymis et humilitate *in tuo amore*
> *ferventibus.* Haec sunt miracula nostra quae praecipue cordi
> sunt nobis, *pro his glorificamus te, Domine Jesu, laudamus et*
> *adoramus,* quia iste totus fructus qui permanet in vitam
> aeternam, pietas et humilitas quae *in te* fervescunt.[111]

A spiritual rejuvenation is concomitant with the miracles at Saint-
Pierre-sur-Dive. Many " videntes signa et mirabilia quae fiebant,
non solum a timore sed etiam *ab amore Dei* " [112] are moved to contrition and endeavor to expiate their sins in the performance of
good works:

> . . . haec etenim multo majora sunt, multo gloriosiora, quia
> spiritualia. Ibi depelluntur aegritudines corporum, hic men-
> tium; ibi salutem languidorum moritura corpora consequun-
> tur, hic animae in aeternum victurae salutare remedium
> exhibetur.

Herman of Tournai makes the observation that no one is cured
unless he is of the diocese in which the travellers happen to be
with the reliquary and has first confessed his sins to the priest.
He frequently refers to this preliminary step. Moreover, it is
tacitly understood that no miracle can be performed unless there is
a forgiveness of enemies. One man who has been bed-ridden for
six years promises to God the restitution of all the money which
he has obtained by usury. He is cured and when comments are
made as to the small amount he contributes to the building fund in
gratitude, he replied:

> . . . se ad praesens nolle amplius dare, donec usuras, quas a
> debitoribus suis acceperat, redderet, *sicut Deo promiserat.*[113]

He is represented as a second Zacchaeus by the people who rejoice
" plus de usurarum redditione animaeque ejus salvatione quam de
corporali curatione *Deum laudantibus.*"

The tribulations sent by God are regarded as trials to test the

---

[111] *Op. cit.*, 6 (cols. 1780-81).   [112] *Op. cit.*, no. xvi, p. 137.
[113] *Ibid.*, ii, 7 (col. 979). See also Helinand, *op. cit.* (col. 1014).

love of the just and as chastisements to bring the sinner to repentance.[114] The judgments of God are inscrutable, but He can
deliver them. Here, the Virgin Mary is decidedly in the background:

> Verum quia *judicia Dei* profunda sunt ut abyssus multa [Ps.
> 35 : 7] quare fiant ista et ista minime non est judicare, *nisi
> cum Dominus voluerit revelare.* Nulli tamen fidelium ambi-
> gendum est quin multe sint tribulationes justorum, set *potens
> poterit Dominus eripere* ex his omnibus. Alique [*sic*] ad
> probationem et examinationem, *ut scire* faciat *utrum diligatur,*
> alique infliguntur *ut a malo resipiscatur.*[115]

In the case of a young soldier of Gascony, an epileptic attack is
considered a chastisement for his blasphemies and rapine. So it
happens " ut *Ille qui potest omnia, potentibus potentior,* potesta-
tem illius minueret." [116] In his affliction he turns to God:

> O bone Deus, totius fons bonitatis, totius dulcedo benignitatis,
> . . . parce miseris, egrotantibus medere, miserere contritis
> corde, . . . Ista est clementie tue, Domine, consolatio nostra
> *solum* istud delinquentibus *refugium* quod proprio humero
> centenariam ovem ad ovile reportasti, et ejus mavis conver-
> sionem quam mortem.

Then he beseeches the Virgin Mary to obtain for him a cure whereby
he may know that he is in the grace of her Son. His prayer is
answered: " Etenim Dei et Virginis *Filius* matris obtentu *sana-
tum dimisit.*" However, seduced by his companions who mock at
his reform, he returns to his former sins; the malady returns in a
more malignant form. The soldier would have despaired, had he
not been sustained by the " benignitate Spiritus sancti." His
friends attempted to encourage him:

> Non est benignus ut Dominus, in ira furoris sui non mortificat
> set corripit; flagello percutit in presenti ut parcere possit in
> sequenti.

They continue with an argument which shows the surprising broad-
mindedness of medieval piety and a liberal attitude toward the

---

[114] Cf. *supra*, pp. 96 and 99.
[115] *Miracles de Notre-Dame de Roc-Amadour*, ii, no. 15, p. 201.
[116] *Ibid.*, no. 24, pp. 222 ff.

generosity of God. He is urged not to fear but to " redire ad fontem medicine qui non reddit pro lapsu vicissitudinem, *quia mortalis pridem passibilitatis nostre condescendit debilitati.*" The worshipers at Rocamadour, touched by his penance and humility, pray fervently for him :

> Omnes affluebant undique, miserie compatientes militis, pro membro male sano quatinus a Christo, *qui caput est fidelium* reformari mereretur instanter orantes et devote.

Their prayer is answered.

Frequently the expressions of gratitude give a clue to the writer's theocentric interpretation of the Virgin's miracles. At Saint-Dié a paralytic is cured by the " Mariae praesidio." [117] All the clergy and the people hasten to the church to give praise to the Physician, Who the poet says is God :

> Mariae praesidio statim fit sanata.
> Ad templum conveniunt populus et clerus,
> Hunc collaudant *qui bonis est medicus verus.*

Through the intercession of Notre-Dame of Saint-Dié life is restored to a child and thanksgiving is rendered to the God of all :

> Mariae subsidio vita restauratur,
> Inde votis *omnium Deus collaudatur.*[118]

At Coutances a cripple hopes to regain her health through the " meritis " of the Virgin. One day her benefactor, Bishop Geoffrey hears shouts coming from the direction of the church; such a jubilation he knows to be " *divinae* virtutis indicium." [119] He discovers that he is correct and with all the clergy unites to sing a " hymnum jubilationis et laudis *Domino.*" At another time as they are chanting hymns before the crucifix, an individual afflicted by the " igne putrido," is cured by the grace of God : " Gratia *Dei* liberatus est." [120] Although the miracle occurs before an image of the Blessed Virgin, the clergy chant the *Te Deum* before the crucifix and during this hymn of thanksgiving another sufferer is cured :

[117] *Op. cit.*, no. xiv, p. 49.   [119] *Op. cit.*, no. xii, p. 375.
[118] *Ibid.*, no. xxvi, p. 58.   [120] *Ibid.*, no. xxix, p. 382.

Dum statim ibidem ante crucifixum *Te Deum laudamus in laudem Dei* concinerent, *divina benignitate,* statim quidam alter contritis pedibus, ante eamdem Virginis imaginem sanus erectus est: sicque sub una cleri et populi gratiarum actione elevata, *gratia Dei dignata est* eorum gaudia *duplicare.*

One woman, who for several years has been afflicted with blindness and a paralysis of the ocular muscles, regains her vision while the *Benedictus Dominus Deus Israël* is being sung. The miracle is attributed to divine efficacy: " *Motus oculorum et visus efficax divinitus* ei redditus est." [121] John of Coutances adds that it is God who makes the sanctuary of the Virgin illustrious: " Clerus ergo et populus . . . glorificaverunt *Deum, qui* tanto miraculo *decorabat* Virginis habitaculum et festum."

Haimo tells us that when a man received his sight, " laetabantur singuli et magnificabant *Dominum in opere suo.*" [122] Their *Te Deum* has not ceased when another miracle follows: " Et ecce in conspectu omnium *magnificavit Dominus misericordiam suam* et pietatis suae consuetam gratiam declaravit." Indeed in the church of Saint-Pierre-sur-Dive in which so many prodigies are wrought through Mary as " Operatrix," [123] the people in their simplicity deem the very ground holy, " quam *dignabatur Dominus* ad nominis sui sed et matris suae gloriam tantis virtutibus illustrare." [124] According to Hugo, the Christ who went about doing good, still walked the earth. Commenting on the emotion of those who heard a little mute boy utter his first words, " Sancta Maria ! " he writes:

Domine Jesu, quis tunc a lacrymis temperavit? Quorum pectora vel saxea non scindebantur, cum videbant *te iterum inter homines deambulantem* ? [125]

No statement could be more theocentric. It is particularly significant since it follows a miracle obtained through the intercession of the Virgin, and therefore, offers reasonable proof that in spite of Mary's prominent rôle of Mediatrix, the presence of Christ, " walking the earth," was a symbol of the invisible power of God in the performance of miracles.

---

[121] *Ibid.,* no. vii, p. 372.
[122] *Op. cit.,* no. xii, p. 131.
[123] Cf. *infra,* pp. 122-30.
[124] *Ibid.,* no. xvii, p. 138.
[125] *Op. cit.,* 15 (col. 1789).

Mary as Mediatrix

No less theocentric are those accounts in which God performs the miracle for the honor and praise of the Mother:

> Proxima autem nocte quae sabbatum secuta est tot et tanta mirabilia *Christus* ad laudem et gloriam suae matris *est dignatus ostendere* ut numerum paene et fidem nisi his qui omnia possibilia Deo esse non dubitant videantur excedere.[126]

In the collection of Rocamadour it is related that a blind woman who has perseveringly prayed to the " Star of the Sea " that she might recover her vision, suddenly finds that her sight is restored; it is evident that she attributes the miracle to God, from the words of her thanksgiving " pre gaudio *Deum* deorum in Syon speculantis, *qui* meritis misericordis Domine *sanat et salvat* sperantes in se." [127] Hugo Farsit tells of a woman, similarly afflicted, who has heard " famam virtutum quas *faciebat Dominus* Suessionae, ob gratiam beatae Virginis matris suae." [128] She promises to make the long journey barefoot and immediately recovers her sight.

When prayers are addressed to Mary, she is not made an end in herself. It is expected that she will use her power of intercession at the throne of God. Thus when a knight, whose wife attempts suicide because of a misunderstanding, appeals to the Blessed Virgin, the prayer is introduced by the words, " preces *ad Dominum* convertit, ejus misericordem Matrem interpellans." [129] And again, when a man, unjustly accused of crime, must undergo the ordeal of fire, " orationem fudit *ad Dominum* his precibus interpellans Matrem pietatis." [130]

It is more clearly stated in the following anecdote that God grants a prayer, though it be addressed directly to Mary. A very zealous priest is at the point of death. His devoted parishioners pray to Our Lady of Rocamadour for his recovery:

> Verum quia *filius Dei unigenitus* dicit discipulis suis " quicquid petieritis in nomine meo dabit vobis [John, 16:23]" *preces eorum,* meritis ipsius Genitricis, *exaudivit.*[131]

---

[126] " Lettre de l'Abbé Haimon," *loc. cit.,* no. x, p. 129.
[127] *Op. cit.,* ii, no. 36, p. 246.   [128] *Op. cit.,* 26 (col. 1797).
[129] *Miracles de Notre-Dame de Roc-Amadour,* i, no. 7, p. 85.
[130] *Ibid.,* no. 10, p. 92.   [131] *Ibid.,* no. 2, p. 74.

The Son of God hears the prayer; His Mother is the suppliant. The omnipotence attributed to Mary in the statement, " quando et ubi et quantum [Maria] vult operatur," [132] is that of one who petitions, for " a Filio suo quicquid vult meretur." [133] And we read elsewhere: " *Nihil* enim *negabit Filius* quod Mater *impetrare* voluerit." [134] If she had divine power, impetration would be unnecessary.

In the following anecdotes God grants the prayer and effects the miracle because of the petitions of Mary. Little Huguette spends the entire night in the church dedicated to Our Lady of Rocamadour. As morning dawns, " respexit eam Dei genitrix," [135] and she hears and speaks for the first time:

> Audientes . . . voce magna laudabant *Deum qui per suffragia matris sue* gloriosissime Domine nostre tot et tanta stupenda fidelibus suis *confert beneficia.*

The cripple Gerbert, living two leagues from the shrine, has himself carried in a basket to the place of pilgrimage, because he has heard of the miracles " quot et quanta *filius* gloriosissime Virginis, per intercessionem sue matris . . . *faciat.*" [136] Stephen, the Abbot of Cluny (1161-1173), upon his deathbed invokes " *Deum* deorum in cubili cordis," [137] and prays to Mary as the " mediatricem inter se et nobile onus suum Redemptorem nostrum." His prayer becomes more and more ardent and because a " cor contritum et humiliatum *Regi regum complacet,*" he is cured. To the monks who are astonished at his recovery he says: " Enimvero Dei genitrix, perpetua Virgo de Rocamador, *impetravit a Filio* me saluti reddi." Guillaume Boyer is a very sympathetic figure in the collection of Rocamadour. A simple, hard-working man, he is suddenly stricken by blindness. For six years his wife suffers the miseries of poverty and the realization that the children are in want. However, she hears recounted " quanta *Dominus,* universorum reparator, per gloriosam Virginem, Dominam de Rochamador, *dignetur largiri beneficia,*" [138] and she begins to urge him to pray with confidence:

[132] *Ibid.,* ii, no. 41, p. 254.
[133] *Ibid.,* no. 21, p. 216.
[134] *Ibid.,* Prologue I, p. 63.
[135] *Ibid.,* no. 33, p. 127.

[136] *Ibid.,* no. 38, p. 137.
[137] *Ibid.,* ii, no. 38, p. 249.
[138] *Ibid.,* no. 18, p. 210.

> Ut quid nos soli expertes erimus *beneficiorum Dei?* Ut quid
> nobis existet durior ceteris qui dicit: " Petite et dabitur vobis,
> querite et invenietis [invenietis], pulsate et aperietur vobis?
> . . ." Petamus igitur instemus orationi, emundemus con-
> scientias nostras ut exaudiri mereamur. De residuo substan-
> tiole [substantione] nostre *honoremus Dominum.*

They will invoke Mary, " *post Deum* mortalium solam spem et
efficacem." Her words are persuasive and he, " ardens . . . toto
desiderio *divino vivificante spiritu,*" agrees. His cure is immediate.

Hugo Farsit presents Mary as a suppliant obtaining from God
the cessation of the plague. According to his anecdote, a child
is cured of the holy fire but by the " nutu divino," [139] entreats his
mother to allow him to make another pilgrimage to Soissons.
Upon her refusal he is again afflicted with the plague. When he
is finally brought to the church, he has a vision:

> Narrat . . . se raptum fuisse ante Deum, et Dominam nostram
> Dei Genitricem pro populo *supplicantem* vidisse, ut *dignaretur
> Deus* hunc morbum a populo *evertere* et hanc scintillam quae
> acciderat *auferre,* et ad hoc a filio suo responsum benigne
> accepisse: Mater, tu es maris stella, fiat omnis voluntas tua.[140]

Under the year 1129 Anselm of Gembloux records that when
many are stricken with the plague in Paris, one man has recourse to
Saint Martin. The saint appears to him and orders that he go to
the church dedicated to the Blessed Virgin. When the man is obsti-
nate, the saint speaks plainly:

> Sanat te dominus Jesus Christus precibus matris suae. Et
> hoc tibi signum: tu primus, post te sex in hac domo sana-
> buntur. Ceterum quicunque advenerint, frustra laborabunt.[141]

The same writer tells of the miracles wrought in many of the other
cities of France. He ends his account for the year with the words:

> Hec precipua loca conscripsimus; sed si per alia loca in
> memoriam ejus dicata vellemus evagari, ubi *inedicibili poten-
> tia* cunctos inibi confugientes mirabilis *Domini sanavit poten-
> tia,* nec sensus, nec ratio ad hec sufficere posset.[142]

---

[139] *Op. cit.,* 9 (col. 1783).

[140] See also Vincent of Beauvais, *op. cit.,* xxvii, 4; Helinand, *Chronicon,*
xlviii, an. 1129 (*PL,* CCXII, 1031) ; Gautier de Coincy, *Miracles de la
Sainte Vierge* (Paris, 1857), cols. 150-51.

[141] *Op. cit.* (col. 252).   [142] *Ibid.* (col. 254).

In the " Auctarium Ursicampinum " attached to the chronicle
of Sigebert of Gembloux under the year 1094 is narrated the history of a woman condemned to be burned for murdering her son-
in-law. Before being put to death, she is permitted to stop at
the church where she commends herself to the " meritis et *pre-*
cibus [143] of the Virgin Mary, making a public confession of her
guilt. The prayers of Mary are effective, for she is preserved from
the fire by God:

> Deinde missa in ignem, incendium nullatenus sensit, sed
> *divina protegente gratia* consumpto igne, ipsa permansit
> illaesa.

At first the spectators do not ascribe it to the " divinae virtuti,"
and more combustible material is added to her pyre:

> Iterato enim miraculo *servavit eam Deus* incolumem ab exus-
> tione ignis, ad laudem sui nominis suaeque genitricis gloriam
> et honorem.

However, God wills her death in another way: " et post laudes
Deo redditas, *volente Deo*, paucis diebus transactis transiit ab hoc
seculo."

In the account of the same event by Herman of Tournai, the
attributes of God are in the foreground: " Cui tantam *miseri-*
cordiam precibus suae Matris *praestiterat omnipotens Deus.*" [144]
The writer adds that all, therefore, should place confidence " in
auxilio sanctae Mariae "; from the word *precibus* used above, one
concludes this assistance to be one of mediation. Elsewhere, Herman relates an anecdote in which both the mercy of Christ and
of Mary are referred to. The monks of Laon have begun to intone
the *Te Deum* in thanksgiving for a miracle in behalf of a fifteen-
year-old boy, a deaf-mute from birth. They have more occasion
for joy when the father whose rapacious ferocity is a matter of
fear to all his neighbors, becomes completely subdued. Indeed,
" idem raptor, misericordia Dei Genitricis animatus," [145] goes so

---

[143] *PL*, CLX, 405; for the same story, as narrated by Guibert of Nogent,
cf. *supra*, p. 37; for the version in the " Auctarium Laudunense " to the
chronicle of Sigebert of Gembloux, cf. *infra*, pp. 120-21.

[144] *Op. cit.*, iii, 27 (col. 1011).   [145] *Ibid.*, i, 6 (col. 969).

far as to accompany the monks with their reliquary to the strong-
hold of a knight who is his enemy. His humility and the report
of the miracle so disarm his rival that he graciously receives the
party who praise " *Christi misericordiam* qui *per suam Matrem*
hostes hostibus occurrere pacifice fecerat." The direct attribution to Christ would seem, in this case, to mark a distinction between the source of mercy and that of the suppliant.

This is even clearer in the account of Hugo Farsit concerning a
woman whose nose is miraculously restored. A victim of the
plague, she has hope of relief " per eamdem matrem misericordiae." [146] Yet, when the miracle takes place, the writer remarks:

> Quid mirum si tunc recens recognoscentibus se fecit miracu-
> lum, quae in tota vita sua *circumferens tantam Dei miseri-
> cordiam,* testimonium *divinae gratiae* publice exhibuit? . . .
> Ardor igitur fervensque fides populorum non erubescebat
> nasum et ora ejus osculari, quasi quod modo recenter *manibus
> ipsius Dei esset factum.*

In Hugo's story the woman has prayed to the Virgin Mary; in
that of Anselm of Gembloux she appeals to the " mater misericordiae " and then addresses her petition to God:

> *Deus,* qui factus es filius feminae *propter misericordiam, sana
> me* per feminam matrem tuam *propter tuam misericordiam.*[147]

The attributes of God are not in the background in the collection
of Coutances, which relates the many favors wrought by the gratia
Dei et meritis Virginis Mariae.[148] Here it is recounted that Bishop
Geoffrey by the " Dei nutu " finds what he believes to be a relic
of the Mother of God. One man proposes that they place it upon
his eyes which are losing their sight and causing him constant
pain, inasmuch as he has confidence in the " clementia *Dei* et ejus
piissimae Genitricis virtute." [149] To this the Bishop answers:

> Oremus ergo *prius ad Dominum,* qui est *justus judex, fortis
> et patiens,* cujus solius judicia sunt vera, justificata in seme-
> tipsa, indicio ut hoc judicio declaret in nobis judicii sui veri-

---

[146] *Op. cit.,* 7 (col. 1781).   [147] *Op. cit.,* an. 1129 (col. 252).
[148] *Op. cit.,* no. xiii, p. 376; no. xxvii, p. 381; cf. *supra,* p. 106.
[149] *Ibid.,* no. xxii, p. 378.

tatem, scilicet, ut, si capillus iste, de quo agimus veraciter
fuit de corpore suae sacratissimae Matris.

This prayer, accompanied by an invocation of the Holy Trinity
and the application of the relic to his eyes, produces the cure
desired.

The brevity of most of the accounts in the collection of Saint-
Dié precludes any conclusions as to the relative emphasis on the
attributes of God and Mary; however, in the first miracle the poet
is quite prolix. A woman, hopelessly crippled, is carried halfway
to the shrine by her husband, who dies on the journey. In her
intense suffering,

> Fame, siti, frigore pestis eam stravit,[150]

she turns to God:

> O Deus *omnipotens, dulcis* atque *mitis,*
> *Qui* tuum *praesidium* quibusvis *immittis,*
> Et personas hominum nequaquam admittis;
> Qui tamen consideras intellectum mentis,
> Miserorum gemitus, et lacrymis flectis,
> *Da mihi subsidium* ad modum medentis.
> Nam quod digne petitur, dignanter impendis.
> Sed fortassis miseram, abjectamque spernis,
> Nam plenam flagitiis, indignamque cernis.

She continues to lament her unworthiness and then has recourse to
Mary:

> Huc, O Dei Genitrix, moestorum solamen,
> Impotenti veniam praestas et juvamen
> Sicut precanti expedire scis. Amen.

A voice commands her to continue her journey to the church where
she will receive the grace which she solicits.

During the plague of Soissons when human aid can be of no
avail, the people turn to the Virgin as a Mediatrix. They accompany their prayers by penance, hoping to move God to mercy.
Hugo Farsit describes the penitent people as bare-foot " exemplo
Ninivitarum armati humilitate, et adjunctis sibi poenitentiae copiis,
ut congrederentur *cum pio et misericorde Deo.*" [151] For the word

---

[150] *Op. cit.*, p. 34.   [151] *Op. cit.*, 1 (col. 1778).

" extorquere " used by Haimo,[152] he substitutes an even more expressive word—" vincere." Moreover, it is God in His mercy, who is conceived as being " conquered " by their penance:

> . . . congrederentur, inquam, et *vincerent. Pius* est enim, et non potest diutius sufferre impressiones praecordialis doloris et immensae miseriae, sed statim cedit et *vincitur, quia pius est.*

When Senorez, a knight of Longay [153] in Perigord, is stricken with paralysis because he ridicules the offerings at Rocamadour, the grace of repentance for his blasphemies is said to be a gift of God's mercy:

> *Dignetur Dominus noster Jesus Christus* militi suo *facere misericordiam,* dignetur hunc sanare *potenti virtute* . . . *miserator Domine,* . . . per hujus etenim fidei tarditatem quam plures reddentur certiores, *opus tue* benignitatis verentes.

He has recourse to Mary because of her proximity to her Son, " quia posse tibi adjacet." He is cured: ". . . laudans Dominum, glorificans et pietatem Matris ejus *advocate* de Rocamador longe lateque predicans."

The Virgin is frequently given the title of " Advocata " in the collection of Rocamadour.[154] Haimo refers to her as " Interventrix." On the way to Saint-Pierre-sur-Dive a certain Odo is run over by a cart so heavily loaded with rocks that it crushes the very stones of the roadway: " Nulla certe spes vitae ejus esse poterat, nisi ille *divinitus* servaretur." [155] All call upon the name " *interventricis* suae matris Jesu," and the man rises unhurt. Haimo concludes: " Sic ad cultum et venerationem matris *bonus filius* fidelium animos *provocabat.*" At another time a huge stone slips from the wagon and is about to fall on the foot of one Andrew: " Sed *protegente* eum *Jesu,* suae matris interventu, minime laesus est." [156] The term is also found in the " Auctarium

---

[152] Cf. *supra,* pp. 97-98.

[153] The editor identifies Longay in the present day as a commune of Sainte-Foy, canton of Lalinde, arrondissement of Bergerac. *Miracles de Notre-Dame de Roc-Amadour,* p. 290, n. 3.

[154] *Ibid.,* i, no. 4, p. 78; no. 49, p. 156; ii, no. 2, p. 178; no. 9, p. 189; no. 17, p. 208; iii, no. 11, p. 292; no. 14, p. 294; no. 22, p. 308.

[155] *Op. cit.,* no. v, p. 125.   [156] *Ibid.,* no. iv, p. 124.

Laudunense " of the chronicle of Sigebert. A woman, who has her son-in-law strangled, repents and asks Mary " in tanto discrimine interventricem sibi affore." [157] In the collection of Rocamadour a soldier who has exposed himself with temerity is mortally wounded by the Basques. He is beyond human aid : " Eger autem auxilium sperans *a Domino qui* per interventum matris ejus generose multos *ad vitam* noverat *rediisse* se adhuc spirantem non ambigebat vita posse donari." [158] His confidence in the " celesti virtute " is rewarded.

Even more frequently Mary is given the title of " Mediatrix." [159] Christ is always the Redeemer,[160] and therefore, the source of grace. One afflicted soul, in addressing God, cries out that we have all need of His grace : " Nam, cum omnes peccaverimus, *omnes egemus* gratia tua, quia nemo mundus a sorde, nec infans unius diei." [161] Mary is the Mother of the Redeemer : " Verum mediatrix Dei et hominum, Mater illius qui tulit peccata mortalium, qui mortem non pessimorum set magis conversionem." [162] Elsewhere it is said that through her the gate of Heaven opens for us, because from her was born the One Who reconciled us to the Father, that is, the Mediator Jesus Christ : " Quia ex te natus Deus nos Deo patri suo confederat." [163] She is invoked by mankind " quia filio tuo Domino nostro complaces in omnibus." [164]

Her rank in the celestial court is clearly stated : " *Super sanctorum milia*, illam que *post Filium* in celesti prepollet curia." [165] Above the saints but below her Son,[166] she is a mere creature : " *Creaturarum omnium dignioris*, post Filium altioris." [167] More poetically described, " Sicut sol lucidior est luna et luna clarior est syderibus, sic Maria *dignior creaturis omnibus*." [168]

[157] *Op. cit.*, an. 1096, col. 359.   [158] *Op. cit.*, i, no. 51, p. 160.

[159] *Ibid.*, ii, no. 15, p. 205; no. 22, p. 219; no. 33, p. 239; no. 38, p. 249; no. 42, p. 256. See also " Lettre de l'Abbé Haimon," *loc. cit.*, no. xvi, p. 136.

[160] Cf. *supra*, pp. 108-109.   [163] *Ibid.*, no. 34, p. 242.

[161] *Ibid.*, ii, no. 24, p. 223.   [164] *Ibid.*

[162] *Ibid.*, no. 11, p. 195.   [165] *Ibid.*, iii, no. 22, p. 308.

[166] See also *ibid.*, ii, no. 17, p. 208; no. 18, p. 211; iii, no. 18, p. 301; no. 24, p. 317; in the collection of St.-Pierre-sur-Dive, *op. cit.*, no. i, p. 121; iii, p. 124.

[167] *Ibid.*, iii, no. 20, p. 305.   [168] *Ibid.*, ii, no. 34, p. 242.

Yet Mary is not all in the lives of these simple folk. There are some like the good pastor, Bernard of Lesvaux in Quercy, " Cui vivere *Christus* fuerat et mori lucrum," [169] and at the point of death, " cupiebat dissolvi ut *Christo* viveret." There are some, too, like Guillaume Boyer and his sympathetic neighbors," quibus *Deus erat omnia.*" [170]   And there were thousands, according to Haimo, " ducente eos Domino," [171] like the cart-haulers of Saint-Pierre-sur-Dive, who knew well Who would forgive the sins for which they were doing penance, and the creature, though the most powerful of creatures, who would intercede—an army which the Abbot designates by the theocentric title " Domini exercitus." [172]

Mary as Operatrix

The appellation " Operatrix " [173] as applied to the Blessed Virgin in the very theocentric collection of Saint-Pierre-sur-Dive seems at first to border on mariolatry. That we may not so interpret this title is evident from Haimo's use of the word and his presentation of Mary as an active agent or mediatrix in the accomplishment of God's will.

In one of the accounts he proposes to tell " quid in ipso sabbato circa quamdam famulam suam misericordiae *mater operari dignata sit.*" [174]   Emma, a hopeless invalid, has been brought to the shrine. The Blessed Virgin appears to the girl, who is lying " ante crucem benigni ejus filii," and utters these significant words:

> Noli, . . . noli, filia de salute desperare; *potens est Dominus* tibi in proximo subvenire, et ego hinc nunc quidem abiens non post multum revertor, et cum rediero salutem simul affuturam simul polliceor.

And because God is powerful, as Mary herself asserts, she returns

---

[169] *Ibid.,* i, no. 2, p. 73, according to Paul, *Phil.* 1: 23. This is also said of Géraud, lord of the Château Saint-Míchel in Quercy, *ibid.,* iii, no. 3, p. 276.

[170] *Ibid.,* ii, no. 18, p. 210; see also *supra,* pp. 115-16.

[171] *Op. cit.,* no. ii, p. 122.   [172] *Ibid.,* no. iii, p. 122.

[173] Mary Mediatrix may appear both as suppliant and as an active agent in the performance of a miracle. When she acts in the latter capacity, Haimo applies to her the title " Operatrix." Cf. *supra,* p. 70, n. 39.

[174] " Lettre de l'Abbé Haimon," *loc. cit.,* no. ix, p. 129.

as His visible agent or "operatrix" to complete the cure, and the girl "in conspectu astantium, laetantium et in ea *Dominum glorificantium*, de lecto surrexit."

At another time a deaf-mute receives his hearing. The people rejoice "de dono *Dei*," [175] but one woman, full of faith and confidence that the sufferer will recover the gift of speech also, proposes to take him with her as she helps draw a cart to Saint-Pierre-sur-Dive. She is mocked. Perhaps she will make the child a tongue! Undaunted, she answers:

> Non insanio certe, . . . sed domina mea quae auditum dedit dabit et linguam. Certa sum, secura sum *quia possibilia sunt omnia apud Deum.*

The reply is paradoxical unless the distinction between the source of power and the agency of Mary is accepted. Halfway on the journey the boy begins to feel a new tongue growing and gradually increasing in size, "sed paulatim in majus crescebat, ut scilicet et miraculum augeretur et *Dei* in eo *magnificentia amplior haberetur.*" With joy his companions pull the heavy cart, for "nihil asperum prae ardore fidei et laetitiae magnitudine refugiunt." When they arrive his tongue is entire, but he does not as yet speak, and their prayers continue: "*Misericordia Domini* propensius exoratur." The boy is brought to the attention of the priest, who chides him for his inattentiveness as he merely gazes with a fixed stare at the tower of the church:

> Et ille, statim laxata *divinitus* lingua: "Nonne, ait, videtis dominam meam sanctam Mariam ibi stantem . . . puerulumque sub veste tenentem?

According to Haimo, he sees her standing,

> quia *adjuvantem*, bene *cum puero*, sed *puero Verbo, Verbo carnem facto*, quia et puer erat qui videbat, et *qui videbatur* in ore ejus qui nunquam locutus fuerat, *verba formabat.*

The multitude give full vent to their joy: "Tota in *Dei* laude ecclesia personat, gratiarum et laudum *Deo* praeconia offeruntur." They wish to see his tongue, because "in ea speciale *Dei* cernere se et venerari gaudebant." Haimo concludes:

[175] *Ibid.*, no. xiii, p. 132.

> In ipsa ecclesia praecipue, tantas *Christus ad* honorem et laudem gloriosissimae suae matris virtutes *est dignatus osten-dere,* ut eas enarrare omnino nobis sit impossibile.[176]

It is to be observed that in the case of the cripple, Murieldis, and the man with a withered hand, Haimo writes:

> Statim misericordiae *mater* . . . mulierem incurvam *erexit* et homini praedicto manum *restituit.*[177]

However, he continues:

> Cum hymnis et laudibus multoque tripudio eos ad ecclesiam, *agentes Deo gratias,* deduxerunt.

He uses practically the same expressions in relating a miracle which occurs when a loaded cart, drawn by pilgrims, passes through Trun,[178] and a well-known cripple, " in conspectu eorum pia Domini mater potenter erexit. . . . Tunc iterata laetitia laudes universi et gratias *Deo* referunt." [179] And he immediately adds: " Tum certe *in opere suo Deum praesentem* laetarique *agnoscunt.*" This last statement seems to render impossible any mariolatrous interpretation of the words " mater erexit." Moreover, it is to be noted that when Haimo gives the simple fact of a miracle, he is most theocentric. Thus he writes: " Contractam quamdam, . . . ante altare, *Dominus,* astante populo, relevavit." [180]   Or again, "Ad Sanctum Leonardum cum venissent, contractum . . . *Dominus* matris suae precibus ita *restituit.*" [181]

In the following miracle Mary is said to defend the city, but a consideration of all details shows that the miraculous protection is attributed to God.   The bands of adventurers who roved from village to village had by 1164 become a veritable scourge.[182]   What terror an approaching army of Brabançons [183] could inspire in the townspeople is vividly described in the collection of Rocamadour:

[176] *Ibid.,* p. 134. For a similar statement, cf. *supra,* pp. 107 and 114.
[177] *Ibid.,* no. x, p. 129.
[178] Trun (Orne), arrondissement of Argentan. *Ibid.,* p. 135, n. 2.
[179] *Ibid.,* no. xv, p. 135.   [181] *Ibid.,* no. xv, p. 135.
[180] *Ibid.,* no. xiv, p. 134.   [182] Albe, *op. cit.,* p. 277, n. 2.
[183] The Brabançons were in the pay of Raymond V, Count of Toulouse, in his war against Alfonsus, King of Aragon. *Ibid.,* p. 277, n. 1; iii, no. 17, p. 298.

Exterius plaudebatur, interius lugebatur; exterius assultus et insidie, omne denique genus dolositatis perquirebatur; interius vero pro patria, domo, pro suorum exterminio, pro virginum exsecranda defloratione, et conjugum odibili violatione civiliter resistebatur. Videres matres in lugubri veste, juvenculas incompto crine debachantes clamare, plorando plateas circuire, lapides jactandos ad munitionem deferre, viros ad bella procedentes animare, senum et imbellium manus extendere ad alta, *incessanter Domini querentes suffragia.*[184]

Humanly speaking, they are no match for the band of *routiers* and they ask for divine assistance:

Sciebant etenim quod *de celo* pendet victoria, ut sicut Moyse orante vincebat Israel et vincebatur Amalehc [sic] ita clamosa oratione, ferventi devotione *ad aures Omnipotentis* lacrimose clamabatur, ut ducti penitentia exaudiri mererentur.

The women then address themselves to the Virgin of Rocamadour and she "cives exaudiens mirabiliter et manifeste *defendit.*" According to the wording of the narrative which follows, however, it is not the Virgin who defends but God Himself. For we are told that the air is serene and calm; there is no rain nor wind nor earthquake. Yet, when the wall falls upon the enemy, the populace ascribe the disaster to the avenging hand of God:

Ut *Potentis potentia* luce clarius clareret omnibus, in longum amplius quam sexaginta cubitos de ambitu murorum funditus dejecit, barbaros interficiendo. . . . Quippe exercitus qui in sui ferocitate et innumerositate confiderat, *sentiens manum Domini super se aggravari* [I Reg. 5:6] . . . et inexpugnatam fugiens civitatem quam citius recessit, in monimentum *divine ultionis* cadaverum fetentium relinquens vestigia.

The people in gratitude for the divine protection obtained through the mediation of Mary, go in pilgrimage to Rocamadour.

The Virgin takes an active part in the following miracle which, however, is theocentric. Hugo Farsit tells of a boy, Christian by name, who for eighteen years has been a deaf-mute. He comes to Soissons, and there in the crowded church, "sola mente et nutibus *ad Deum clamans,* nam lingua non poterat,"[185] he prays patiently, awaiting the time "quando respiceret eum *gratia divina.*" In the

[184] *Ibid.,* iii, no. 4, p. 278.   [185] *Op. cit.,* 11 (col. 1785).

words of Hugo, " respexit *Deus*," for he sees the Blessed Virgin resplendent with light:

> Tunc vero dulci manu sua fauces aegroti pertractans et ora vinculum linguae et aurium resolvit.

The youth silently withdraws from the church, but his cure is quickly perceived by his companions. The pastor, hearing of the miracle, treats Christian as an impostor, until the youth is led into his presence, and the priest's incredulity gives way to the deepest contrition, " quod . . . ausus fuit de potentia Domini et matris ejus dubitare." There is no public thanksgiving, however, until neighbors testify that he has been a deaf-mute from birth, and he himself " testimonium perhibente *gratiae Dei*." Then the joy of the people knows no bounds: " Tunc vero laudes canuntur *Deo altissimo* . . . *et gloria Dei* in commune praedicatur." Mary, who has been instrumental in the cure, receives no recognition in the thanksgiving.

However, she has a share in the expressions of joy when a little crippled boy is seen to walk for the first time; nevertheless, her praise does not overshadow that of her Son:

> Tum nomen beatae Virginis millies replicatur, ita ut clamore hominum et clangore tympanorum fragiles adhuc parietes ecclesiae a fundamentis everti viderentur. *Jesu bone,* nunquid non praesenseras huic spectaculo, quale tu ipse plurimum diligis, cum ardens fides et furor diligentium te certatim rapiebant te, et sacrificium contriti spiritus libamine dulcium lacrymarum condiebatur.[186]

Mary is also the active physician in the cure of Robert de Joüy. Because of the stench from his gangrenous foot, he is forced to leave the church, but in his prayer to the Virgin he assures her that wherever he is " a *Filio tuo* salutem mihi *potes impetrare*." [187] Then he addresses Christ:

> Domine Jesu, respice in servum matris tuae, ecce recedo et morior, quoniam a te devellor, *summe Deus*, recordare servi tui et servi matris tuae. Iteratis doloribus affligitur cor meum qui *a te* recedo.

Later when the Virgin Mary appears and restores the amputated

[186] *Ibid.*, 13 (col. 1787).   [187] *Ibid.*, 31 (col. 1799).

foot, Robert joyfully runs to the church—into the very "Holy of Holies"—and gives vent to his emotions: "Hic est pes dominae meae Sanctae Mariae." But, says Hugo, God Himself inspired his words: "Melius ipse novit Deus, qui verba devotionum format."

Mary also appears in the collection of Rocamadour as "Operatrix." It is narrated that a knight named Peter is taken prisoner at the siege of the château of Anjou in Vienne.[188] He does not lose courage, "fiduciam habens *in Domino* qui erigit contritos corde et sanat contritiones eorum."[189] However impregnable the fortress, and high the walls, the captive persists "ut eum non meritis set precibus *Liberator omnium Dominus de carcere educeret* et ad propria *reduceret.*" He likewise invokes Notre-Dame of Rocamadour, assuring himself that she has most power in the celestial court "post Filium." He falls asleep from fatigue but is awakened by a voice which commands him to arise and leave. He passes through the doors of the prison, slides down a dangerous wall without accident, and at last by the "Virginis auxilio" breaks with a turn of his hands the last chain. He delays in going to Rocamadour to acknowledge the favor, and when war is renewed he and his brother are again taken prisoner. He confidently boasts that the Virgin who delivered him once will again exert her power. In his dungeon cell he fasts and prays, "non nisi *in Domino* quiescebat." The brother, because of his wounds, has been placed in an upper part of the fortress; the more he suffers, "tanto amplius *opem divinam* et *opus* misericordie expetebat." Peter is finally allowed to share his brother's cell and the writer attributes the leniency of the guards to God: "*Dedit* itaque *Dominus* utrique gratiam in conspectu custodum." They spend the entire day in prayer and invoke the aid of the Blessed Virgin. That night, "Operatrice magnalium operante," they are certain that escape will be possible. Their confidence is rewarded. One cannot but remark, despite references to the kindly offices of Mary Operatrix, that trust in God is primary; the expression "post Filium" is evidence of her secondary position.

[188] As the editor indicates this is a château of Anjou, today a commune of the canton of Roussillon, arrondissement of Vienne (Isère). Albe, *op. cit.*, p. 307, n. 2.

[189] *Ibid.*, iii, no. 22, p. 308.

The writer of the *miracula* of Rocamadour more frequently has
recourse to a circumlocution which has the same connotation as
Operatrix: he would write of the miracles " que *per Filium suum
Dominum nostrum, Salvatorum* [Salvatorem] *omnium* florida
Virgo et Immaculata brevi temperis [temporis] intervallo *fieri
voluit.*"[190]   He merely substitutes for the one word *Operatrix*,
" Virgo per Filium."

Accordingly, when all the pilgrims pray for the cure of Gervaise,
the Virgin of Rocamadour hears their petitions,

> *per filium suum* Dominum nostrum Jesum Christum qui cum
> patre sanctoque Flamine per immortalia vivit et regnat secula
> Deus.[191]

A soldier, Géraud Tosez, wounded in the neck, can no longer speak
and breathes with the greatest difficulty.   After a night spent in
prayer, he is being taken home from the shrine, when he declares
himself well, praising our Lady " que *per filium suum* Dominum
nostrum curans languentes reddit sanitati."[192]   A woman, re-
covering the gift of speech, thanks "mundi Dominam, omnium
per filium salvatricem."[193]   Guillaume Fouquier spends eight
months as a captive of the Saracens.   Before the Feast of the
Assumption his mother redoubles her prayers for his deliverance.
On the vigil the young man falls asleep, tired from his labors and
prayers: " Frequenter in cubili cordis se mactabat *Domino*."[194]
His chains are broken when he awakens and he goes to Rocamadour to render thanks to Mary " qui *per filium suum Salvatorem
omnium* salvat sperantes in se, qui trinus et unus vivit et regnat
in secula."[195]   A similar prodigy occurs in favor of a prisoner,
Pierre le Bègue, who returns home " gratificans Virginem virginum que *per Salvatorem omnium* unicum Filium suum Dominum nostrum operatur salutem in medio terre."[196]   When a fire
threatens the homes of the people of Saint-Geniès in Rouergue,[197]
the inhabitants have recourse to Notre-Dame of Rocamadour, and
the wrath of God changes into a " dew of refreshment ":

[190] *Ibid.*, Prologue II, p. 167.

[191] *Ibid.*, i, no. 41, p. 142.

[192] *Ibid.*, no. 48, p. 155.

[193] *Ibid.*, ii, no. 5, p. 182.

[194] *Ibid.*, i, no. 53, p. 162.

[195] *Ibid.*, p. 164.

[196] *Ibid.*, iii, no. 18, p. 302.

[197] Saint-Geniès-d'Olt,   arrondissement   d'Espalian (Aveyron).   *Ibid.*,
p. 256, n. 2.

Clamore lacrimantium Beatam Mariam de Rochamador simul invocantium celum penetratur et *ira corripientis Domini* non in furore omnia exterminantis, *conversa est in rorem refrigerii.*[198]

The wind suddenly dies down and the catastrophe is averted:

Incontinenti peritura conservante Domina, super omnes propitia, *per Filium suum* Dominum nostrum Jesum Christum, qui trinus et unus, per immortalia secula vivat et regnat Deus.

More unusual is the account of a Gascon woman, falsely accused of poisoning her relatives and friends. She is to be burned alive but the flames are miraculously extinguished. Delivered, she goes to Rocamadour,

. . . et gracias ei reddidit, que operatur in omnibus *per unicum Filium suum* Dominum nostrum Jhesum Christum cui est honor et imperium in secula seculorum.[199]

According to Géraud, lord of the château of Saint-Michel in Quercy, Mary can do all things through the grace and power of her Son: " Non ambigo Dominam meam *omnia posse in Filii sui* beneficio et virtute."[200] Guibert of Nogent, after relating a miracle wrought through the reliquary of Laon, in addressing God, exclaims: " Ecce, quae in Maria *praestas.*"[201] It is remarkable that in relating the miracles, the writers do not lose themselves in the spectacular and leave to implication a truth which needed no expounding and which was almost a platitude. Mary is an efficient instrument of God in the *miracula*, but merely an instrument, and depending for her efficiency solely upon Him. Certainly this attitude towards Mary Operatrix is not mariolatrous.

The rôle of the Blessed Virgin in the local collections is primarily one of mediation, for the hope of the medieval man is that of an age of metaphysical security in which one has recourse to divine aid and to the intercession of Mary:

Omne ope humana destituta et desperata, contulit se *ad divinum auxilium* et ad propitiam matrem misericordiae, quae spiritu contritos exaudire solita est.[202]

---

[198] *Ibid.*, ii, no. 43, p. 257.
[199] *Ibid.*, iii, no. 24, p. 317.
[200] *Ibid.*, no. 3, p. 276.
[201] *Op. cit.*, iii, 12 (col. 939).
[202] Hugo Farsit, *op. cit.*, 26 (col. 1796); *ibid.*, 7 (col. 1781); *ibid.*, 13 (col. 1786).

Famines, floods, pestilences, and other scourges are, in the opinion of the people, a punishment for sin, but the Virgin is always approachable and is ready and powerful to appease the divine wrath. By their flagellations and humiliating penance they literally " extorted " an answer to their petitions. Few of the other types of miracle collections present such an interest or such a deep religious spirit. The writers assert that all is well-attested fact.[203] The vogue of the *miracula* as literature is partially explained by the beginning of wonders in the local shrines.

---

[203] In the collection of Coutances the writer says that he could hope for no reward from God for his labor, were he to exceed the truth, since He is " pura veritas," *op. cit.*, p. 364; in that of Laon, " teste Deo ejus Filio, sine ulla falsitate retulimus narratione veracissima," *op. cit.*, ii. 22 (cols. 986 ff.) ; in that of Soissons, " certiore omnium gentium testimonio," *op. cit.*, 31 (col. 1800) ; in that of Rocamadour, " cuncta que cotidie videmus, cotidie audimus," *op. cit.*, p. 165; in that of Saint-Dié, the author says that the miracles occurred " sub oculis nostris," and he cites as canonical witnesses: " Domino Johanne de Fontenai, magno Praeposito, Tullensis Ecclesiae tunc electo; magistro Werrico de Darnolio decano, . . . domino Symone de Parroya, cantore constituto; Nicholao de Amantia, scholastico," *op. cit.*, pp. 29-31.

CHAPTER IV

THE VERNACULAR COLLECTIONS

The unknown writer of the Theophilus legend referred to by Adgar,[1] and a certain Guiot designated by the author of one of the miracles in MS *Arsenal 3518*[2] were probably the two earliest writers to treat the Marial legend in the vernacular. Unfortunately their writings are not extant. The manuscript fragment, containing four miracles found at Orléans, which was written in the second half of the twelfth century, is the oldest specimen so far discovered.[3]

Since there is still question as to the Norman or Anglo-Norman authorship of the Orléans fragment,[4] one may include only three collections under the latter category: first, the miracles of Adgar, translated at the end of the twelfth century from the work of a certain Mestre Albri[5] and preserved in the incomplete MS *Egerton 612*,[6] in a fragment in the library of Alleyn College at Dulwich[7] and in a manuscript of Sir Henry Hope Edwardes;[8] second,

[1] *Marienlegenden*, ed. Carl Neuhaus, p. 81.

[2] Paul Meyer, "Notices sur un manuscrit d'Orléans contenant d'anciens miracles de la Vierge en vers français," *Not. et extr.*, XXXIV, 2 (1895), 34.

[3] *Ibid.*, pp. 31-35.

[4] J. Morawski, "Mélanges de littérature pieuse," *Romania*, LXI (1935), 163.

[5] According to Mussafia, the work of Mestre Albri is based, either directly or through the intermediary of other copies, upon a collection of William of Malmesbury, preserved in MS 97 of the Library of Salisbury. *Studien*, IV, pp. 29 ff.

[6] The forty miracles have been published by Neuhaus (cf. n. 1); also the Latin miracles of MS *Cotton Cleopatra C. x.* of the British Museum in *Die lateinischen Vorlagen zu den altfranzösischen Adgar'schen Marienlegenden*. There is not yet conclusive proof that the story of the Abbess at the end of the manuscript was not written by Adgar. See Rolfs, "Die Adgarlegenden," *Rom. Forsch.* I (1883), 179-236; J. A. Herbert, "A New Manuscript of Adgar's Mary-Legends," *Romania*, XXXII (1903), 415-16.

[7] *Das Dulwich'er Adgar-Fragment*, ed. Neuhaus (Aschersleben, 1887). This edition is rare and has been inaccessible to the writer. Fortunately, Herbert has printed the introduction to the *Gracial* (cf. *infra*, p. 134) collated with the Dulwich text. Mussafia has done the same for the Vision of Wettin (*Studien*, IV, p. 34 ff.); there remains only the latter fragment of the Theophilus legend which is equivalent to lines 559-1102 of *Egerton* no. 17 in Neuhaus, *Adgars Marienlegenden*, p. 79 ff.

[8] The prologue and ten miracles which are lacking in the *Egerton* manuscript have been published from this copy by Herbert, *loc. cit.*, pp. 394-421.

an anonymous collection of sixty miracles, composed between 1230 and 1250 and contained in a single manuscript *Old Royal 20 B XIV* of the British Museum;[9] third, the *Miracles de la Vierge*, written by Everard de Gateley in the thirteenth century, a collection of three miracles and a prologue in an Oxford manuscript, *Rawlinson Poetry 241*.[10] One may add to these a single miracle at the end of MS *Ee. 6, 30* of the University of Cambridge, dating from the thirteenth century.[11]

Among the French collections the most remarkable, according to Paul Meyer,[12] is the *Miracles de la sainte Vierge* of Gautier de Coincy. One may judge of its success by the survival of seventy-nine manuscripts,[13] of which Abbé Poquet has published that of Soissons.[14] Gautier's work is also the most extensive, consisting of fifty-four miracles related in thirty thousand lines, and was written between the years 1218 and 1227.[15]

The *Vie des Pères*, dating from the middle of the thirteenth century, survives in over thirty manuscripts. It is the work of two writers; the first poet lived in the Marne district, not far from Paris, while the second was a Picard.[16] In six manuscripts the

---

[9] *Deuxième collection anglo-normande des miracles de la Vierge et son original latin*, p. xvi. The editor, Kjellman, includes variants from *MS 375* and *818* of the Bibliothèque nationale.

[10] Paul Meyer, " Notice du MS. Rawlinson Poetry 241," *Romania*, XXIX (1900), 27-47.

[11] Paul Meyer has printed seventy verses of this legend—the vision of the flowering field. " Les manuscrits français de Cambridge," *Romania*, XV (1886), 272-73.

[12] *Loc. cit., Not. et extr.*, XXXIV, 2, p. 31.

[13] Arlette P. Ducrot-Granderye, " Etudes sur les Miracles Nostre Dame de Gautier de Coinci," *Annales Academiae Scientiarum Fennicae*, Series B, XXV, 2 (1932), 16 ff.

[14] While Abbé Poquet assigns this manuscript to the beginning of the thirteenth century on the authority of Michel Germain, Alfred Darcel and E. Fleury place it in the fourteenth century. *Ibid.*, p. 21.

[15] Ducrot-Granderye distinguishes three successive periods: in 1218 he composed the first book; towards 1222 he added songs, developed miracle 12-13 and wrote the poems of St. Leocadia; from 1223 to 1227 he drew up the second book and changed the arrangement of poem 46, which he had revised, to 82. *Ibid.*, p. 171.

[16] E. Schwan, " La Vie des anciens Pères," *Romania*, XIII (1884), 259 f.

two *Vies* are found as one collection at the end of the thirteenth century. No critical edition has as yet appeared.[17]

In 1262 Jean le Marchant translated a Latin manuscript which he found at the cathedral of Chartres.[18] Written in 1212, the original has been identified with the Vatican manuscript *Reginensis 339* and contains all but five of the vernacular miracles.[19] *Le Livre des miracles de Notre-Dame de Chartres* is composed of thirty-two miracles related in 6400 lines, and while the collection does not possess the same literary value as that of Gautier de Coincy to a naïveté which distinguished the writers of the epoch, Jean le Marchant joins " une certaine facilité de style qui n'est pas indigne d'être remarquée." [20]

In the second half of the thirteenth century a writer from the district of Lyons [21] composed the legends found in MS *Bibl. nat. fr. 818*, the last part of which includes some of the miracles found in the collection of Gautier de Coincy and in the *Vie des Pères*.[22] Kjellman has published thirty-five as variants in his edition of MS *Old Royal 20 B XIV*.[23] Fourteen more were published by Mussafia,[24] who indicates their sources in Pez, MSS *lat. 14463, 5257, 5268* of the Bibliothèque nationale. Only twenty-three remain unpublished.[25]

In this study the six larger collections prior to the fourteenth century are treated in detail. Fragments, the three miracles of Everard de Gateley, legends inserted in works such as the *Roman de Rou* [26] and the *Conception de Nostre-Dame* [27] of Wace or the *Miserere* [28] of the Renclus de Moiliens are referred to incidentally.

[17] *Ibid.*, pp. 232-33. Cf. *infra*, p. 178, n. 171.

[18] *Le livre de miracles de Notre-Dame de Chartres*, pp. 210-11.

[19] " Les miracles de Notre-Dame de Chartres," ed. Antoine Thomas, *Bibl. de l'Ecole des Chartes*, XLII (1881), pp. 504-550.

[20] Jean le Marchant, *op. cit.*, p. viii.

[21] Paul Meyer, " Notice sur le recueil de Miracles de la Vierge, renfermé dans le MS Bibl. nat. fr. 818," *Not. et extr.*, XXXIV, 2 (1895), 58 ff.

[22] *Ibid.* Cf. Morawski, *loc. cit.*, pp. 175 ff.

[23] *Op. cit.*, Appendix, pp. 269-306.　　[24] *Studien*, V, pp. 19-74.

[25] Morawski, *loc. cit.*, pp. 207-208. We would add to Morawski's list of published legends, no. 30. Cf. Kjellman, " La légende de Saint Jean Damascène," *Studier i Modern Språkvetenskap*, VIII (1921), 103-20.

[26] Ed. Hugo Andresen (Heilbronn, 1877), I, 68 ff.; II, 43 ff.

[27] Ed. William Ray Ashford (Chicago, 1933), pp. 1-11.

[28] Ed. A. G. Van Hamel (Paris, 1885), pp. 265-73.

Adgar

In the prologue to the " Gracial " [29] found in both the Dulwich [30] and Edwardes MSS, Adgar says that he intends to relate the miracles for the purpose of attracting men to God:

> Meillur uvre ne put hume fere
> Que sei et autre *a Deu atrere.*
> Qui suls i vient, mene a dreite vie,
> Mieldre ki i meine cumpanie.
> Pur ço qui set se deit pener
> Que plusurs puisse *a Deu mener.*   (3-8) [31]

Were he not to do so, he would be worthy of reproof:

> Ki ben set et ne s'entremet,
> Mielz li venist estre muet,
> Kar *de Deu* li ert repruvé
> Pur quei sun saveir ait celé.
>
> .   .   .   .
>
> Qui sages est ne l'a de sei;
> *De sul Deu* l'ad, sachez en fei.
>
> .   .   .   .
>
> Endreit mei m'en sui purpensé
> Que aukune chose voil treiter,
> Que *de Deu* ne aie repruver.   (9-22)

In his dedication to the Trinity he definitely assigns Mary the status she is to occupy in the legends which he relates:

> El nun del pere faz l'escrit,
> Del fiz et del saint esperit,
> De la dame sainte Marie
> *Ki desuz Deu est nostre aïe.*   (27-30)

------

[29] Adgar so terms the book of miracles which he dedicates to " Dame Mahaut ":

> Estreite est d'icele reïne
> Ki est pleine de grace fine;
> De la Deu grace est replenie,
> Cume sa mere et sa duce amie;
> Pur ço est " Gracial " numez
> Cest escrit, si l'apelerez.   (42-47)

Herbert, *Romania*, XXXII, 400.

[30] *Ibid.*, p. 397. Cf. *supra*, note 7.

[31] Herbert, *loc. cit.*, p. 400.

The poet gives expression to the theocentric conception of a miracle in the first lines of his prologue in *Egerton MS 612*:

> Suuent *fait Deus merueilles* maintes
> Pur tuz sainz e pur tutes saintes,
> Ensurquetut pur la reine,
> Dunt il nasqui, e est meschine.
> Bien demustre par sa neissance,
> Ke de tute rien ad puissance,
> K'il sa mere aime plus ke rien.   (1-7) [32]

Moreover, the Anglo-Norman poet asserts that he has no doubt as to the miracles which he proposes to translate because of the power of Mary as a suppliant Mediatrix:

> N'est rien, si ele le ueut preier,
> Dunt ne puisse bien espleiter.
> Pur ceo ne uus esmerueilliez
> Des honurs ne des amistiez,
> *Ke Deu fait pur sa duce mere*
> Cum sis chier fiz, cum duz pere.
> De mei ne redeuez duter,
> Ki m'entremet de translater.   (11-18)

In the eleventh legend he reiterates his design to translate " en romanz le faz de latin " and acknowledges divine assistance:

> E beneit seit de Jhesu Crist
> *Cil*, ke comencier le me fist
> E *par ki* iol faz en auant.   (21-23) [33]

When his task is half-completed, he does not tire:

> Kar bel m'est si trauailler,
> *Pur Deu seruir* e uus plaisir.   (12-13) [34]

In the forty miracles which " Deu fait pur sa duce mere," as contained in the Egerton manuscript,[35] Mary mediates as an active agent, although Adgar never applies to her the vernacular equivalent of the Latin " Operatrix." The theocentric statement with which he opens his prologue is repeated in only a few of the legends. In " Love through Black Arts " the clerk's amendment is so perfect, that his purity at death is made known to those

---

[32] Neuhaus, *op. cit.*, p. 8.

[33] *Ibid.*, pp. 58-59.

[34] *Ibid.*, no. 17, p. 82.

[35] Cf. *supra*, p. 131.

whom he had formerly scandalized by a dove which issues from his mouth as he yields up his soul:

> E si que *Deu fist* pur s'amur
> grant miracle al suen derain jur,
> *pur amur sa mere Marie*, . . .   (269-71) [36]

Many miracles are performed in the rustic church near Bury St. Edmund's, rebuilt according to the dimensions which the Virgin Mary had specified in an apparition to a poor farmer:

> *Deus* i *fait* merueilles asez
> D'icels, ki unt enfermetez,
> Malade n'i uint, que ne seit sains.
> Prodhom deuint icil uilains,
> Macun deuint des icel tens,
> Mult enginnus e de granz sens.   (261-66) [37]

In the one legend which treats of the *Mal des ardents* God is the direct author of the miracle which, according to the narrative, is performed by Mary. Thus, Adgar preludes his account:

> Mult fait Deu miracles souent
> Par tut le siecle diuersement,
> Pur l'amur sa mere chere;
> Mustre l'ad en meinte maniere:
> Par ses mustiers, par ses ymages,
> Rent il souent des desuez sages,
> Si cum uus iert ici mustre.   (1-7) [38]

In the story, however, all prayers are addressed to Mary, and it is she who restores the amputated foot. Hence, Adgar conceives her in the function of " Operatrix," and attributes the miraculous cure to the power of God, working through her. The happy man,

> Dunc comencat a esioir
> E *Deu* loant en piez saillier
> .   .   .   .
> Loat *Deu* e sa duce mere, . . .   (90-94)

Her tardiness to relieve the sufferer is in conformity to God's will:

> A son cher fiz graces rendi,
> Ki a la feiz fiert durement

---

[36] Mussafia, *Studien*, IV, p. 71.
[37] Neuhaus, *op. cit.*, no. 30, p. 193.   [38] *Ibid.*, no. 12, p. 63.

> Les sons, pur lur amendement,
> Purluigne lur sante atens,
> Pur amender els e lur sens.
> Ke il requirgent sa duce grace
> Tut tens, desque merci lur face.   (97-103)

The dependence of a cure upon divine volition is also exemplified in that of the monk whose ulcerous sores are healed by the Virgin's milk.   By God's will he is afflicted with a malignant disease:

> Mais, granz sunt li Deu iugemenz,
> Que ameinet entre ses genz.   (18-19)[39]

The Bishop tries to comfort the dying monk:

> Dit lui souent, ke Deu flaele
> Ses amis, k'il aime e apele.   (56-7)

When the stench of the ulcer becomes more and more offensive, few visit the monk's cell:

> Mais, *quant Deu ueut*, tost ad turne
> Home malade en grant sante.
> Ensement uolt cel son ami,
> Ki de si greuus mal langui.   (70-73)

First, however, he is granted a vision in which he is led by an angel to a flowering field where he beholds twenty-three plants. His guide explains their symbolism: twenty-two signify the same number of divisions in the 118th Psalm which he is accustomed to chant with devotion; one flower more beautiful than the others represents the 53rd Psalm:

> Ceste salme senefiout:
> ' Deus in tuó nomine
> ' Saluum me fac per ta bunte,'
> Ke cil out chaun ior chante
> *En l'onur de la trinite.*   (145-49)

The flowers on this plant also have their signification:

> Les set duns de saint esperit
> Par unt Deus ad les suens eslit.

---

[39] *Ibid.*, no. 6, p. 29.

> Les uit flurs des herbes entur,
> Ki rendirent si grant fleirur,
> Vit boneurtez senefioent.   (154-58)

When he has seen the entire field " par Deu et par sa grant vertu," the angel directs the monk to a temple where he is cured.

In another group of legends Mary is asked to intercede but in the language of the poet God performs the miracle. In the attack of Chartres the inhabitants

> Par l'aie e *par la preiere*
> De sainte Marie la chere
> Eurent il aie e cumfort.   (9-11) [40]

The Virgin's garment is placed in a prominent position upon the wall. Weapons are directed at the relic:

> Mais aneire sunt auogle
> E saillirent halt cum desue:
> *La Deu ueniance,* sa uertue,
> Si que chaun perdi la ueue.
> Issi est *Deu* te tuz uengie
> Ke n'i pout returner un pie
> Auant n'ariere remoueir.   (49-55)

By the will of God Rollo escapes:

> Lur prince a grant peine eschapa,
> Pur ceo ke *Deu* alkes l'ama.
> Co fud Rollun, que orainz numai,
> *Par Deu* eschapa, bien le sai.   (65-68)

In another legend Adgar relates that the Saracens are devastating the country in the vicinity of Ascalon.[41] They enter a church in which many people have taken refuge. They are unable to deface an image of the Virgin and leave the Christians unmolested:

> A la Dame firent lur cri;
> Tuit crierent a li merci.
> *Deu lur mustra bele uertu;*
> Kar un sul n'i fu retenu.   (55-58) [42]

---

[40] *Ibid.,* no. 20, p. 127.

[41] For further indications as to the historical background of the legend, cf. Ward, *Catalogue of Romances,* II, 715-16 (35).

[42] Neuhaus, *op. cit.,* no. 35, p. 212.

Adgar's version of the " Jew Lends to a Christian " is also of this type. The merchant suddenly finds himself poor but does not lose confidence in God:

> Mais tut le suffri bonement,
> Si ama Deu parfitement.
> *En li out tute sa fiance;*
> D'aueir grant bien out esperance.
> *Deu dune tut bien ueirement.*   (63-67) [43]

In his predicament he turns to Mary in prayer and gives her picture in security to the Jew. Later, when he is unable to meet his obligations, he takes the casket,

> Dedenz mist *l'aueir de part Deu*
>
> .   .   .   .
>
> Puis depris sainte Marie,
> Que ele le receust en baillie.   (215-24)

The treasure is rescued from the waves by the Jew, but

> Del miracle, que *Deu out fait,*
> Ne tint li fel Jueu nul plait.   (263-4)

Before the image he denies receiving the money which the merchant claims to have transmitted to him " de part Deu." God, not Mary, gives speech to the image:

> Mais *cil*, que fist parler iadis
> La beste desuz Balaam,
> Pur ateindre cest Abraham,
> *Duna* dunc a cel' ymage
> Cert *sermun e entier langage,*
> Pur icele mencuinge ateindre
> E pur le fel Jueu cunstreindre.   (282-88)

In the legend of the miraculous supply of mead the prayer is also addressed to Mary who answers it:

> Nostre Dame li fist merci
> E bien l'en otria sun pri.   (83-4) [44]

Yet when the noblewoman of Glastonbury [45] first perceives that

[43] *Ibid.*, no. 29, p. 179.
[44] *Ibid.*, no. 33, p. 208.   [45] For identity, cf. *supra*, p. 47.

she cannot entertain her royal guest properly, Adgar refers only to her confidence in God to supply the deficiency:

> *En Deu del ciel out sa fiance*
> E dist: " D'iceo n'aiez dutance!
> Saciez, iceo ne uus faldra,
> Mais a plente uus suffira." (71-74)

In another group of tales prayers are addressed to God and the Virgin Mary carries out their fulfilment. The legend of Jerome is of this type. It is related that at the death of the Bishop of Pavia,

> Li clerc del pais tuit i uindrent
> E un grant parlement idunc tindrent.
> Les prodhumes tuit acuillirent;
> A ieuner treis iorz establirent,
> *Ke Damnedeu lur demustrast*
> Euesque, ki bien les guardast.   (17-22) [46]

God's choice is made known to them through the Virgin who appears to a brother after the third day and says:

> . . . 'Ua tost a la gent
> *Ke requerent Deu* si forment.
> Ne lor estut ia plus preer;
> Mes prengent tost mun chanceler,
> Sil facent euesque e pastur
> De la cite, de l'autre honur.'   (27-32)

That Mary intervened to obtain this honor for Jerome is apparent from the poet's words:

> Par le uoleir, *par la preere*
> De nostre duce Dame chere
> Vint icil a mut grant honur.   (47-49)

In another legend when the apostate Julian threatens Basil and the inhabitants of Caesarea, the saint commands

> . . . que tuz iunassent
> Treis iors, e *Deu* forment *preiassent*
> *Ke il lur fust defensiun*
> Cuntre Julien, le felun.   (35-38) [47]

---

[46] *Ibid.*, no. 3, p. 14.   [47] *Ibid.*, no. 16, p. 77.

In a vision Basil sees the Virgin Mary surrounded by the " cheualerie " of Heaven, commanding Mercury to slay Julian:

> Icil Mercurie esteit martir,
> De bon cuer *soleit Deu seruir,*
> E fud pur amur Deu ocis
> De Paens, de Deu enemis. (57-60)

Basil is certain that his vision is no illusion when he finds that the arms from a statue of Mercury have disappeared:

> Dunc solt bien k'en Deu ueire esteit. (69)

The people join with the Saint in his fervent " Deo gracias " and

> A la Dame graces rendi. (78)

Adgar has a very vivid conception of the activity of the devil.[48] Against the infernal power the Virgin is "nostre escu" (21).[49] This protection, however, is essentially different from Christ's power over the evil spirits:

> Mais *cil* nus reinst par sun sanc,
> Si nus deliuerat del Diable
> E de la mort pardurable.
> Ceo ert nostre Seignur Jhesu Crist. (48-51) [50]

Through the mysteries of the Incarnation and Redemption Christ withdrew man from the power of Satan:

> Nostre frere en humanite.
> Est li Sires, par sa merci,
> *Pur nus tolir de l'enemi,*
>
> .   .   .   .   .   .
>
> *Icil Sires,* par sa merci,
> *Nus defende* de l'enemi,
> Pur l'amur sa chere mere. (156-63) [51]

Those who violate the vow of chastity are protagonists in several

---

[48] Adgar writes:
> Saciez, ke entre humaine gent
> Regnent diables ueirement,
> Kis aticent de mal faire. (13-15) *Ibid.,* no. 40, p. 224.

[49] *Ibid.*
[50] *Ibid.,* p. 225.   [51] *Ibid.,* no. 21, pp. 134-35.

of the legends in Adgar's collection; however, they are the same stock characters who appear again and again in legendaries. As in other versions the nun (Beatrice) succumbs " par l'engin de l'enemi (100)." [52] She is miraculously prevented from leaving the convent until she deliberately neglects to salute the Virgin Mary. After seven years her sense of remorse becomes so keen that she resolves to return. In his sympathetic interpretation of the sinner's repentance Adgar is not original and merely paraphrases Gospel texts:

> Ici poet l'em bien oir,
> Ke, ki se uoldra repentir
> E guerpir trestuz ses pechiez,
> *Deu en est ioius e liez.*
> *Kar repentance de pecheur*
> *Aime mult nostre Seigneur.*
> Kar n'ad suz ciel pechie si grant,
> Purquei que l'en seit repentant,
> Ke ne face uerai pardun,
> Par fei e par cunfessiun.   (288-97) [53]

God alone has the power of forgiving sins:

> Ki li fra puis amendement,
> *Fors sul Deu,* ki la cria.   (314-15)

Mary's part is one of mediation:

> La nunain, dunt io uus di,
> Mult cria *a Deu merci*
> E a sa mere, la reine,
> Ke de ses mals li fust mescine,
> E *uers Deu tant li feist,*
> *K'en ses pechiez ne peresist.*   (348-53)

---

[52] Neuhaus, *op. cit.,* no. 40, p. 226.

[53] Adgar would not have the sinner presume on God's grace; he adds:
> Mais ne purquant bien garder
> Se deit chascun de pechier.
> Kar nul ne poet sauer l'ure,
> Quant la mort li curra sure.
> Ne nul de uiure n'ad espace,
> Se par Deu nun e par sa grace.
> Pur ceo se deust l'em cuntenir,
> Cum l'endemain quidast murir,
> E nient penser, qu' en auant
> S'amendera; . . .   (298-307)   *Ibid.*

In the legend of the drowned monk the devils are striving for the soul when Mary intervenes:

> Cument osez uus trauailler
> Cels, *ke mis fiz achata chier*? (107-8) [54]

They confidently boast that they will appeal to the higher Court of her Son, but the Virgin assures them that He is merciful as well as just (146-54). The devils claim that the monk had died in their service. Mary proves a clever advocate and demands that he repeat his dying words:

> Cum li clers sa buche ouri,
> *Quant a Deu plot*, sue merci,
> Dunc dist li clers: ' Aue Marie,
> ' Pleine de grace, Deu amie! ' (197-200)

Then she turns upon the evil spirits and proceeds to berate them for their warfare against the human race:

> E pur quei as dunc tel enuie
> Enuers humaine cumpaignie?
> A quei as tu dunc ioie e hait
> De ceo, *que hoem uers Deu mesfait*? (243-46)

The clerk's fate still depends upon the success of her petition before her divine Son, for she finally announces to him:

> *Tant ai enquis uers mun fiz cher*
> K'ariere t'estoet reparier;
> A tun cors t'estoet reuenir
> E tes pechiez espenir.
> E tu pren guarde nuit e ior
> *De seruir mun fiz cum seignor.* (263-68)

In the version of the same legend, contained in the Edwardes' manuscript, the angels first become aware of his plight:

> Li angles Deu, ki ço virent,
> *Par la Deu grace* i descendirent,
> Kar il pensent par aventure
> Sucurre icele creature. (35-38) [55]

There is the same verbal strife between Mary and the devils. It is

---

[54] *Ibid.*, no. 8, p. 45.   [55] Herbert, *loc. cit.*, no. 2, p. 403.

she who proposes to take the case " devant mun fiz qui est puis-
sant " (68). By the command of God the soul and body are to be
reunited:

> Si *plut a Deu, la sue merci,*
> Pur l'amur sa mere chere,
> Ke l'alme au cors venist ariere. (70-72)

In pleading for a soul before her Son, Mary's attitude is that of
a suppliant creature. She kneels with her virgins when she asks
for mercy towards the monk of St. Peter's at Cologne, but " il
encuntre eles leva (58)." [56] In the vision of Wettin, she approaches the throne of God with her retinue of virginal saints:

> . . . si se voleit *agenuiller,*
> mais nel volt suffrir sis fiz cher. (231-32) [57]

In the legend of Theophilus, she says:

> Pur la pitie, que de uus ai,
> A Jhesum, mun fiz, m'en irrai.
> *A sez duz piez charrai de gre*
> Que il te receiue en saluete. (777-80) [58]

Adgar's account of this legend presents the same theocentric
traits noted in other versions. The conversion of Theophilus is a
gift of God:

> Deu, li glorius creatur,
> Ki ne uelt la mort de pecheur,
>
> .   .   .   .   .
>
> Ne despist pas sa creature
> Compunctiun li dona pura. (333-44)

As he meditates upon the greviousness of his sin and the serious
consequences of the denial, he would have been tempted to despair,
but

> Li *pius Deus,* li bons iustisires
> Li merciable e dreituriers,
> Ne despist pas sa creature;
> *Duna li esperance seure.* (437-40)

---

[56] *Ibid.,* no. 7, p. 408.
[57] Mussafia, *Studien,* IV, p. 46.
[58] Neuhaus, *op. cit.,* no. 17, p. 105.

When the Virgin Mary reprimands him for his temerity in calling upon her Son,

> Ki sire est de ciel e de terre,   (536)

her rebukes only serve to inspire respect for those attributes of God which first make Theophilus flee to her as Mediatrix. Undaunted he proceeds to recite the history of God's mercies from the time of the Ninevites to Cyprian and then entreats her:

> Pur ceo espeir aueir pardun
> E des pechiez remissiun,
> Si me uoillez, Dame, aider
> *E uostre fiz pur mei preer.*
>
> .   .   .   .
>
> Comment le oserai io preier
> Od la buche, u sun nun tucher?   (645-88)

Mary yields but makes one more demand in words which reveal the difference between the mercy of the Savior and her benevolence towards Theophilus in acting as a Mediatrix:

> Ore regeis tant sulement
> K'il seit ueirs Deu omnipotent,
> K'il te defende del Diable,
> Kar mult est pius e merciable.
> Il receuera ta penitence,
> Tes lermes e ta cunscience.
> Si fait il de tuz, ueirement,
> Ki le requerent bonement;
> *Kar pur ceo prist Deu char en mei*
> *Ke pecheurs saluast en fei.*   (697-706)

His credo made, the Blessed Virgin departs and announces on her return:

> Li criaturs de tute rien
> Ta penitence prent en bien.   (805-806)

In his joy Theophilus declares that "apres Deu" (818) he has no other refuge. The same status is also given to her by the Bishop when he invites all to join Theophilus in his thanksgiving:

> Enloum Deu, nostre Seignur,
> Ensemblement od cest pecheur,
> Ki oi si benignement

> La uoiz d'icest pechur dolent
> Par la preire e la requeste
> Sainte Marie, ki est preste
> A presenter nos ureisuns
> A Deu, e nos afflictiuns;
> Ki est *desuz Deu* cheuetaine
> E *entre Deu e nus* funtaigne, . . .   (957-66)

Their praise is redoubled when they behold his transfigured face after he has received the Eucharist:

> Loerent Deu par mult grant hait,
> *Ki sul par sei merueilles fait.* (1051-52)

The secondary position which Mary holds in relation to God is reaffirmed by Adgar elsewhere in the *Egerton* manuscript. In the legend of the monk buried outside of the churchyard, he writes:

> D'icele Dame uoil traiter,
>
> .   .   .   .
>
> Ki *desuz Deu* ad poeste:
> Kar sis fiz regne en maeste.   (141-44) [59]

In the Edwardes MS Adgar refers to Mary,

> Ki *desuz Deu* est nostre aïe.   (30) [60]

She is superior to the Saints in her power of mediation:

> Que overer put la mere Jhesu
> Sur tuz seinz et [sur] tutes seintes
> Ki a sun cher fiz funt lur pleintes,
> Ki Sires est de ciel, de terre.   (124-27) [61]

This preëminence, Adgar explains simply:

> . . . estes mere, fille e espuse
> A *celui, ki tutes riens fist*:
> Ceo est li sires Jhesu Crist.   (1092-94) [62]

Yet He who " tutes riens fist " also created her:

> *Deu la fist,* tuit puissant pere.   (24) [63]

In relation to men Adgar proclaims her " Nostre Dame ":

[59] *Ibid.*, no. 26, p. 156.
[60] Herbert, *loc. cit.*, p. 400.
[61] *Ibid.*, no. 7, p. 409.
[62] Neuhaus, *op. cit.*, no. 17, p. 115.
[63] *Ibid.*, no. 40, p. 224.

> Se plurelment ne la numast,
> Si que 'nostre' la clamast;
> S'il die sulement 'ma Dame'
> E nient 'nostre,' dunc ad tel blame
> Ke de tuz est huniz e gabez
> E al dei de tuz demustrez. (135-40) [64]

Although the Blessed Virgin in the Anglo-Norman collection, is a very attractive figure, her sympathy and charity towards the sinful and unfortunate does not eclipse entirely the mercy and love of God toward creatures. He is "mult pius uers tute gent" (120).[65] God loves all:

> Deus aime tuz; nul ne despit,
> Quel que seit, u grant u petit;
> Clers e cheualirs e uilains,
> Tute gent forma de ses mains. (31-34) [66]

Adgar, like the author of the Pez collection,[67] does not marvel at the cure of the monk by the Virgin's milk since God has shown greater mercy to men:

> Grant merueille est ueraiement.
>
> .   .   .   .
>
> Mais si nus uolum entendre
> Cum Deu deigna del ciel descendre,
> E naistre e estre circumcis,
> Estre asaez e en croiz mis
> De pecheurs, de Phariseus,
> De Sarazins e des Hebreus;
> Puis se laissa enseuelir,
> De mort leua a sun plaisir;
> Puis munta la sus a son pere,
> La regne en ioie, nostre frere.
> Ki creit iceo par bone creance,
> De cel lait crerat sanz dutance;
> Dit del lait suuent senefie
> Misericorde en bone uie. (107-27) [68]

In an anecdote which is similar to the "Mater misericordiae" legend,[69] the dying monk prays:

[64] Ibid., no. 21, p. 134.
[65] Ibid., no. 40, p. 201.
[66] Ibid., no. 30, p. 187.
[67] Cf. supra, p. 86.
[68] Ibid., no. 13, p. 70.
[69] Cf. supra, pp. 18 and 25.

> . . . " *Jhesu,* bel pere,
> *Aidez* me a uostre plaisir;
> Kar bien uei que io dei murir."
> *Mult requist Deu,* si cum ore dis,
> Ke maindre peust en pareis,
> E mult requist sainte Marie
> Ke ele li fust uerai aie.   (6-12) [70]

When the Virgin appears to the monk, she quiets his fears of death by recommending that he call upon the mercy of her Son:

> Dist li, se il requere uoleit
> La misericorde a espleit
> *De son fiz,* de sei ensement,
> Il la trouereit ueirement.   (29-32)

Her rôle is that of Mediatrix:

> Pleine de grace e de pitie,
> Pleine de la Deu amistie;
> Kar n'ad suz ciel tel pecheur,
> K'il ait uers li ferm' amur,
> K'ele nel face ueraiement
> *Vers Deu aueir acordement,*
> E aueir en grant haur
> Les mals, u ainz out amur,
> E uiure a honur **entre gent,**
> E apres murir saintement.   (55-64) [71]

In the legend of the " Devil in Beast-shapes " she tells the monk that she has no power of herself:

> Dist k'ele portad le fiz Deu,
>
> .   .   .   .
> Dist ke *par li* poet si sauuer
> Tut cels, ki la uolent clamer.   (123-26) [72]

God, however, can do all things and hence for Adgar there are no legends beyond the limits of credulity:

[70] *Ibid.,* no. 15, pp. 74-75.   [71] *Ibid.,* no. 40, p. 225.
[72] *Ibid.,* no. 9, p. 54. In the story of the abbess attributed with question to Adgar, the subordinate character of Mary's power is evident:
> Ke cele, ki ad *suz Deu* poeir
> De faire trestut sun voleir.   (187-88)
Herbert, *loc. cit.,* p. 420.

Deu put certes et jur et nuit,
Fere quant ke il vult sanz cunduit.   (141-42) [73]

Adgar places no restrictions upon divine omnipotence—a proof of his theocentrism and significant evidence in respect to the subordinate character of Marial mediation.

THE SECOND ANGLO-NORMAN COLLECTION:

MS *Old Royal 20 B XIV*

MS *Old Royal 20 B XIV* of the British Museum resembles the collection just considered inasmuch as it derives from a Latin source analogous to that used by Adgar.[74]   It is divided into three books, each of which is preceded by a prologue.   The general introduction gives an indication of the anonymous writer's theocentric position:

Deu pur ces seins fet grant vertu,
Ke pitus est & tus jurs fu;
Mes tuz deit passer la duce mere,
Cum al jur solal dune lumere.
Ci fet ele, kar ceo est ben dreit.   (25-29) [75]

Through her God " comforts " humanity:

. . . loent Deu omnipotent,
Ke de une jofne virgine purre
Conforte humeine creature.   (20-22)

In the prologue to the second book the author presents her as a Mediatrix, telling his audience not to despair, but to call upon her,

Ke Deu donist a vus la sue grace.   (12) [76]

His introduction to the third book is a personal appeal theocentrically stated:

Deu ke meint en trinité
Pur la sue seinte pité
Cest ters livere nus lest ci commencer
Ki pussum estre tuz parcener

---

[73] *Ibid.*, no. 7, p. 409.
[74] Cf. Mussafia, *Studien IV*, pp. 7 ff.; Kjellman, *Deuxième collection anglo-normande des miracles de la Sainte Vierge et son original latin*, pp. xx ff.
[75] *Ibid.*, p. 5.   [76] *Ibid.*, p. 75.

> De la joie & de la vie
> A la duce franche Marie;
> E force nus doint & entendement
> De lui servir a sun talent;
> Si nus tramette en cest escrit
> La grace del seint espirit,
> Ke nus pussum a chef venir.   (1-11) [77]

As in Adgar's version God performs miracles in the rustic church at Bury St. Edmund's:

> *Deus* i *fet vertuz* meinte manere
> Pur le amur de sa duce mere.
> Icele mere a l'Omnipotent
> De pecché, mal & de encombrement
> Nus defende par sa duzur
> E nus doint la grace nostre Seignur.   (151-56) [78]

The account of the amputated foot restored by Mary also contains an explicit statement of the divine potency effecting the miracle:

> En la cité de Yvorie
> Out une eglise de seinte Marie;
> Mult i *fist Deu* sovent *vertuz,*
> La s'asemblerunt les druz
> Ke amerunt la gloriouse,
>
> .   .   .   .
>
> Meint malade, meint peccheor
> I fu gari par sa duzur.   (23-32) [79]

In this quotation one has the author's conception of a Marial miracle: the power of God working through the visible instrumentality of the Blessed Virgin.

This theocentric concept is also found in the legend of the Jew Boy. When the child is found untouched by the flames, the miracle is attributed to God:

> *Ce fist Jhesu li trespussant,*
> ke en Babilone en la furneis' ardant
> les treis enfanz deigna garir,
> ke Nabegodonosor voleit hunir.   (193-96) [80]

Yet the child tells the astonished onlookers:

[77] *Ibid.,* p. 135.

[78] *Ibid.,* no. xlix, pp. 216-17.

[79] *Ibid.,* no. xxxiii, p. 143.

[80] Wolter, *Der Judenknabe,* p. 120.

> Cele bele dame, ke jeo vus di,
> od sa manche me defendi
> de la flambe enmi le fu
> ke unke ne senti mal n'ennu. (215-18)

In the legend of " Childbirth in the Sea," a woman overtaken by the tide is in great danger and beyond human help:

> Kar securs ne veit ne entend
> Fors de Deu omnipotent. (63-64) [81]

Moreover, God shows His power by a miracle:

> Issi l'out Dampnedeu *purveu,*
> *Ke* a nus *mustrat sa grant vertu.* (73-74)

In the shelter of the Virgin's sleeve she brings forth a child. By the virtue of God this miracle is wrought through the agency of Mary:

> E *Deu mustra sa grant vertu,*
> Cum il fist Jonan de grant peine,
> La prophete dedenz la baleine,
> E sun poeple, kant le fist passer
> Trestut a pe la ruge mer. (118-22)

When man cannot aid, " Deus socurt " (145). The *Te Deum* is sung and according to the poet, there is no one who does not say:

> Beneit seit Deu, le fiz Marie. (164)

Mary is also an instrument of the divine power in the legend of Julian the Apostate. Here Mercury at the command of the Virgin deals the Emperor a mortal blow:

> Dunke si aparceit ben l'amperur
> Ke ceo fu *par Deu le Creatur.*
>
> . . . .
>
> E dist cum cil ke fu plein de fel:
> " Vuz, *danz Deu apelé Jhesu,*
> " De tut en tuz *me avez venku.* (193-200) [82]

---

[81] H. Kjellman, " Une version anglo-normande inédite du miracle de S. Théophile. Avec un appendice: Le miracle de la femme enceinte retirée par la Sainte Vierge," *Studier i modern språkvetenskap,* V (1914), 219.

[82] *Deuxième collection anglo-normande,* no. iv, p. 12.

God's will made manifest to Mercury through Mary does not identify her with the Power behind the act but merely as an agent of that Power. Further evidence of this interpretation is contained in Basil's message to his people:

> Si lur cuncta de la pité
> Dunt *Deus les averat tost visité,*
> Par sa mere & par sun duz nun
> Des mals lur frad garisun.   (241-44)

The account of the siege of Chartres by the Normans accords to God the credit for the miraculous events. Bishop Waukelin is described as

> Prodom en Deu, ceo sacez ben,
> E Deus ama sur tute ren.   (31-32) [83]

He places his confidence in supernatural aid:

> Mes de tuz ad sa grant fiance
> En Deu & en sa seinte pussance
> E enz la gloriuse mere.   (43-45)

At his suggestion the Virgin's garment is raised as a standard, and the people cry out:

> . . . .   " Seinte Marie,
> " Vus nus seez oi en aïe! "   (69-70)

At Mary's petition God performs the miracle:

> *Deus* i *fist* vertue mult grant
> Pur sa mere demeintenant.   (77-78)

The people of Chartres are quick to perceive the confusion of the Normans:

> Ore sunt en engusse grant
> *Par la vertu del Tutpussant.*
> De Chartres veient cil & entendunt
> Ke cil n'en fuent ne defendent;
> Dunke sevent ben ke *Deus les lie*
> Par le voler de la Marie.   (93-98)

However, God does not approve of their cruel pursuit of the Normans and in punishment, " Deu mustra sa grant vertu " (126); the relic disappears:

[83] *Ibid.,* no. v, p. 15.

> Si fu ravie ne sai coment
> Par le pecché de la gent,
> Ke malveisement aveint usée
> *La vertue Deu ke i fu mustré.*   (145-48)

The theocentrism implied in Adgar's version [84] of the miraculous supply of mead receives direct expression here. Athelstan's hostess is not disconcerted when she discovers that she cannot fittingly entertain her royal guest:

> . . . dit entre ces dens en bas:
> " *Si Deu plet,* ceo n'i faudra pas." (45-46) [85]

She prays to the Blessed Virgin to save her from embarrassment. According to the poet, God performs the miracle:

> Par tut ala la merveile clere,
> Ke ceo *fist Deus* pur sa duce mere. (81-82)

Both the just and the sinner are recipients of favors in the *miracula* of this collection. Saints Bon, Ildefonsus, Jerome, and Dunstan are rewarded in a particular way as clients of the Virgin Mary. Bon, Bishop of Clermont, spends the greater part of the night absorbed in prayer:

> E pria Deu le fiz Marie
> Ke li doint pardurable vie,
> *E Deu* pur sun seintime nun
> *Li face* de ces pecchez *pardun;*
> De merci crier ne quist ja terme,
> Sovent i lessa meinte lerme
> Devant Deu & sa duce mere. (25-31) [86]

Humbly he kneels in a secluded corner, unseen by human eyes; nevertheless,

> De Deu & sa mere fu ben veü,
> E de sun cors fist sacrifise
> A Deu par itel servise. (40-42)

Suddenly the church is ablaze with light. Unable to withdraw, he witnesses a heavenly procession:

---

[84] Cf. *supra*, pp. 139-40.
[85] *Ibid.*, no. lii, p. 225.   [86] *Ibid.*, no. xxxvi, p. 161.

> De ceo ne vus esmerveilez mie;
> Ke sert Deu le fiz Marie,
> Kant il desert la haute coroune,
> Si la pere lui li done.   (74-77)

At the command of the Virgin Mary he is brought forward and clothed with her own vestments. After he has sung the Mass, she rewards him with these. His successor is not so favored. He, too, keeps vigil but each time sleep overcomes him and he awakens in his bed:

> Quant iceo vit, ne volt reprover
> Aver maimeis pur Deu esprover.   (200-201)

Ildefonsus also receives " un albe bele de paraïs." [87]   At Pavia the choice of a Bishop falls upon Jerome. For three days the people fast and pray:

> *Ke Deu* pur sa grant duzur
> Lur purveit un bon pastur.   (21-22)

Mary appears to announce that her " chanceler " is to be appointed:

> Ceo est Jeronime, le mon ami,
> Ke mult me sert devoutement
> E mun cher fiz tut ensement.   (38-40)

Dunstan is entertained by the choir of the Virgin who, herself, intones a hymn,[89] inviting her virginal train to unite in praise of the Lord. The Anglo-Norman writer thus renders her song:

> Compaygnes, chauntum par amur,
> Dium, compaignes, *a Deu honur,*
> Conisum le *duz Creatur,*
> *Ke nus ad salvé* par sa duzur.   (84-87) [90]

Dunstan is then urged to sing and his song like the Virgin Mary's is theocentric praise:

> Sire rei de gloire, le fiz Marie,
> Salvez, ke merci vus crie,
> Tun people humble & cristiene,
> De de paraïs est waine.   (118-21)

---

[87] *Ibid.*, no. xv, p. 77.
[88] *Ibid.*, no. xxvii, p. 119.
[89] Cf. *supra*, p. 47.
[90] *Ibid.*, no. xxxvii, p. 169.

MS *Old Royal 20 B XIV* also contains the legend of Saint Thomas.[91] The priest in this version is suspended because of his perversity, and, having followed Thomas into exile, pleads that the order be retracted:

> E dist ke ver Deu & li
> Freit mult bon amendement. (70-71) [92]

Finding his attempts fruitless, he turns to the Virgin Mary, reminding her,

> . . . n'estut for vus *requere*
> *Vostre cher fiz Jhesu Crist,*
> *Ke cel & terre & homme fist*
> *Et chescune creature,*
> Kar tant vus aime & honure
> Ke il ne vus deneie ren. (124-29)

As Mediatrix, Mary has already appealed to her Son:

> Sachez que tant ai fete
> *Ver mun fiz* par requeste
> Ke par confessiun
> De tes pecchés averas pardun. (155-58)

He is to go to the Archbishop and ask to be absolved from his sins:

> Kar *Deu* tes [pechés] ad tut pardonés. (164)

As a sign Thomas will find his hairshirt mended,

> " Des meins dunt jeo Deu maniai. (192)

The priest promptly delivers the message and falling at the feet of the Archbishop, begs for absolution, humbly admitting that the prelate has been justified in his removal. He is reinstated in his parish where " il chantout le Deu servise (299)."

Like other collections this manuscript contains a great number of legends which depict Mary mediating between Christ and the sinner whether he is still on earth, in purgatory, or awaiting the judgment. Here, too, the religious is described as subject to many temptations:

---

[91] *Ibid.*, Introduction, p. lxxiv. Morawski has published a variant from MS *Bib. nat. fr. 12483, loc. cit.*, p. 345.

[92] *Ibid.*, no. lix, p. 257.

Mes n'ad homme en religiun
Ke ne face akun mesprisiun,
N'ad desuz le Creatur
Homme ke ne pecche set fez le jur,
Ja tant ne seit seinte sa vie.   (17-21) [93]

Even the Pope has recourse to Mary's mediation. Unable to enter the Church of St. John Lateran because he has permitted the Emperor to stop the custom of burning a lamp of balm in St. Peter's honor—a custom inaugurated by Constantine when he founded the church—he realizes the wrong he has committed in yielding to the bribe of the avaricious ruler:

E pria a Deu remissiun,
De ces pecchez cria merci,
Ke Deus en eit merci de li.   (176-78) [94]

He appeals to Mary to intercede and enjoins all the people to unite with him in prayer:

E prient Deu omnipotent
Et la duce mere Marie
Ke en cest bosoin li soit aïe.   (194-96)

After three days of prayer and fasting, the Virgin Mary appears to report his reconciliation:

Ai ore fet *pra ma preere*
Vers mun cher fiz & vers son pere
Ke le pecché te volent pardoner,
E entrer pussez en muster.   (217-20)

The next day he enters the church in procession:

Kar *Deu* par sun seintime nun
Li fist de sun pecché *pardun*.   (257-58)

The hand of God stays the entrance of Mary of Egypt into the temple:

L'entré escundit li fu
Par Deu del cel & sa vertu,

.   .   .   .

Ele se efforci, ne poet avant,
Deu la destent li tut pussant.   (84-103) [95]

---

[93] *Ibid.*, no. xlii, p. 190.
[94] *Ibid.*, no. ix, pp. 37-38.   [95] *Ibid.*, no. xii, pp. 51-52.

As in other versions she is about to despair when she sees the image
of the Virgin Mary and entreats her intercession:

> Jeo n'ay esperance si en vus nun,
> Ore me purchacez verai pardun,
> Sicum vus estes virgine pure
> E Deus en vus fu creature
> E Deus fu homme veraiment,
> Kant de vus prist encharnement. (128-133)

She promises full amendment, if she is allowed to adore the Cross,

> U *pur la vostre alme* & la meye
> Tun cher fiz espandi sun sanc
> De sun cher cors gentil & blanc;
> A hunte se mist pur peccheürs,
> Vers lui me seez, dame, succurs. (147-51)

The italicized phrase is a clear indication of the Virgin's creature-
status. The legend contains many theocentric traits worthy of note.
Of Mary of Egypt's communion, it is written:

> A la *volunté del Creatur*
> Fu acuminé cum cristiene. (207-8)

She is assailed by many temptations:

> Ke jur & nuit ne l'angusseit,
> Tant ke *Deus en out pité*,
> Si l'ad fors del travail juté. (229-31)

Towards the end of her life " Deus envea un sun privée," Zosimas,
who in accordance with the will of God, brings her the Eucharist:

> Ele se genoile, si receit
> Le cors celi *ke savé l'aveit*. (326-27)

She makes Zosimas promise to return within a year,

> . . . . pur esgarder
> Ceo ke Deus lui mustera. (339-40)

The lion which mysteriously appears at her interment is also sent
by God:

> *Deu* lui *envea* un liun grant,
> Fort & hidus ke li fust aidant.
> Zosimas el nun de Jhesu Crist
> Comanda ke il la fosse fist. (369-72)

The poet concludes the legend by referring to the first grace received through Mary's mediation:

> Deu converti la Magdaleine,
> Ke fu de ordure & de pecché pleine.
> Ceste peccherese benuré
> Est par sa duce mere savé.   (387-90)

By the will of God a robber chances to meet Odo, the Abbot of Cluny, and is so struck by his appearance that he begs for admittance into the monastery in order to expiate his sins. Finally the Abbot consents, and introduces the robber to the monks as one whom the " Salveür . . . enveit." [96] The thief-monk becomes most fervent in the service of God:

> Le convers met so peine mult de jur en jur
> *A servir Deu sun pere, sun gentil Salveür,*
>
> .   .   .   .
>
> Mult aveit mal fet, les bens après se fist
> *Par la grace ki li dona le seint espirit.*   (59-66)

He is particularly devoted to the Virgin Mary. She appears to him when he is dying, and calming his fears, says:

> Ceo sui jeo, cele ke claiment tute gent
> Par mai fu formé humeine concordee,
> E mere sui apelé de misericorde.   (118-20)

Odo, hearing these words, praises her in her rôle of Mediatrix:

> Beneite seit ore la mere de misericorde,
> Ke *a sun trescher fiz* peccheürs acorde.   (127-28)

While still living, Wettin is granted the vision of the Mother of God pleading for his soul before her Son:

> ' Bel fiz,' fet ele entreshet,
> ' s'il poet estre, eyez merci
> de cest moigne, ke veez ici.
> Les angeles e seins m'unt tant requis!
> Fayle le malfé, Deus eit le pris.
> Beal fiz, ke estes charité,
> a vostre figure facez pité.'   (132-38) [97]

---

[96] *Ibid.*, no. vi, pp. 19-20.   [97] Mussafia, *Studien*, IV, p. 46.

Christ answers:

> Ma duce mere, e jeo le vus grant;
> ta preere si m'est comand.
> Face amendes, a ceo ke il poet,
> de males ensamples ke de li moet.
> Tut seit il fols e pecheür,
> pardoné seit pur vostre amur.   (138-43)

In those tales dealing with souls who await judgment or who suffer in Purgatory, Mary has not the power, which is the exclusive right of the Divinity, to pardon. As in the legends of Wettin, of the pope,[98] and of Saint Thomas [99] she pleads for the forgiveness of the soul or announces that through her prayers she has obtained this grace. After the apparition of the Prior of Saint-Savior's at Pavia to Hubert, the latter dies and the poet comments:

> E *Deu* li *face* vŕai *pardun,*
> Et de nus pur la priere
> De la duce seinte mere.   (116-18) [100]

In another legend angels come to the rescue of a poor peasant who had been seized after his death by devils on the charge that he removed landmarks. They severely rebuke the evil spirits:

> *Ne place a Deu omnipotent*
> Ke en vus seit le jugement
>
> .   .   .   .   .   .
>
> Alum, si orum tute dreiture
> Devant la mere virgine pure.   (69-74)

Through the intercession of Mary he is saved:

> Ke a tut dis mes seit honuré,
> E sun cher fiz pur sa duzur,
> *Ke tant pardone a peccheür*
> *Pecché,* si sunt mesfesant,
> Pur sa mere ke il eyme tant,
> Cil nus pardoint nos folies,
> Nos pecchez & nos vileinies.   (86-92)

---

[98] Cf. *supra*, p. 156.   [99] Cf. *supra*, p. 155.
[100] *Deuxième collection anglo-normande,* no. xxvi, p. 118.
[101] *Ibid.,* no. xxv, pp. 114-15.

A priest who for a year has said Mass and performed penance for the soul of a friend is assured by Mary that God has granted pardon:

> . . . Mult m'as travaillé,
> Chapelein, tant, m'as sovent clamé
> Pur le alme de tun cher compaignun,
> Ke *Deu* li *fist* verray *pardun*,
>
> .   .   .   .
>
> E mun cher fiz ad tel duzur
> Ke il est asouz pur la meie amur.   (69-80) [102]

In the legend of the " Nun's Penance Left Unfinished " a religious appears to an abbess, telling her that she hopes for a speedy delivery from the pains of Purgatory according to a promise of the Virgin Mary who has told her:

> *Mun fiz te mettra hors de labur*
> Unkore pur la meie amur.   (99-100) [103]

In the version of the drowned sacristan Mary's power is limited to the influence which she has with her Son. She reprimands the evil spirits for seizing the soul of a man who died saying the " Ave Maria." She leaves the case to the judgment of Christ:

> E *Dampnedeu* pur sa duce mere,
> Ke a bon dreit deit aver chere,
> *Comanda* ke l'alme fu remenée
> Al cors & ke ne fu pas penée,
> Mes ke il amendast après sa vie
> De sun trespas & de sa folie.   (97-102) [104]

Restored to life the monk relates,

> Coment *Deu* par sa mere
> *Comanda* l'alme repeirer arere
> Al cors pur amender sa vie
> Par les preeres de la Marie.   (133-36)

In the legend of the two brothers in Rome St. Prejectus begs Mary to intercede for his client Stephen:

[102] *Ibid.*, no. xlvii, p. 203.
[103] *Ibid.*, no. li, p. 223.   [104] *Ibid.*, no. xvi, p. 82.

> La reine franchement l'otrie:
> *A sun fiz* vent & tent *li prie*
> *Ke* l'alme *commanda* remener
> E le cheitif resusciter.   (127-30) [105]

The devils are enraged,

> Quant vint le *contremandement*
> *De Dampnedeu omnipotent*
> Ke l'alme fu remené arere
> Par preere de sa chere mere.   (181-84)

Just as the authority of Christ is not encroached upon here by Mary and the counter-command is given by the Judge whose good pleasure, though compliant to her desires, determines the issue, the dependence of a miracle upon the will of God is sometimes revealed in an occasional phrase of the narrative concerning lesser circumstances which are connected with the miraculous incident. The thief-monk receives his first grace of conversion from his meeting with Odo, " cum le volt Deu de cel." [106]   Mary of Egypt, in accordance with the " volunté del Creatur," [107] receives communion. A great famine and pestilence ravage Constantinople and are attributed to the heresy of the Emperor Justinian and his wife:

> Kar ne plout *a Deu* sun afere.   (30) [108]

The cancer of the monk is not a punishment but a trial sent by God:

> Mes si cum *Deu le out purveü,*
> Chancre l'ad en la buche feru.   (23-24) [109]

The poet attributes to the divine succor the cure which is later wrought through the ministrations of the Virgin:

> U tost u tart Dé le sucure.   (42)

A further distinction between the mercy of God Who wills the miracle and the aid offered by Mary is made in the legend of the resuscitated monk at St. Peter's in Cologne. The monks

---

[105] *Ibid.*, no. xxiv, p. 110.
[106] *Ibid.*, no. vi, l. 15, p. 19. Cf. *supra*, p. 158.
[107] *Ibid.*, no. xii, l. 207, p. 55. Cf. *supra*, pp. 156-57.
[108] *Ibid.*, no. lvii, p. 238.   [109] *Ibid.*, no. lviii, p. 245.

rendent graces a Jhesu Crist,
Ke tant de misericorde fit,
E mult honuerent la Marie,
Ke en cest besoin li fist aïe.   (148-51) [110]

The Virgin is an active protagonist in the legend of the erring abbess; nevertheless, the latter in her confession to the Bishop, relates that she has been saved by the mercy of God:

Coment *la merci Deu li savad*
De la folie & de sa hunte.   (174-5) [111]

The Virgin's charity toward suffering humanity makes her a very attractive figure in the legends. However, the poet also portrays the love and providence of God toward men. God loves all but particularly the poor:

Kar en Deu sunt & Deus en eus
Plus ke en nuls altres mortels;
Kar tut fut il haut rei de cel,
Il en devint pore mortel.
Pur ceo n'est pas hunte poverte,
Kant Deu del cel l'ad tant sufferte;
Pur ceo serrunt li pore haut,
Al jugement justise haut,

.   .   .   .

Deus salvera tuz; s'il ben prent,
De Deu seient pores honuré.   (3-17) [112]

Moreover, the power of God " ke tut le munde guie," [113] extends over all creatures and the elements. In the miracle of the fire at Mont-Saint-Michel the poet writes:

Deus eime le lu Seint-Michel;
Mult i unt *miracles del cel,*

.   .   .   .

La out un ymage ben entailé
De la duce seinte benuré.
Issi avint, cum *Deu ben guie*
Tut le munde en sa ballie,
E fu & vent, mer & terre
A sun voler movent lur guere

---

[110] *Ibid.*, no. xxi, p. 98.   [112] *Ibid.*, no. xix, pp. 88-89.
[111] *Ibid.*, no. xii, p. 66.   [113] *Ibid.*, no. xi, l. 50, p. 45.

> En lur seisun par sun voler,
> Atant avint ke en ical eir
> Munte un turment de toneire,
> Si kay le fuidre ardent & neire
> Sur le eglise ke ai nomé.   (13-28) [114]

Mary refers to Christ in one legend as her " cher fiz ke tut est sire." [115]   Christ is the " gentil Salveür " [116] and as if to strengthen His claims upon the love of mankind, the poet adds that His suffering was " pur nus ":

> . . . Deu soffri hunte meinte
> *Pur nus* peccheürs salver.   (16-17) [117]

Christ through His Passion has merited the graces which Mary in the legends is merely asked by her servants to dispense:

> Icele mere a l'Omnipotent
> De pecché, mal & de encombrement
> Nus defende par sa duzur
> *E nus doint la grace nostre Seignur.*   (153-56) [118]

He is the Creator, attracting all Christians to Himself, in the theocentric prelude to the account of the Feast of her Nativity:

> La duzur del Seignur Jhesu Crist,
> *Ke tuz nus furma & tuz mist,*
> Molt se peine, si cum jeo crei,
> Des cristiens *trere a sei.*   (1-4) [119]

Evidently, the poet does not conceive that God might look upon honor shown to Mary as derogating from His own.   The quotation just given, as well as the narrative, would lead to such a conclusion, for, the poet relates that God Himself sends an Angelic messenger to explain to a hermit the reason of the music heard on the Nativity of the Virgin Mary.   In obedience to the command of the angel the hermit makes the feast known to others:

> . . . fist par seint eglise mander
> Ceo ke *Deu le volt commander.*   (91-92)

---

[114] *Ibid.*, no. xxix, p. 124.

[115] *Ibid.*, no. xvi, p. 81.

[116] *Ibid.*, no. vi, l. 60, p. 21.

[117] *Ibid.*, no. xli, p. 186.

[118] *Ibid.*, no. xlix, p. 217.

[119] *Ibid.*, no. vii, p. 24.

In the legend of Murieldis, the miracle is performed in a church dedicated to Mary rather than in the Church of the Holy Trinity where the demented woman has been brought by her friends:

> Mes *Deu ke meint en trinité*
> *Ne li volt* unkore sancté doner
> Pur sa pussance avant mustrer,
> Kar *il estua la mestrie*
> A sa duce mere Marie. (60-64) [120]

If God reserves the " mestrie " to the Virgin, in this version of the legend He grants the cure to her prayer:

> *Pur la priere* seinte Marie
> Ceste muiller devint garie. (109-10)

In two of the legends of this collection God honors the image of the Virgin Mary by miracles. In the anecdote " Saturday," her picture is miraculously unveiled:

> Trestut par sey sanz mettre main
> *Par la vertu al Soverain;*
> Nul hom ne sout coment ceo fu.
> *Si louent Deu & sa vertu.* (53-56) [121]

In another tale it is related that her image protects the Christian against the Saracens. Heraclius carries it with him in his expedition against Chosroes, King of the Persians, and completely defeats his enemy:

> . . . sa seinte duce figure
> Poet tant conforter la gent
> *Par la vertu de l'Omnipotent.* (70-72) [122]

The poet leaves no doubt as to her status. He refers to her as " la meillur creature " [123] and " sur tute ren." [124] While she is addressed by the title

> La *mere Jhesu, le Tutpussant,* (110) [125]

in the same legend she is scolded,

> Cum a sa seor de sa mere née. (70)

---

[120] *Ibid.*, no. xxxi, p. 132.

[121] *Ibid.*, no. liv, p. 231.

[122] *Ibid.*, no. lvi, p. 236.

[123] *Ibid.*, no. xx, l. 4, p. 91.

[124] *Ibid.*, no. xvii, l. 6, p. 86.

[125] *Ibid.*, no. xxxiii, p. 145.

This familiarity is undoubtedly shown because she is a creature. Exalted though she is, says the poet in the general introduction, she does not forget her human nature:

> Une ren me fet si curagus;
> Tut seit ele reïne coroné,
> *Si est ele de ma lignée,*
> *E de ma char e de mun sanc*
> Est eschaucé en si halt banc;
> *Tut passe ele tute creature,*
> *Ele n'ublist mie sa nature.* (66-72) [126]

In the legend of the "Jew Lends to a Christian" she is "après Deu":

> . . . . la dame seinte Marie
> Ke as cristiens est al grant fiance
> *Après Deu* & la esperance. (42-44) [127]

"Desuz Deu," [128] she is neither "arere" occupying the place accorded to the devil by the poet, nor "avant" usurping as chief protagonist the position of the Deity:

> Le deble arere & Deus seit avant
> Ennoré, beneit & tut pussant. (1-2) [129]

Gautier de Coincy

To celebrate the praises of the Virgin Mary was not a mere exercise of literary skill for the prior of St. Médard. His great devotion to her was the one passion which dominated his life,[130] and has been compared to that of Ildefonsus.[131] It is to be expected, then, that Mary will be the central figure in the *Miracles de la Sainte Vierge*.

An investigation of the theocentric phases of Gautier's work discloses that he does not attribute to her any direct power. In the prologue he states very explicitly that if God performs miracles for the saints, He will do as much for His Mother:

---

[126] *Ibid.*, p. 6.

[127] *Ibid.*, no. xlviii, p. 207.

[128] *Ibid.*, no. xli, l. 60, p. 87.

[129] *Ibid.*, no. xxvi, p. 115.

[130] A. Ducrot-Granderye, "Etudes sur les Miracles Nostre Dame de Gautier de Coinci," *Annales Acad. Scientiarum Fennicae*, Series B, XXV, 2 (1932), p. 5.

[131] *Loc. cit.*, note 2.

> Comment feroit pour Saint Eloy,
> Pour Saint Joce ou pour saint Romacle
> *Le rois du ciel* nul haut miracle
> *S'il nes fesoit pour la pucèle*
> Qui l'aleta de sa mamèle,
> Quand pour les autres ne fine oncques.
> Qui me dira, que fera donques
> Por la puissante dame célestre,
> Qui jour et nuit siet à sa destre?   (75-83) [132]

It does not seem plausible that the active connotation of the verb " puet " in the following verses derogates from the primary source of power:

> La mère Dieu puet assez plus,
> Que tuit li saint du ciel lasus,   (89-90)

for toward the end of the collection the same thought is repeated with slight variations:

> La lettre dit en moult de leus
> Qu'en ses sainz est Diex merveilleus;
> Et quant li *Roys puissanz et pius*
> Et loinz et près en moult de lius
> Miracles et merveilles maintes
> Fait por ses sainz et por ses saintes,
> Bien est buisnars qui se merveille
> Se mainte merveillant merveille
> *Fait* jor et nuit *por la pucèle*
> Qui l'aléta de sa mamèle,
> Qui le nourri, qui le berça.   (7-17) [132]

In describing the tour of the pilgrims of Laon through England, he more clearly refers to the Father as the source of power than Herman of Tournai.[134]

> Tant biau miracles avenir
> I *fist li Sires, li douz Père*,
> Pour essaucier le non sa Mère,
> Q'un moult grant livre en porroit faire
> Qui les vourroit dire et retraire.   (12-16) [135]

When the ship is threatened by pirates and the reliquary is to be raised aloft, he writes:

[132] Poquet, *Miracles de la Sainte Vierge*, col. 5.
[133] *Ibid.*, col. 557.   [134] Cf. *supra*, pp. 90-91.   [135] *Ibid.*, col. 209.

Se Diex par sa Mère *n'i veille,*
Tuit seront mort sanz delaier.   (110-11) [136]

During the plague which ravaged Arras and its environs in 1105, Mary's rôle of " sainte phisiciane " does not seem to obscure that of the " piteus Père." Great would have been the havoc,

Se li piteus Père de gloire
Tramis n'eust à ce tempoire
Une sainte phisiciane,
Pour sauver la gent crestienne.   (179-182) [137]

The efficacy of the cures is due to their divine origin :

La lettre dit où trouvé l'ai
Que *li douz Roys,* li très douz Père,
A sa très douce sade Mère
Donna a donc si grant pooir,
Que nus ne la venoit véoir
A Arraz, à son bon moustier,
Estainz ne fu sans détrier
De la doulereuse arsion ;
Mais qu'il eust contriction
De ses pechiez et repentance.   (186-95)

These two passages are a prelude to the story of the " Maid of Arras." From them one may conclude that Mary's power is a delegated one, when she heals the girl and " donna adonc tel efficace " [138] to the kiss of the woman that she, too, may cure others. Further indication as to the correctness of this deduction lies in the fact that Gautier repeats his initial thought, this time, without reference to the "lettre " :

Nus n'est tant fous, tant chuleure,
Qui bien ne sache sanz doutance
Que tant parest de grande puissance
Et tant par est de haute affaire
La Mère Dieu qu'ils fait faire
Au roy des roys qui lassus siet,
Quanqu'il li plest, quanqu'il li scet,
Li très douz *Diex,* li très douz Père,
Tant hauz *miracles por sa Mère*
Fait . . . .   (496-505)

---

[136] *Ibid.,* col. 213.   [137] *Ibid.,* col. 265.   [138] *Ibid.,* col. 270 (l. 394).

Gautier does not charge the skeptic with incredulity because the latter questions the possibility of the Virgin's performance of a miracle; rather, he accuses him of disbelief in the existence and power of God—a proof that Gautier's conception of the miracles of Mary was theocentric:

> Et ses miracles bien ne croit,
> *Il ne croit mie que Diex soit*
> *Ne que Diex ait point de puissance.*
> Mescréanz est tous sanz doutance,
> Qui bien ne croit qu'ele ait tel grace,
> *Qu'il n'est chose que Diex ne face,*
> En ciel, en air, en mer, en terre,
> Cèle un petit l'en vint requerre.
> Nostre Dame est de tel mérite,
> Que Diex meismes s'i délite
> En faire quant qu'il li agrée,
> Dès les plantes jusque en la grée.   (537-48)

Elsewhere he makes the same accusation:

> Petit ont foi et pou créance,
> Quant il *à Dieu de sa puissance*
> Ne veulent rendre gré ne grace,
> Ne dire bien de rien qu'il face.   (673-76) [139]

The miracle of " Lucerna " has its origin in the desire of God to honor Mary:

> A Bisance la cité noble
> Qui dite or est Constentinoble,
> *Fait li douz Diex*, li très douz Père
> Por honnourer sa douce Mère,
> La douce Virge, la piteuse,
> Une merveille merveilleuse.   (1-6) [140]

The miraculous unveiling of the image of the Blessed Virgin, from Friday before vespers until Saturday after Mass, is done by God:

> Si beau miracle com je di,
> Si biaus affaires, si biaus giez
> *Fait* por sa Mère *li douz Diex*.   (116-18)

God desires reverence to be shown to her:

[139] *Ibid.*, col. 664.   [140] *Ibid.*, cols. 671-72.

> *Li puissant Roys* bien *moustre* en ce
> Qu'il veut par grant révérence
> Et tempre et tart et jor et nuit
> Sa douce Mère servons tuit
> Méesmement le samedi.   (139-43)

To disparge Mary or even her relics is to dishonor God and it is for this that Boson is punished. While the villagers make the miracles of Soissons a topic of conversation,

> Que des miracles moult parloient
> Que *Diex faisoit à Nostre Dame.*   (20-21) [141]

Boson joins in to deride. As he writhes in pain, Abbess Mathilda blesses him, now contrite, with the holy Slipper,

> Por cui *Diex fait* tantes merveilles.   (129)

He is cured, but Gautier warns those who would insult the Mother:

> Diex partout boute feu et flame
> Et tout abat et acravante,
> Lorsque sa Mère voit dolente.   (330-32)

Moreover, Mary has a champion who will defend her rights:

> Cist Champions est Ihesucris,
> Ce dist David en ses escris,
> Qu'il est *tant granz, puissanz* et *fors,*
> Que nus tant soit de grant effors,
> Por rien qu'il die ne qu'il face,
> Fuir ne puet devant sa face.
> A lui ne puet champir nule ame.
> Ce grand champion Nostre Dame.   (551-58) [142]

Mary is more frequently a peacemaker,

> Qui accorde à Dieu et au monde.   (306) [143]

The sinner, fleeing from the just wrath of God, may find shelter beneath her mantle:

> Si très douz est li très douz Sire
> Si très douz est li très douz Père,
> Que desouz le mantel sa Mère
> Souz le secors la douce Dame
> Ne ferra jà home ne fame.   (322-26) [144]

---

[141] *Ibid.*, col. 155.
[142] *Ibid.*, col. 122.
[143] *Ibid.*, col. 612.
[144] *Ibid.*, cols. 612-13.

He may find in her, also, an advocate to plead his cause. Thus, Mary adds her support to that of Saint Peter in favor of the monk of Cologne:

> " Filz," fait ele, " por péchéeurs
> Retraire d'enfer et de poine,
> Char en mes flans preis humaine.
> Pour ce, biau filz, de toi me fi
> Tant que por eus touz jors te pri." (114-18) [145]

In answer to her persuasive argument Christ replies:

> Vos vouloirs sont mes volentez,
> Que mon cuer est ou vostre entez.
> Ma douce Mère vos prières
> Sus toutes autres ai je chières?
>
> .   .   .   .
>
> Mère du ciel estes et porte,
> Qui que vous siet y poves metre. (125-33)

Indeed, Gautier gives to her the unique title of " plederesse." [146]

More frequently Mary is asked, not to work a miracle, but to intercede before God in a seemingly hopeless case which demands divine intervention. Germanus prays when Constantinople is besieged:

> La mère Dieu, la doce dame,
> Deprit que prit a son chier fil
> Jeter les daint de ce peril. (74-76) [147]

When the pagan, Muselinus, sees this " grant dame merveilleuse " receive into her mantle the projectiles of his army, he is converted:

> Bien set que c'est oevre *devine*. (153) [148]

---

[145] *Ibid.*, col. 458. See also the miracle " Du chevalier a cui la volente fu contee pour fait apres sa mort," where Mary uses a similar argument (*ibid.*, ll. 141-43, col. 497 or Ducrot-Granderye, *loc. cit.*, p. 203).

[146] He writes:

> Devant Dieu est si enramiée
> Tex plederesse et tex parlière
> Qui de li fait sa amparlière,
> Il a la court et s'a le plait. (375-78)

Ibid., col. 697.

[147] Ducrot-Granderye, *loc. cit.*, p. 219.

[148] *Ibid.*, p. 222.

So too, a blind Saracen has confidence in her intercession, because he has heard,

> Que li haut *Diex* as crestiens
> Qui touz est sires et pères
> Por l'ymage sa douce Mère
> *Faisoit miracles si granz.*   (496-99) [149]

He comes to Sardenay with the firm belief

> Que *li granz Diex*, que li *grant Père*
> Se l'en prie sa douce Mère,
> *A bien vertu, force* et *pooir*
> D'un aveugle faire vooir
> .   .   .   .
> La douce Mère Ihésuscrist
> Prie et requert ententilment
> Qu'à son doux Filz déprit piument
> Que ses prières daint entendre
> Et sa veue il daint rendre.   (503-14)

Likewise, the merchant boldly ventures to borrow money from the Jew, and after making the pact, prays God that through the mediation of Mary, success may attend his plans:

> Beaus sire Diex, qui piex et doz
> Et puissanz ies seur tote chose,
> Je te depri a la parclose
> A jointes mains, beaus tresdoz pere,
> Par les precés ta doce mere.   (199-203) [150]

He has recourse to Mary's intercession again, when the Jew refuses to acknowledge the receipt of the casket:

> En Dieu ot tote s'esperance
> .   .   .   .
> Devant l'image nostre dame.
> De tot son cuer, de tote s'ame
> En sospirant li quiert et proie
> Que son doz fil deprit qu'il l'oie.   (431-39) [151]

---

[149] Poquet, *op. cit.*, col. 660.

[150] Erik Boman, *Deux Miracles de Gautier de Coinci*, p. 13; Poquet, col. 547.

[151] *Ibid.*, p. 25. When he intrusts the casket to the waves, he commends it,
> Au grant Seigneur et au grant Dé
> Qui tot le monde a en sa guarde,
> Qui terre et mer governe et guarde.   (334-36)

Ibid., p. 20.

When he stands before the image, he calls directly upon Christ to
give testimony of the truth:

> Et si a dit: " Rois, Jhesu-Criz,
> Si voir com ies li vrais fiz Dieu,
> Tesmoigne moi vers cest ebrieu
> La verité si com ele est.
> Vrais Diex, vrais Diex, di de cest prest
> Por essaucier toi et ton non,
> Se j'aquitez m'en sui ou non."   (440-46)

In the story of the " Chaste Empress " Gautier of Coincy definitely consigns the Virgin Mary to the subordinate position of
Mediatrix. While the Empress is being dragged by her execution-
ers to the woods to be beheaded, because of a false accusation of
unchastity on the part of her brother-in-law, a constant prayer is
on her lips:

> . . . . Diex! il me semble
> Que tu dou tout m'as obliée.
>
> .   .   .   .
>
> Doz Diex! doz Diex! ce dit la dame,
> Garde que ceste lasse fame
> De cels ribauz ne soit soillie:
>
> .   .   .   .
>
> E, tres douz Diex, fet-ele, é, é!
> Par ta douçor soffrir ne daigne
> Ma chastéé mie ne fraigne.   (976-1030) [152]

She addresses Mary as a Mediatrix:

> Hé, douce Virge, douce Mere,
> Qui Dieu portas en tes douz flans,
> Sequeur moi tost, il en est tans;
> *Prie ton Filz qu'il me sequeure,*
> Il m'est avis qu'il trop demeure.   (1032-36)

The Empress is rescued by a nobleman who places her in charge
of his son. Another trial awaits her for his brother is so impressed
by her beauty and purity that he, too, makes unwelcome advances.
She spurns him:

> Sire, fet-ele, si mespensez,
> Set Diex moult miex que nus ne face,

---

[152] Méon, *Nouveau recueil de fabliaux et contes* (Paris, 1823), II, 32-34.

> Diex voit el cuer et en la face,
> Diex voit el cuer lou vis li hom;
> Diex qui bien set m'entencion,
> Meillor me face que ne dites.
> Si me consaut Sainz Esperites,
> De tex paroles pou me chaut. (1484-91)

The brother seeks retaliation and contrives that the murder of his nephew be laid to her charge. Banished to a ship, she is left to the mercy of mariners and again her virtue is imperiled:

> La lasse crie, bret et plore,
> Et prie Dieu qu'il la secore:
>
> .   .   .   .
>
> Reclaime et prie Nostre Dame
> Qu'ele de s'ame preigne cure, . . . (1877-83)

Since she is not cowed by their threats of death, the sailors leave her upon a rock in the sea. Her prayer is theocentric:

> Or me deffende, or me consaut
> Et daint sauver sor ceste pierre
> *Cil qui* en mer *sauva Saint Pierre.* (1932-34)

Then, addressing Notre-Dame, she asks that she " proie ton Fil " and obtain her request. However, she accepts her tribulations as coming from the hand of God:

> Diex sueffre persecution,
> Ce dit al letre et fet savoir,
> A cels qu'il aime plus avoir. (2130-32) [153]

She is finally comforted by an apparition of the Virgin Mary who shows her an herb growing upon the rock. " Com Diex volt," a ship comes to her rescue. With the miraculous plant, she cures many. Moreover, the herb has its virtue from God:

> Ainz *li douz Diex mès ne dona*
> A nule herbe si très grant force. (2382-83)

In treating of the herb, Gautier de Coincy's words concerning the Virgin as Physician are significant:

---

[153] Gautier develops this idea in some thirty lines. Compare with a similar passage in the *Vies des Pères*, cf. *infra*, pp. 184-85.

> Phisicienne est Nostre Dame,
> Loier ne prent de riens que face,
> *Tot fet por Dieu, tot fet par grace.*   (2464-66)

With the plant the Empress cures her slanderers of leprosy, after having made them confess their guilt and her innocence.   In the presence of the Emperor she reveals her identity:

> Je sui la lasse Empereriz
> Qu'a *getée Sainz Esperiz*
> *D'aversitez* teles et tantes.   (3317-19)

When he is able to express his joy, his words are in divine praise:

> . . . Merci, merci, douz Diex,
>
> .   .   .   .
>
> Qant m'*as rendue et ramenée*
> La riens el mont qu'ai plus amée.
>
> .   .   .   .
>
> Dame, fet-il, il m'est avis
> Que *Diex vos a resuscitée,* . . .   (3345-72)

However, his joy is short-lived, for the Empress, convinced of the fickleness of human affection, is determined to consecrate herself to God alone:

> *Diex est si larges* de merir,
> Nus en lui perdre en nule guise
> Ne puet s'amor ne son servise.
> Il n'est *fors Dieu nus vrais amis.*   (3472-75)

After a tribute to the immutability of divine love (3480-93), the Empress once more ascribes her protection from peril to God:

> Qant tot li mondes m'assailli,
> *Adonc m'aida li tres douz Diex.*   (3512-13)

Therefore, Mary had merely served as a messenger in her apparition upon the rock.

The Virgin acts as a Mediatrix in those legends which treat of sinners.   A worldly clerk mocks his uncle who has counseled him to cultivate devotion to the Virgin Mary:

> Plus volentiers chant pastorèles
> Et d'Olivier et de Roulant.   (90-91) [154]

---

[154] Poquet, col. 365.

Later, when he is excommunicated and ostracized by society, he repents. On his deathbed he does not despair of God's mercy but begs for it through the intercession of the Mother:

> " Douz Diex," fait-il, " miséricors,
> Si voirement com ton saint cors
> Livras por nous à passion,
> Daigne hui avoir compassion,
> Par la prière de ta Mère,
> De cest chétif qui a misère
> Et a douleur fine et trépasse." (175-81)

The contrite Guibourc appeals to her as Mediatrix when she is about to be burned for having caused the death of her son-in-law. The fire dies down and the woman says to the spectators:

> Quant *par les preces* Nostre Dame,
> Qui Dame et Royne est des ciex,
> *Espargnié m'a li doux Diex,*
> Espargniez moi, si ferez bien.
> Sachiez por voir que nule rien
> Ne sent de chose que me face;
> Quar *Diex me garde* par sa grace
> Et par les preces de sa Dame. (512-19) [155]

Gautier's comment is theocentric:

> Cest miracles n'est pas mains granz,
> Ce m'est avis, que des enfanz
> Que *Dieu sauva* en la fournaise. (573-75)

He does not marvel that God should perform a miracle as a reward for faith, but Guibourc, he reasons, is condemned " por crime," and therefore,

> Cist miracles bien nous esclaire
> Que moult parest *Diex débonnaire*
> *Miséricors, piteus* et *douz;*
> Quar les péchiez pardonne touz,
> Tout maintenant qu'on s'en repent. (677-81)

From this one may conclude that Mary's mediation is not used by Gautier to detract from the splendor of God's mercy. In the legend of " Incest" the Pope counsels the repentant woman to meditate upon this divine attribute:

[155] *Ibid.,* col. 250. Cf. *supra,* p. 117.

> ' Sachiez,' dist il, ' ma douce amie,
> Qu'il a merci qui mercie crie,
> Que dieus est douz et debonere
> Plus que ne puet langue retraire.
> Qant saint Pere merci cria
> Qui par trois foiz dieu renoia,
> Il ot merci, ma douce suer.
> Qui merci crie de bon cuer
> Et qui dou tout set son mesfet,
> Il a merci que qu'il ait fet.
> Dont merci ot la Madelaine.' (459-69) [156]

This is likewise evident in the miracle of Theophilus, where the
grace of sorrow for sins is a gift of God:

> La Dame, en cui pitiez est toute,
>
> .   .   .   .
>
> Son piteuz, filz le roy de gloire,
> Piteusement en dépria,
> Et *li douz Diex*, qui tout cria,
> Par les prières sa douce mère
> *Out tiel pitié* de sa misère
> Qui ne vout mie geter puer,
> Ainz li rendit les yex du cuer. (641-50) [157]

When Mary appears after his penance of forty days, he is undaunted by her apparent harshness:

> Haute Royne, en es-tu cele
> Dont Dex daingna sa mere faire
> Pour péchéeurs à lui retraire? (1002-4)

The words of the Virgin, when she returns in three days to announce his forgiveness, indicate that her rôle has been one of
intercession and that his pardon depended upon the divine will:

> Par mes prières, biau douz amis,
> Cil qui en croiz à tort fu mis
> Tes chaudes lermes a véues
> Et tes prières a reçéues. (1289-92)

Gautier refers to her, elsewhere, as a mere instrument in the salvation of souls:

[156] J. Ulrich, " Drei Wunder Gautiers von Coincy," *ZRPh.*, VI (1882), 331.
[157] Poquet, col. 44.

> Maint esgaré a par toi ravoié
> Le roys qui est véritez, vie et voie.[158]

The Child-Christ does not appear in this collection of miracles; rather, He is Judge and Savior. As Judge, the poet softens any traits of severity and refers to Him as the " doux Seigneur qui tout justice." [159] As Redeemer, he recalls that He suffered " pour nous." The remembrance of the passion incites feelings of self-reproach and contrition in the heart of Theophilus:

> Ame chetive que feras?
> Di moi que tu responderas
>
> .   .   .   .
>
> Quant te dira li pussanz sire
> Voici la honte et le martire
> Voici le costé et le flanc,
> Voici les plaies et le sanc
> Que je *por t'amour* respandi!
> Que diras-tu? .   .   .   .   .   .   (763-76) [160]

In the legend " De l'enfant que le Deables vouloit enporter," the child salutes the hermit,

> Tout en plorant, à basse voiz,
> Du haut Seigneur qui en la croiz
> *Por nous* ses membres estendi, .   .   .   (271-73) [161]

The clerk whom Mary cures with her milk, in addressing Christ, acknowledges Him to be the Savior:

> " Nos sires es et nos sauverres,
> Et de tuit le mont racheterres." (29-30) [162]

It is apparent from Gautier's presentation of Christ as Savior that Mary's mercy is directly dependent upon her Son. Her influence, " Devant celui *qui la cria* " (1227),[163] lies in the dignity of her motherhood:

> Que de ta char vout li Roys estre faiz,
> Qui de nient toute chose avoit faite.[164]

---

[158] *Ibid.*, " Chansons pieuses," I, col. 385.

[159] *Ibid.*, l. 51, col. 518.

[160] *Ibid.*, cols. 46-47.

[161] *Ibid.*, col. 449.

[162] *Ibid.*, col. 341.

[163] *Ibid.*, col. 104.

[164] *Ibid.*, " Premières Chansons," I.

The devil laments

> L'eure que Dieu en fist sa Mère.   (196) [165]

Gautier exalts her as

> La Mère au Roy qui tout cria   (446) [166]

or

> Sus toutes riens es gracieuse
> Sus toutes riens es déliteuse,
> Sus toutes riens es bèle et sage.   (1663-65) [167]

but he also depicts her

> Humble Dame, humble pucèle
> En qui Dieu prist humanité.   (2002-2003) [168]

Gautier metaphorically indicates the relative position of Christ and Mary, when he writes concerning the Virgin birth:

> Quant Diex vout nestre de s'ancèle
> Qui tant est granz, puissanz et hauz,
> De l'*estoile* issi li *solaus*
> *Qui toutes choses enlumine.*   (981-84) [169]

However much Gautier exalts her, he nevertheless depicts her as a creature,

> Por cui *Diex fait* toutes merveilles.   (23) [170]

The *Vie des Pères*

Most of the legends of the *Vie des Pères* are not concerned with the Virgin Mary, and therefore, are not considered here.   Of the strictly Marial legends which have been published from this collection,[171] the greater number treat of sinners.   Hence their theo-

---

[165] *Ibid.*, col. 466.

[166] *Ibid.*, col. 84; l. 107, col. 519; l. 38, col. 316 *et passim.*

[167] *Ibid.*, col. 66.   Elsewhere he refers to her: " La Mère Dieu sus toute *chose* " (467), col. 87.

[168] *Ibid.*, col. 73.   [169] *Ibid.*, cols. 670-71.   [170] *Ibid.*, col. 651.

[171] According to Morawski, there are twenty-eight Marial legends in the *Vie des Pères. Romania*, XLI, 194 ff.   Méon inserts six which are strictly Marial in the *Nouveau Recueil*, II.   His text is that of " MS C: *Bib. nat. fr. 23111 (anc. Sorb. 309)*, fin du xiii⁰ ou commencement du xiv⁰ siècle.''

centrism is based on the principle that forgiveness of sins is the
exclusive right of God, and that in procuring pardon the Blessed
Virgin may act merely as a Mediatrix. In his prologue the writer
calls upon the Trinity for assistance:

> *Aïde* Diex rois Jhesu Criz,
> Peres et fils, sainz Esperiz,
> *Dieu qui tout puez et tout crias,*
> Qui en la sainte croiz crias:
> " Je muir de soif," ce fu a dire
> Que despit avoies et ire
> De ceus qui en enfer estoient
> Sanz ce que forfet ne l'avoient.[172]

He continues with lines which exalt the " bonté " of Christ in
paying the price of redemption by His death:

> De ton seint sanc les rachetas
> Et de la prison les gitas
> Par ta grant debonneireté.
> Moult fet a home grant bonté
> Qui de mort le tret et delivre
> Et a la mort pour li se livre;
> Diex, cete bonté nous fëis
> Car a mort nos te meïs.[173]

So great is the divine mercy that God works a miracle as a sign
that He has pardoned the Queen, slayer of the Seneschal who robbed
her of her virginity and of her cousin who would have betrayed her.
Condemned to be burned, she prays to Mary:

See Schwan, *Romania*, XIII, 233, n. 6 and 235. The *Ave Maria* legend is
printed from MS *657* (*anc. 139*) of the Bibliothèque d'Arras. Cf. " Petites
pièces de vieille poésie," *Mémoires de l'Académie d'Arras*, XXVIII (1855),
297. Indication of the manuscript is given by Schwan, *loc. cit.*, p. 239.
The present writer does not include here the fifth miracle of an interpolation
of ten found only in three fourteenth century manuscripts. It is the legend
" Du chevalier qui ooit messe et Nostre Dame estoit por lui au tournoie-
ment," published by Bartsch-Wiese, *Chrestomathie de l'ancien français*, 12th
ed. (Leipzig, 1919), no. 59, p. 207. For interpolation, see Morawski, *loc.
cit.*, pp. 194 ff.

[172] Paul Meyer, " Notice sur deux anciens manuscrits français ayant
appartenu au Marquis de la Clayette," *Not. et extr.*, XXXIII, 1 (Paris,
1890), 67.

[173] *Ibid.*

> Dame, que j'ai amée et aim
> Et amerai toute ma vie,
>
> .   .   .   .
>
> Que vos aiez merci de moi,
> Qu'à mort de feu serai livrée,
> Se par vos ne sui delivrée. (544-58) [174]

Together with a confidence in the Virgin is a trust in God; for she is led forth, stripped of her clothing, and in great confusion and shame,

> . . . de bon cuer à Dieu se tint. (567)

Moreover, God delivers her, using as His instrument, an old hermit who tells the King that she is under the special protection of God:

> Cil li dist: *Diex* à toi *m'envoie*
> *Qui* la Roïne *velt sauver;*
> Dampner ne la puez ne grêver
> Quant *Dame Dieu la prent en garde.* (596-99)

Thereupon orders are given to bring the condemned woman forward.   God Himself preserves her from shame:

> Mès *Diex* la *deslia* tantost
> Que li sainz hom véue l'ot,
> Et un autre cas li avint,
> Q'un vestement des sainz ciex vint,
> Et un voil qu'il mist seur son chief.
> Desus le voil avoit un brief
> Qui devisoit son errement. (611-17)

The garment which she miraculously receives and the letter sent from Heaven convince the King that her contrition has restored her to the friendship of God:

> Sot-il de voir que *Diex l'amoit*
> *Quant einsi sauvée l'avoit.* (625-26)

He greets her with joy and declares that her preservation from death is to be attributed solely to divine aid:

> . . . vos fussiez morte et perie
> Se de Dieu n'eussiez aïe. (631-32)

---

[174] Méon, *op. cit.*, 273. For the history of this legend, see R. Koehler, " Le conte de la Reine qui tua son sénéchal," *Romania*, XI (1882), 581-89.

The wife of a senator at Rome, in spite of her sins of incest and the murder of a child, is also protected by God because of her repentance. In the first and last lines of this legend, which are identical, the writer says: " Bien est gardez cil *que Diex garde.*" [175] In spite of her sins the noblewoman in this tale continues to pray and give alms:

> La Mere Dieu toujorz avoit
> An sa memoire et son chier fil
> Por garder son cors de peril.
> *De Dieu servir* moult s'esforça.   (140-43)

When she is denounced by the devil before the Emperor, she confesses her crimes to the Pope. She appears for trial, but the evil spirit does not recognize her nor the Virgin who accompanies her. The noblewoman is acquitted and attributes her deliverance to the intercession of Mary (" por la *priere* de sa Mere ").[176]   At death she faces another judgment where the Virgin again mediates in her acquittal:

> An la fin *à soi* l'apela,
> *Diex en paradis l'ostela,*
> Et ses filz quant il s'aperçut,
> Ses pechiez dit et reconut.
> Por un touz les autres douta,
> Tant fit que *vers Dieu* s'aquita
> Par la *priere* de sa Mere.   (471-77)

In the legend of the erring abbess Mary is the visible instrument used by God to deliver her from shame. The religious then spends the remainder of her life in expiating her sin:

> Tant jéuna, tant se bati,
> Tant servi Dieu, tant se mati,
> Et tant servi la Dame sainte,
> Que sa mesprison fu estainte,
> Et *que Dieu* du saint paradis
> *Li fist doaire à son devis,*
> Por que où monde s'aquita
> Et de son pechié se jeta.   (419-26) [177]

In the tale of the sacristan who leaves her convent the Virgin Mary impersonates the erring nun during her absence. However,

[175] Méon, *op. cit.*, ll. 1 and 522, pp. 394 and 410.
[176] *Ibid.*, l. 469, p. 408.   [177] *Ibid.*, p. 327.

it is the thought of God's mercy which first prompts her to leave a life of sin:

> *Mès Diex n'est malades ne mors,*
> Se je de li servir m'effors
> Et mon pechié veille guerpir,
> *A merci* porrai bien venir.
> Qui son pechié pleure et gemist
> *A merci vient, si com Diex dist.*   (211-16) [178]

Her confessor's words of advice confirm her in the desire to live purely once again. He assures her that God guards those who turn to Him:

> Alez vous en, je vous di bien
> Que vostre fet vendra à bien:
> *Celui garde Diex et soustient*
> Qui à li s'atant et se tient.   (315-18)

She returns to the convent and tells the story of her life to the nun who admits her. She then asks the portress her name:

> Dame, or vous ai dit qui je sui,
> Si vous requier-ge *por celui*
> *Qui as pechéors fet pardon,*
> Que vous me dites vostre non.   (471-74)

The astonished sacristan receives the reply: " Je sui la Mere Dieu Marie " (477). The poet evidently attributes the pardon of the sinner to the Virgin's intercession, for he says in his conclusion to the legend that Mary is " nostre enparliere " or advocate,

> Cele qui sanz faintise *prie*
> *Son chier Filz que pardon nous face*
> *Non par merite* mès par grace.   (546-48)

The legend " De celui qui espousa l'ymage de pierre " is somewhat similar to the anecdote of the ring given to Venus as told by William of Malmesbury.[179] A newly-married man puts his ring on

---

[178] *Ibid.*, p. 161.

[179] *Gesta Regum*, I, 256. See also Helinand of Froidmont, *Chronicon*, xlvi, an. 1051 (*PL*, CCXII, 945-46). For the history of the legend, cf. Arturo Graf, *Roma nella memoria e nelle immaginazioni del medio evo* (Turin, 1915), pp. 665-78; Gédéon Huet, " La légende de la statue de Vénus," *Revue de l'histoire des religions*, LXVIII (1913), 193-217.

the finger of a pagan goddess so as to join in the sport of his companions. The hand of the statue closes upon it and the image continually intervenes between him and his bride. A hermit whom he consults sees in this the will of God: " Croi-ge que Diex te voille avoir." [180] The recluse further proposes that he live a chaste life and honor the Blessed Virgin. This the young man does, and at the end of a year Mary appears to him and orders that her image be made and placed in honor. He confers with the Pope who believes that such is the will of God:

> Li Papes de par Dieu li dist
> Que l'ymage fere féist.
> De voir sot que *Diez le voloit,*
> Qant par trois foiz mostré l'avoit.   (457-60)

The statue is made and placed over the altar. One day to the young man's dismay it disappears. As he is praying to the Virgin, it suddenly reappears with the ring in hand:

> Du miracle apert que tuit virent,
> Dont maint mescréant s'amenderent,
> Et *à la loi Dieu* se donerent.   (540-42)

The image of Venus had been one " en qui *Diex n'ot part* " (264) ; the statue of the Virgin, according to the Pope, was willed by God. There are no other theocentric traits in this legend.

There is no mention of Mary in the version of the Jew boy, who tells his father:

> . . . *un enfant* mangié avoit
> ausine con chascuns fet avoit.
> ' Et uns grans sires le donoit.   (190-92) [181]

Other details of the miracle are also theocentric. The child is thrown into the oven but God shows His power:

> *Nostre sire* illec *mostra*
> La poissence que partout a.   (219-20)

Not Mary but the Child Whom he received in the Eucharist protects him:

> ' As tu nul mal? ' ' Nannil, par foi,
> que *cil* ci est avecques moi,

---

[180] Méon, *op. cit.*, l. 324, p. 303.   [181] Wolter, *Der Judenknabe*, p. 95.

13

que j'ai hui mangié au mostier.
et *m'a fet bone compagnie.*

.   .   .   .

Ensi en son samblant estoit
diex avec lui, qui le tenoit.
Tuit cil, qui le miracle virent,
a dame dieu graces rendirent.   (249-62)

The legends considered here are but a small part of the twenty-eight [182] contained in the *Vies des Pères.* However, in the relatively few treated, it is obvious that Mary is not made equal or superior to God since the author's principles of perfection make God the center. Both prologues and epilogues to these tales contain digressions in which the love of God, the attainment of Heaven, the divine mercy, or His ever-sustaining Providence are themes.

In the legend of the " Ring and the Image," the author writes:

Si doit chascun *pro Dieu avoir*
Metre et cors et ame et avoir.   (661-62) [183]

In striving for the love of God, hope of reward is to be a stimulus:

A *l'amor de Dieu devons tendre*
Por le grant guerredon atendre
Qui en vient à pou de servise.   (47-49) [184]

He is wise who strives to

.   .   .   .   conquerre le saint hostel
Que Diex a ses amis pramet, . . .   (18-19) [185]

All trials and sufferings are to be endured,

Por avoir repos et coronne
Que Diex en saint paradis *donne*
A cels tant com il sont en vie,
Qui de li servir ont envie,
Et *par œvres* de bon renon
Connoissent et li et son non.   (13-18) [186]

In application of the proverb that he who spares the rod, " het son enfant," God also chastises His children:

---

[182] Morawski, *loc cit.,* p. 417.   Cf. *supra,* pp. 178-79, n. 171.
[183] Méon, *op. cit.,* p. 313.   [185] *Ibid.,* p. 293.
[184] *Ibid.,* pp. 155-56.   [186] *Ibid.,* p. 314.

> Nous somes tuit fius Jhesu Crist
> qui de son cors bonté nous fist,
>
> . . . .
>
> Nostre sire sens estoutie
> ses fiuz et ses filles chastie,
> en penitance les enbat,
> ou par maladie les bat. (25-32) [187]

The author does not fail to see the will of God in misfortunes great or small—chastisements in which the ultimate motive is the salvation of the victim:

> A l'un tolt son buef ou son arne,
> ou sa nef li afondre en Marne;
> por ce le fet: se plus avoit
> que par le plus se dampneroit.
> L'autre tient court par maladie,
> *por ce que perdre nel velt mie;*
> de son pechie l'oste et retorne
> Par l'infermete qu'il le donne,
>
> . . . .
>
> Ensi *dame diex les siens plesse.* (33-45) [188]

Love of God is such a great good that one should be ready to relinquish all earthly possessions to attain it:

> C'est la fonteinne de largesce,
> C'est le solaz, c'est la richesce
> Que tuit crestien doivent querre
> En eschivant les biens de terre,
> Que l'en ne puet, si com moi semble
> Dieu et le monde avoir ensemble.
> *Si se doivent a Dieu tenir*
> Et les biens terriens foïr
> Cil qui sevent la verité. (53-61) [189]

Finally, no more theocentric simile could be made than to liken the assistance of God to that of the " roche fort " and to find that the rock may fail, but divine aid, never:

> Mout valt miex à vie et à mort
> *Diex aïe que roche fort.*

---

[187] Wolter, *op. cit.*, p. 87.
[188] *Ibid.*, pp. 87-88.   [189] Méon, *op. cit.*, p. 156.

> Cil qui *à Dame Dieu se tient,*
> *Dame Dieu par tout le sostient,*
> Et à touz ses besoinz li vaut
> Là où la roche fort li faut.   (561-66) [190]

The author places no emphasis on service to the Virgin in the legend of the Queen who murders her Seneschal:

> *A Dame Dieu* servir devez,
> *Au Roi des cieux, au Roi de gloire*
> Qui en croiz conquist la victoire
> *Par quoi tuit sauvement avons,*
> Et por ce servir le devons.
> Bien fet son preu, bien fet s'oneur
> Qui s'avoue par tal seigneur,
> *Qui par tout le garde et norrist.*   (690-97) [191]

Because of such theovergent statements in the Marial legends which have been treated, these *miracula* may be considered theocentric.

Jean le Marchant

Jean le Marchant will not treat of " Rolens ne de Paris." [192] He prefers " voire estoire " [193] and which, he may be sure, is founded on fact.   He writes:

> Ge ne cont pas les auentures
> De Gauuain ne de Perceual. [194]

However, in the work of Gilon of Chartres, [195] he finds a source which satisfies his desire for truth:

> Ou il na riens fors verite
> Par le tesmoign dantiquite
> Cil qui fist en latin le liure
> Dit quo ses iaulz vit a deliure
> Les miracles certeinement
> *Que Dieu oura apertement*

---

[190] *Ibid.*, p. 277.
[191] *Ibid.*, pp. 277-78.
[192] *Livre des miracles de Notre-Dame de Chartres*, no. 13, p. 83.
[193] *Ibid.*, no. 3, p. 17.   [194] *Ibid.*, no. 12, p. 80.
[195] Morawski, *Romania*, LXI (1935), 165.

A lenneur de sa douce mere,
A cui il est et fiz et pere,
En Chartres en sa mestre iglise.[196]

The rebuilding of the cathedral of Chartres, destroyed by fire in 1194,[197] was an impossible task for the parishioners alone. The work was begun, but funds soon became low, and in this predicament divine aid came:

De dieu sera tost auanciee
Cest oeure qui est commenciee,

. . . .

Humaine aide y failli toute,
De par dieu conuint que venist
Aide qui le soustenist.[198]

Moreover the assistance of God was obtained through the importunities of Mary:

La haute dame glorieuse

. . . . . .

Son douz fils pria doucement
Que miracles apertement
En son iglise a Chartres *feist*
Que touz le pueples le veist
Si que de toutes pars venissent

. . . .

Li rois des rois, li tous poissans
Fu a sa mere obeissans,
Doucement oi ses prieres,
Miracles de meintes manieres
Fist por sa mere apertement.[199]

---

[196] *Ibid.*, no. 3, p. 17. The Latin text reads: " Cum plerosque et scriptorum quam plurimos sepissime videam vana quedam ac prorsus inutilia litteris exarare . . . honestius michi visum est et utilius *mirabilia quedam ao memorabilia Dei opera*, que *ad laudem et gloriam nominis sui* in ecclesia Carnotensi palam *exercere dignatus* est." Cf. A. Thomas, " Les miracles de Notre-Dame de Chartres," *Bibl. de l'Ecole des Chartes*, XLII (1881), no. 1, p. 508.

[197] The year 1020 given by Jean le Marchant has been falsified. Thomas, *loc. cit.*, pp. 504-505.

[198] *Livre des Miracles* . . . , p. 31.

[199] *Ibid.*, p. 32. The Latin for the entire account shows that Jean le Marchant followed his model closely: " Quid plura? *humano* penitus *deficiente a[u]xilio*, cum necessarium esset *adesse divinum*, beata Dei

The renown of the miracles performed at Chartres quickly spread and soon, as at Saint-Pierre-sur-Dive, carts full of building materials and supplies for the workmen arrived, drawn by the pilgrims. The crowds, keeping vigil each night, were so large that the monks were unable to enter the church for matins.[200] Psalms, hymns, and the " loanges de Dieu " were sung,

> Mes sus tot ce que vos dion
> Acroissoit leur deuocion
> Et les fesoit plus fors creanz
> Que tote ior leur ialz voicanz
> Miracles espers auenoient
> Que deuant els souent vaient
> Que *Dieu* por sa mere essaucier
> Et por siglise auancier
> *Fesoit* li rois qui vit et regne
> Et sans fin durera son reigne.[201]

Those who drew the carts enjoyed the special protection of God. Three of the miracles which Jean le Marchant relates illustrate the providence of God in their behalf. The first, which the author says has " seignorie " over all the others, concerns the people of Château-Landon.[202] They are on their way to Chartres with a load of wheat, which is to be sold and the money used for the reconstruction of the church. Their provisions fail and in this predicament the Son of the Virgin has pity upon them:

> *Le Filz* de la verge ennoree
>
> .   .   .   .
>
> Voult alegier *par sa pitie*
> Et voult *par vertu demostree*
> Que sa mere fut ennoree

---

genitrix novam et incomparabilem ecclesiam sibi volens fabricari ad facienda ibidem miracula, *ejusdem filii sui potentiam meritis suis et precibus incitavit,* et ut major illuc concursus fieret populorum . . . inauditum miraculum cunctis . . . evidenter *ostendit* " (*loc. cit.,* no. 1, p. 511).

[200] *Ibid.,* p. 41.

[201] Pp. 41-42. The Latin reads: " Hoc autem fidem precipue omnium et devotionem augebat, quod in eorum conspectibus crebro miracula contingebant, *prestante hoc domino Jhesu Christo* ad laudem et gloriam genitricis sue, qui cum eo vivit et regnat in secula seculorum amen " (*loc. cit.,* no. ii, p. 514).

[202] Château-Landon is in the Département (of) Loiret.

> Et essauciee en tous leus,
> *Miracle monstra* merueilleus
> Qui nest en coustume venus.[203]

Their bread is multiplied by " la vertu dou roi celestre." When the amazed people recognize that a miracle has taken place, they praise the generosity of God and His Mother as Mediatrix:

> A Jhesucrist graces rendirent
> Qui toz biens donne largement
> Et a sa mere ensement
> Qui son chier filz tant ot prie
> Que par lui furent auoie.[204]

The poet concludes that the church of Chartres enjoys great favor with " la haute dame ":

> Quant aus bienfeteurs de seglise
> Monstra amor de tele guise
> Que son *filz* par eulz tant pria
> Que les peins leur mouteplia
> Et *fist* miracles por sennor
> Telz com au tens ancionnor.[205]

A second miracle in behalf of the benefactors of the church is similarly theocentric. Jean le Marchant writes:

[203] *Ibid.,* no. 6, p. 71. The translator follows the original closely: " . . . sed illis sua temporalis providencia profuit, istis vero Dei et genitricis clementia in tanta necessitate non defuit. . . . Attendens igitur gloriose Virginis *filius* vendentium pietatem et fatigate plebis miseratus esuriem, quoddam insolitum et insigne *miraculum dignatus* est inter eos *operari* de celis, quod condam inter discipulos operatus est dum conversaretur in terris. Sicut enim olim in deserto Vque milia hominum satiavit, ita panes in sacculis positos *sua dignatus est* ad honorem matris *multiplicare potentia* " (*loc. cit.,* no. iii, pp. 514-15).

[204] *Ibid.,* p. 72. Jean le Marchant does not translate the phrase " qui facit mirabilia magna solus " in the following passage: " Omnes simul gaudio et exultatione repleti sunt ac *largitori bonorum omnium, qui facit mirabilia magna solus,* nec non et gloriose genitricis sue gracias egerunt " (*loc. cit.,* p. 515).

[205] *Ibid.,* p. 73. In the Latin text Mary has a great predilection for the church of Chartres, " que benefactoribus ejusdem ecclesie non solum consueta et usitata impendit beneficia, verum et insolita et inusitata ejus aliquando exibet filio suo, prout ipsa vult et quando vult antiqua brachii sui miracula suscitante " (*loc. cit.*).

> Ne voill pas mestre en oubliance
> Un autre fet dautel samblance
> Que ge troue ou liure escrit
> Que nostre sire *Jhesu crist*
> Por sa douce mere ennorer
> Et de Chartres liglise ourer
> *Fist* en icelui tens meismes.[206]

The people of Pluviers [207] refuse to allow the villagers of Le Puiset [208] to assist them in drawing a cart of wheat but accept a refreshment of wine:

> Quant mis se furent a la voie,
> *Dex* qui toz biens donne et ennoie
> *Mostra* illec apertement
> Biau *miracle* a lessaucement
> De sa douce mere Marie:
> *Cil dex qui tout a en baillie*
> Li rois poissanz de paradis
> *Qui* cortois *miracles iadis*
> *Fist a la poure fame vueue.*[209]

When the astonished inhabitants of Le Puiset find their barrel filled with wine, they recall the pilgrims that they may see

> Comment dex set bien poruaoir
> Cels qui lui et sa mere seruent.[210]

They are invited to taste this wine " que Dex a fet " and they do so, but not gluttonously as at first, " mes comme vin seintefie," and which " *Dex* la par sa grace *enuoie.*" [121]

---

[206] *Ibid.*, no. 11, p. 73.

[207] Pluviers or Pithiviers in Gâtenais, Département (of) Loiret.

[208] Le Puiset, a commune of the arrondissement of Chartres.

[209] *Ibid.*, p. 77. According to the Latin version He who formerly wrought a miracle for Elias, " ipse idem dolium vacuatum *sua* statim *virtute* vino meliori *replevit*, cujus scillicet dolii liquor peregrinis gloriose virginis ex habundantissima caritate totus jam fuerat erogatus " (*loc. cit.*, no. vi, p. 516).

[210] *Ibid.*, p. 78.

[211] *Ibid.*, p. 79. According to the original, " accedunt omnes rursus ad olium, sacrum poculum libaturi, non de vitis olim germine, sed sola *Dei gracia* noviter et mirabiliter procreatum. Extrahunt vinum novum in calices et degustant non avidius sed devotius quam solebant " (*ibid.*, pp. 516-17).

Another miracle occurs in favor of the people of Bonneval [212] who, while drawing a wagon loaded with lime, are overtaken by a storm and are unable to find shelter. Nevertheless,

> *Dex qui tot puet* le roi celestre,
> Qui daigna de la virge nestre
> Qua lenfanter ne fu maumise,
> En tel maniere et en tel guise
> *Garda les dons* destre maumis
> Qui auoient este promis
> A sa douce mere et voez
> Moillies ni furent nenboez.[213]

One woman is unable to be removed from the wagon during the storm:

> Mais *Dex* par sa mere *y ourra*,
> Car la contreite recouura.[214]

This is " la tierce vertu a Dex feite." [215]

Even those who make small offerings merit favors. When everything in the home of a woman of Villentras in Berry seems to have been destroyed by fire, it is found that by the " vertu de dieu " [216] a cloth which she has made for the altar at Chartres is untouched:

> *Cil* qui en la fornese ardant
> *Fist* les enfanz iadis gardant
> Conques nul ardeur ni senti,
> *Cil dieu* qui onques ne menti
> *Fist miracle* dautre maniere
> A lenneur de sa mere chiere
> Que la touaille fu sauuee
> Qui ert a sa mere voee.[217]

---

[212] Bonneval, a commune of the arrondissement of Château-dun (Eure-et-Loir).

[213] *Ibid.*, no. 12, p. 82. The Latin reads: " Ille enim qui ex intemerato virginis utero sine matris [in]corruptione incorruptus exivit, *ipse* matri sue munera destinata inviolata et integra *conservavit* " (*loc. cit.*, no. v, p. 517).

[214] *Ibid.*, p. 83. The Latin merely says: " Tandem virtute et clementia beate Virginis pristine saluti restituta est " (*loc. cit.*).

[215] *Ibid.*, p. 82.

[216] *Ibid.*, no. 27, p. 176. This is one of the miracles which the author took from a source other than the Vatican MS *Reginensis 339*.

[217] *Ibid.*, p. 176.

The cathedral of Chartres is the scene of most of the miracles which Jean le Marchant relates. One which "les autres passe et seurmonte," [218] concerns a little child who happens to overhear the plans of two lovers and is punished by having his tongue cut out by the knight who takes this cruel precaution to guard his secret:

> A dieu pleiscit ceste auenture,
> Ainsint comme dist lescriture
> Que la *vertu De fust veuc*.[219]

While the poet sees in this the pleasure of God to manifest his power, he attributes the recovery of the boy's gift of speech to the direct action of Mary:

> La douce *dame* de pitie
> Li demostra grant amitie
> Car la parole li *rendi*.[220]

Nevertheless, in the thanksgiving offered by the witnesses and friends of the child, Jean le Marchant specifically says:

> La douce dame mercierent
> Por qui *dieu* en lenfant *oura*
> Que sa parole recoura.[221]

The boy now speaks without a tongue, but on Pentecost the work is perfected:

> En la semblence et en memoire
> Dou fet que fist a ses apostres,
> *Li haus rois tous poissans* qui nostres
> Criator est et nostre pere
> *Fist* par lessaucement sa mere
> Que la langue a lenfant trenchiee
> En celui ior rentheringnee

---

[218] *Ibid.*, no. 3, p. 32.

[219] *Ibid.*, no. 4, p. 34. The Latin reads: "Quod siquidem eo disponente vel permittente factum fuisse arbitror, qui cecum a nativitate ideo cecum frustus(?) est, *ut Dei opera manifestarentur in illo*" (*loc. cit.*, no. ii, p. 512).

[220] *Ibid.*, p. 36. There is the same activity on the part of Mary in the original: "Respexit in eum pia misericordie mater, et loquendi usum, . . . ei contra naturam restituit" (*loc. cit.*).

[221] *Ibid.* In the original one finds: "Quod *meritis ipsius et precibus* [Mariae] fidem ac devotionem eorum *Christus ex alto prospexit*" (*loc. cit.*).

Fu de char nouelle et entiere

. . . .

Ce fist le roy de maieste
Por se quen sa foi plus fors saient
Cil qui en ses vertux craient.[222]

In another miracle in favor of a mute the good dispositions of the recipient are emphasized. Two men come to Chartres: one, who is blind, lingers in a tavern; the other, a mute, seeks first the " reigne dieu " : [223]

Meintenant *dex* le roi celestre
Qui quenoit totes les pensees
Ses prieres ot escoutees:
Si *ouura* por lamour sa mere
Car li mus ot voiz haute et clere
Dez et sa mere gracia.[224]

By the " vertu dieu . . . par la vertu diuine " [225] his tongue is entire. His blind companion arrives from the inn. He, too, sheds tears, but as Jean le Marchant remarks,

Ce estoient lermes de vin.

. . . .

Il ne pria fors que de boucher,
Tel priere a dieu pas ne touche.[226]

The miracle is not performed, not even " por lamour sa mere."

[222] *Ibid.*, pp. 37-38. The Latin reads: " Die Pentecostes, novum . . . miraculum in memorato, puero et in eadem ecclesia *manus Omnipotentis exercuit*, . . . Sicut enim *divine majestatis potentia* olim in die Pentecostes apostolorum linguas sanctum de celis emittendo spiritum innovavit . . . ita (ut) in die Pentecostes memorati linguam pueri, . . . nove carnis immissione *supplevit* et ad enarrandam Dei et genitricis ipsius potentiam mirabiliter reparando *restituit* " (*ibid.*, pp. 512-13).

[223] *Ibid.*, no. 12, p. 115.

[224] *Ibid.*, p. 116. The Latin differs slightly: " Mutus itaque jam non mutus sed eloquens, cum *divinam* sibi primo *sensis*[s]*et adesse presentiam* repletus gaudio inestimabili in vocem laudis et exultationis aperte loquendo perrupit " (*loc. cit.*).

[225] *Ibid.*, pp. 116-17. The Latin writer uses the expressions " virtus divina . . . divine signa potentie " (*loc. cit.*).

[226] *Ibid.*, pp. 118-19. The humor is not Jean le Marchant's own: " Ebrietatis magis, ut reor, quam devotionis lacrimas . . . Quippe probatum est in hiis duobus quantum valeat apud Deum conscientia bona et fides non ficta et quod sine fide placere Deo impossibile est " (*ibid.*, p. 526).

This expression or its equivalent is frequently employed by the poet and is found in the account of the resuscitation of a drowned child. Suspecting that his readers may be incredulous, Jean le Marchant prefaces his account with the warning:

> Ge ne voill mie recreire
> Des miracles qui sont a creire
> Que ge la verite nen die
> Que *dieu fit por sa chere amie,*
> La douce mere glorieuse.[227]

He repeats the same thought in the beginning of the miracle " Dun effant naie qui fu resuscite a Soilli " : [228]

> De verite dire me vant
> Quant cil miracle que deuant
> Vos ai conte orent este
> Que *dex* li rois de maieste
> *Ot fet por lenneur de sa mere.*
> *Cil dex* que reclamons a pere
> *Fist* en cel tens en cel deteire
>
> .   .   .   .
>
> *Un beau miracle* et renomme.[229]

The child is revived,

> .   .   .   .   *par vertu deuine*
> Car la haute *virge raine*
> Qui dautres raines est gemme
> *I oura* por la bonne dame.[230]

After such an introduction, the force of the word " oura " obviously indicates a delegated power or one of intercession.

Jean le Marchant uses the same word to express the intervention of Mary in the miracle, " Dou pelerin que Nostre Dame deliura de prison." The pilgrim has not allowed the war between Richard of England and Philip of France to prevent his yearly journey to

---

[227] *Ibid.*, no. 7, p. 55. This personal remark of Jean le Marchant is not in the Latin.

[228] Sully-sur-Loire in the Département (of) Loiret.

[229] *Ibid.*, no. 19, p. 107. This, too, is an original introduction.

[230] *Ibid.*, p. 111. Both accounts compare the faith of the mother to that of the centurion in the Gospel, " cujus scilicet centurionis fides, pietas et devotio in evangelio plurimum a Domino laudata est " (*loc. cit.*, no. xii, p. 524).

Chartres. He is miraculously delivered from prison and finds that his horse is even saddled and ready: " La mere dieu por lui oura." [231] This time the poet gives the reader a hint as to the proper interpretation of the word in his conclusion:

> Lors sauerti par remenbrance
> Que partout est *la grant puissance*
> *De dieu* nostre souerain pere
> Et que *il deliura* saint pere
> Des liens et deschaenna
> Et par son ange le mena
> Seuls eissist seurement
> Et le gita hors de prison.[232]

Moreover, he states explicitly that Mary was merely acting as Mediatrix when she " gita . . . de prison " her pilgrim:

> Car *dieu* poissant *par la priere*
> De sa douce mere Marie
> Li a fet secors et aie
> Et la de prison hors *gite*:
> La rose de virginite
> Li a feste ceste bonte.[233]

As a suppliant intercessor, Mary is appealed to in a miracle

> Que *Dieu* li peres esperitables
> Li rois poissans li glorieus
> *Fist* a Chartres et en meint leus,
> Por sa douce mere essaucier
> Et por sa besoigne auancier.[234]

---

[231] *Ibid,.* no. 24, p. 148. [232] *Ibid.*, p. 148.

[233] *Ibid.*, p. 148. The passage in the original reads: " Quidem ad beati Petri similitudinem de carcere per angelum liberati hec omnia per visionem estimans se vidisse; sed cum ipse reversus Dei genitricem hec et majora posse facere plenius advertisset sui nimirum *virtute* et *potentia filii* qui eundem Petrum in carcere cathenatum et a multis militibus multipliciter observatum mirabiliter liberavit, ipse tandem Deo et gloriose Virgini, ut pote liberatrici sue, gratias agens " (*loc. cit.*, no. xx, p. 541).

[234] *Ibid.*, no. 5, p. 42. According to the Latin, " mirum non est si divine potestatis magnalia que in ecclesia Carnotensi . . . ad honorem genitricis sue *Dei filius* mirabiliter *operari dignatus est . . . describere . . . satagimus.* Quanto enim divina potentia fragilitate precellit humane, tanto *Dei opera* humanis actibus excellentiora sunt et perhenni magis memoriae commendanda " (*loc. cit.*, no. xxi, pp. 541-42).

A young bride is stricken with paralysis, and being too poor to have medical care, she and her husband have recourse to the Blessed Virgin:

> Que por le son chier filz *priast*
> Que de ce mal la desliast
> Ou a la mort tost la liurast.[235]

The bride goes to Chartres in obedience to a command of the Virgin Mary who has appeared to her in a vision, and is cured.

It is also through the intercession of Mary that a youth of Paleiseau[236] escapes uninjured after three days imprisonment in the bottom of a well, the sides of which have caved in upon him:

> Par trois iors fu ou puis sanz peine
> Comme Ionas en la baleine,
> Car cil qui Ionas senefie:
> Le *filz d*e la virge Marie,
> *Par la priere de sa mere*
> Le sauua de la mort enmere.[237]

When a little girl falls into a well, her miraculous rescue is attributed to the Virgin Mary into whose care the mother had commended the child. Here the poet applies to Mary Mediatrix the figure of " eschielle ":

> Icelle est eschielle celestre
> Par quei montent li pecheor
> Ou ciel a nostre sauueor
> Qui par la priere a la dame
> Nos veille sauuer cors et ame.[238]

Only a few of the miracles in the collection of Jean le Marchant treat of the " pecheor." In one of these, " Dou chancelier de Chartres qui saluet uolentiers Nostre Dame," the poet expatiates upon the contradiction between the clerk's irregular life and his devotion to the Virgin:

[235] *Ibid.*, p. 44.

[236] Paleiseau is a commune near Paris.

[237] *Ibid.*, no. 13, p. 87. The Biblical comparison is also contained in the original (*loc. cit.*, no. vi, p. 518).

[238] *Ibid.*, no. 16, p. 101. The metaphor is not in the Latin account (*loc. cit.*, no. ix, pp. 520-22).

> Volentiers seruoit Nostre Dame
> Ses hores disoit, car de same
> Auoit mise en le sesperance
> Et quauroit par le acordance
> Vers son chier filz de ses meffez
> Quil fesoit et quil auoit fez;
>
> .   .   .   .
>
> Mais ce bien ne sot pas la gent
> Qui le fesoit *priueement.*[239]

The attempt of Jean le Marchant to judge the clerk charitably by emphasizing his efforts [240] to combat his vices through prayer is not usually found in the many variants [241] of the legend in both Latin and vernacular collections.

The omnipresence of God, as well as His mercy, appears in the legend " Dune fame a cui il mesauint porce quel filla au semadi au seir." [242] The woman has forgotten,

> *Dex le set qui voit toutes choses,*
> Les pensees qui sont enclouses
> Ou cuer voit toutes en espert,
> Ja nul segrei niert si couert
> Que *dex nel sache bien et voie.*[243]

A paralysis of the hand makes her realize the seriousness of a broken vow. She debates whether to confess her sin to the " sergent dieu " or not:

[239] *Ibid.*, no. 29, p. 185.

[240] He reiterates his comment:

> Cil chanceliers fist autrement,
> Son mal fesoit apertement
> Com home en vice auiue,
> Et son bien fesoit en priue,
> En priant chacune iornee
> A la mere dieu ennoree
> Quele par sa misericorde
> *Vers son filz li feist acorde.*   (*ibid.*, p. 186).

[241] Cf. Crane's notes to Pez, no. iii, p. 83.

[242] Cf. *supra*, pp. 33, 37-38.

[243] *Ibid.*, no. 25, p. 154. The Latin merely depicts her attempts to perform her work in secret, "magis timens hominem quam Deum (*loc. cit.,* no. xvii, p. 531).

> Dex veult quen moi soit sanz celee
> *Sa haut oeure manifestee.*[244]

Shame prevents her from revealing her punishment but the pain becomes so great that she yields to the importunities of her friends and makes a public confession. She is cured but fails to keep her promise to go to Chartres in thanksgiving. The pastor warns her:

> Toust as la bonte obliee
> Que dex tauoit por le mostree,
> Ge crei tu le comparras chier
> Quant dex velt bien se set venchier.[245]

Again she is afflicted, but her repentance merits for her another cure through the intercession of Mary.[246]

Jean le Marchant frequently refers to his desire for " ordre " in relating the miracles and for this reason he changed the arrangement of the Latin original. In his emphasis on the element of theocentrism his work presents a perfect plan. It soon becomes quite clear that God Himself performs the miracles for the " Dame de Chartres." While this idea is repeated in scattered accounts, it is the central theme of a vision related toward the middle of the collection:

> Miracles de meinte maniere
> *Ouura dex* por sa mere chiere,
> Au tens que len ouureit siglise.[247]

After this introduction he tells that the church, one Saturday, became resplendent with light, whence it was believed,

[244] *Ibid.* The omnipresence of God is brought out in her soliloquy: " Possum diu occultare *mirabilia Dei*? . . . Si non videt homo, in me videt Deus; si non scit vicinus, non nescit Dominus; si percussit me Dominus, nonne meruit? . . . Vivam ita in eternum si Dominus vult opus suum manifestare? " (*ibid.*, p. 532).

[245] *Ibid.*, p. 163. The pastor chides: " Heu! misera, quomodo tam cito facta es immemor tui, oblita beneficii accepti, prevaricatrix mandatorum Dei, transgressa votum, inobediens preceptis? si bene novi opera Dei et gloriose Virginis quam despexisti, non diu inpune feres. Sed modo sit *sicut Domino placuerit*; tamen indulgeat tibi Dominus " (*ibid.*, p. 535).

[246] The original describes the effect of the miracle on her friends: " Erant autem omnes qui aderant mirantes et benedicentes *Deum in omnibus que viderant* " (*ibid.*, p. 536).

[247] *Ibid.*, no. 18, p. 106.

> Que la douce dame en siglise
> Entra et la seintefia,
> Et *son filz requist et pria*
> Que por siglise tost ouurer
> *Volsist miracles demostrer.*[248]

The last miracle in the collection leaves no doubt as to its theocentric emphasis, although the theme is Mary the physician. The mercy of God is not cast into the background by the pity of the Blessed Virgin:

> *Dex qui fontaine est de pitie*
> Monstre au pecheurs amitie,
> Car nuit et ior ses bras leur tent
> Et de ior en ior les atent
> Que il viengnent a penitance.[249]

When "humeine medicine" is of no avail during the plague, the *Mal des ardents,* Mary proposes a remedy. She appears to a sufferer, saying:

> . . . Fei ioie bonne fame,
> Saches que de Chartres sui dame,
>
> .   .   .   .
>
> Que ge sui ci a toi venue,
> *Car ge ai tant mon filz prie*
> Que il ma un don otrie
> Par quoi li ardant esteindront,
>
> .   .   .   .
>
> Fei leur feire ymages de cire
> Chacune . iij . deniers pesant
> *En lenneur dieu le tot puissant*
> *Qui est un dieu en trinite*
> Et est treibles en unite.[250]

Those who make this offering in honor of the Trinity will be cured. The poet tells of the wonderful effects of this heavenly remedy:

> Meintenant la vertu deuine
> Dou ciel enuoia medecine
> Que li ardant tantoust estaindrent,

---

[248] *Ibid.*, p. 107. This differs from the Latin: " Unde credimus quod beata Domini mater suo tunc adventu eamdem illustravit ecclesiam, eo quod super memorata miracula exinde subsecuta sint et alia etiam quam plurima que vel prorsus oblivioni tradita sunt " (*loc. cit.*, no. xi, p. 523).

[249] *Ibid.*, no. 32, pp. 205-206.

[250] *Ibid.*, p. 207.

14

Nul signe de feu ne remeindrent.
Oncore *dex plus i ouura,*
Chacun ses menbres recouura,

. . . .

Cil a qui rien nest impossible
I demostra bien sa poissance
Et que vers lui grant acointance
Ha la virge qui lenfanta:
La mere vers son effant a
Poer dempetrer quant quel quiert.[251]

He concludes with a prayer that through the mediation of the Mother, Christ may lead us into the Father's presence:

La dame quelle par sa grace
Vers son filz soit nostre auocace,
Dempetrer nous dou ciel la ioie
La mere et *le filz* nos en oie
Qui par la priere sa mere
Nos conduie deuant son pere
A cui est royaume et enpire
Ou riens ne perist ne nenpire.[252]

In a final note in prose he restates his theocentric position:

Fist nostre Seigneur les miracles dessus dis a lenneur de sa sainte mere la benoiste vierge Marie pour aidier a ediffier ycelle eglise de Chartres qui est la propre et especial chambre de la dite vierge Marie en terre.[253]

In this collection Mary is subordinate to God inasmuch as Jean le Marchant could not say more explicitly that God "fist les miracles" for the Mother. We may not conclude, because a few of the miracles do not contain such direct statements, that Mary has power of herself.

MS *Bibl. nat. fr. 818*

Written in the second half of the thirteenth century, MS *818* contains many of the legends previously treated. However, this collection which Paul Meyer terms " une sorte de Mariale " [254] in the vulgar tongue offers variety in the presentation of theocentric traits.

---

[251] *Ibid.*, pp. 209-10.   [252] *Ibid.*, p. 210.   [253] *Ibid.*, p. 211.
[254] Paul Meyer, " Notice sur le recueil de miracles de la Vierge renfermé dans le ms. Bibl. nat. fr. 818," *Not. et extr.*, XXXIV, 2 (1895), 57.

The legend of Ildefonsus from the viewpoint of narrative differs little from other vernacular versions; nevertheless, in the introduction to this tale the author does not leave to implication the authority of the Deity ruling Mary's actions, even in the mere bestowal of a reward to one of her clients:

> En nun de Deu l'esperitable
> Vos voil raconter les miracle
> Que *Jhesus*, li rois de pidie,
> *A fait por sa mere Marie,*
> La reine de Paradis. (1-5) [255]

The chasuble is brought from "paradis *mon fil*," and may not be worn by another; otherwise, Mary says: "Mos fiz en prendra grant venjance." (74) During the lifetime of Ildefonsus her command is respected, but his successor, "Poi prisa Deu, lo roi celestre." (95) Siagrius ventures to don the vestment:

> E *Deus* qui orgoil n'ama onques
> Si prit venjance en prit donques;
> Li vestimenz l'estreint si fort
> Que devant toz ceuz chaisit morz. (111-14)

In the legend of the "Amputated Foot Restored" the direct statement found in other collections to the effect that "Deu fait miracles pur l'amur sa mere," [256] is so rendered in MS *818* as to present the Virgin acting through the power of her Son. Hence, there is the same theocentric significance when the poet says that it is Mary,

> Qui de maladi les garoit,
> Celui qui de cuer li queroit,
> *Per la vertu a son douz fil,*
> Qui toz nos giteit de peril. (7-10) [257]

He does not contradict himself when he writes towards the end of the legend:

> La santé trova de son pie
> Par la vertu sainte Marie. (61-62) [258]

---

[255] Appendix to the *Deuxième collection anglo-normande*, ed. H. Kjellman, no. iii, p. 269.

[256] Cf. *supra*, pp. 136 and 150.

[257] *Ibid.*, no. 50, p. 291.   [258] Cf. *infra*, p. 216.

The writer's position as to the *vertu Deu* and the *vertu sainte Marie* is made clearer in the anecdote of the clerk Stephen. During his return from Jerusalem, his ship strikes a rock and while others seek safety in boats, the clerk faces the peril of being drowned:

> ' Ahi' fait il, ' douce reine,
> *apres Deu* tote m'esperance,
>
> .   .   .   .
> douce dame, aide moi.'   (80-88) [259]

Suddenly he is picked up by a wave and cast upon the shore:

> Bien sot la mere Jesu Christ
> l'avoit gite de cel peril.   (99-100)

His companions who despair of his safety look for his body. The words of the poet in describing their meeting make clear the part of the Deity and of the Virgin in the miracle:

> Domentres que serjant l'aloient,
> de loing a euz venir le voient;
> quar *la vertu del roi autime*
> par la *priere* de la Virge
> entra jenz l'ot posse en terre.   (119-23)

In the legend of the Jew boy Mary visibly cooperates in the child's protection; nevertheless, the author says that it is a " grant miracle de Jhesu." Her rôle is not minimized:

> E il tantost lor respondet
> Que celle dame honorable
> Qui desure l'auter itave
> ' Et a nos qui comenjavam
> O tendit a sa nue main;
> Cele cest'ajua me donet
> Et lo feu de sus moi ostet;
> Onques del feu non oi chalor
> Ne del fumez sentui odor.'
> Adonz soront bien li crestin
> Que la virgine genitrix
> Mere al douz roi totpoissant
> Avoit del feu gardé l'enfant.   (60-72) [260]

---

[259] Mussafia, *Studien*, V, no. iv, p. 27.

[260] Mussafia, " Handschriftliches zu Wolters Judenknaben," *ZRPh.*, IX (1885), 413.

Many Jews are converted:

> Et maint del juex qui eront iqui
> La synagoge ont laissié
> *A Jhesu Crist se sont torné*
> Quant li crestiain ont veu
> *Lo grant miracle de Jhesu,*
> Los en rendont a Jhesu Crist
> Et a sa mere autresi.   (80-86)

The cure of the monk by the Virgin's milk is a reward given by God for fervor in His service:

> *Nostre Deus,* nostre droit Salvere,
> *Qui a toz est guiardonere,*
>
> .   .   .   .
>
> *Vout rendre guiardonement.*   (29-36) [261]

His long life, moreover, is due to the mercy of God:

> *Par la merci de Jhesu Crist*
> Mainz jor après iço vesquit.   (87-88)

Mary also appears as agent in the legend of Saint John of Damascus.[262]   When he loses his hand at the command of the Emperor Theodosius (375-95), John turns to God in perfect resignation, although he suffers keenly from his inability to celebrate Mass:

> Molt esses grant, beus sire Deus,
> E ta patience est teus
> Des pecheor as penitence
> E los sainz suffres que hom tormente;
> Semblanz est que aies oblié
> Lor justice e lor bonté;
> Veritez est pure e nete
> Ço que tu diz per la prophete.   (387-94) [263]

---

[261] Kjellman, *op. cit.*, no. liv, p. 296.

[262] Cf. the same legend by Vincent of Beauvais, *supra*, p. 73.   As the editor Kjellman remarks, both MS *818* and the *Speculum Historiale* are identical in details which differ from the original biography by John of Jerusalem (*PG*, XCIV, 429 ff.).   Since it is very likely that the work of Vincent is a later composition than the manuscript, the editor concludes that "l'auteur français et Vincent de Beauvais ont connu le même récit latin."   Cf. "La légende de Saint Jean Damascène," *Studier i Modern Språkvetenskap*, VIII (1921), 107-12.

[263] La légende de Saint Jean Damascène," *loc. cit.*, p. 117.

However, he questions Mary why he should have lost the hand which wrote her praises and daily offered Mass,

> A salu de tot pecheor
> Offroie je *a Deu lo pere*
> Le sanc son fil dont tu es mere.   (428-30)

When she appears to him, she says that God has the power to restore his hand:

> Beuz tresdouz fiuz, or te conforte!
> En nostron Seignor te conforte,
> Tost te *pot restorer ta man*
> Qui forma de niant Adan.   (459-62)

Nevertheless, she brings the hand to him and it is miraculously joined to his arm. The poet exclaims at the greatness of this miracle:

> Oi, Deus, quant grant bonté ci a!
> Oi, Deus, quant benastrua man
> Que la virge tint en sa man!   (468-70)

MS *818* is also of interest in that it contains two versions of the Jew who lends to a Merchant: one is obviously theocentric; the other makes the Virgin Mary a prominent figure. In the first Christ is offered in guarantee:

> Por ce que je gage ne truis
> Voudroies tu mon Salveor
> Que jo ahoro nuit e jor,
> Mon Deu, mon Seignor Jhesu Crist,
> Qui de la virgine nasquit?   (54-58) [264]

Moreover, the Christian confidently prays that if he is unable to pay the debt, Christ will supply the default:

> Sire Jhesu Crist, cui image
> Por cest avoir je doing en gage
> A cest Jueu, e por fiance
> Que je li tiegne covenance
> Supliement e te depri
> Que se par aventura avint
> Que jo al jor que establiz est
> Ne puisse rendre cest aver,
> Que je a toi le puisse rendre

---

[264] *Deuxième collection anglo-normande*, no. liii, p. 294.

> Que *tu por moi a lui lo rendes.*
> Issi com il meuz te plaira,
> Beuz sire Deus, si fait sera. (97-108)

Following his Latin source closely,[265] the poet writes concerning the merchant who commends his treasure to the sea:

> A *celui* qui fist mer e terre
> Lo comande que lo governe.
> Ce est granz merveille a dire,
> Mais *a Deu nule riens n'est grie.* (167-70)

Later to prove to the Jew that his confidence is not misplaced in a Man-God, he demands a miracle, if necessary, to verify the fulfilment of his obligation:

> Beuz, seigner, Deus, rois Jhesu Criz,
> Si te plait, escoute ton serz,
> E si *com Deus e vers hom es,*
> Issi *me porta garenti,*
> De verité je lo te pri,
> Si j'ai rendu a cest Juef
> L'avoir que il m'avoit presté. (227-33)

In the second version the merchant becomes poor " com Deu plaisit,[266] and in borrowing the money offers an image of the Virgin Mary in surety. At first he is unsuccessful, but at length meets a shepherd who is willing to trade for his goods an unknown metal which the merchant knows to be gold. Upon his return he hangs the purse around the neck of the image. When the Jew denies receiving it, the Christian who " mult se fia *en Deu* (132)," adjures Mary to bear witness. Her image speaks:

> ' Bon Crestain, alegrez vos,
> *je pri* toz jorz *mon fil por vos.*
>
> . . . .
>
> Ovrez l'arche, sel troverez;
> ce seit *a la gloire de Crist*
> et a confusion de Juis.' (168-77)

This legend concludes with lines which pointedly designate the part of God in all miracles:

[265] Cf. Pez, *supra*, pp. 55-56.
[266] Mussafia, *Studien*, V, no. xxix, l. 13, p. 45.

> A grant joi et a grant honor
> ont l'ymage porte lo jor
> a l'esglise sainte Marie,
> li *cui fiuz nos soit en aie.*
> *En ses sains est mervillous*
> *nostre syre et poderous,*
> et li sainz et ses bones ovres
> et cel qui lo creira encores.
> Cest seignor devons nos loer
> beneir et glorifier
> et sa douce *mere Marie*
> qui toz jors *por nos merci crie.* (182-93)

The verb " crie " indicates a subordinate rôle of mediation for the Virgin Mary.

MS *818* is also clearer than other versions as to the part of God in the miraculous supply of mead, and the rôle of Mary as Mediatrix. The noblewoman is not disturbed because she is threatened with embarrassment:

> Esperance a *en Deu* pensee
> et en sa mere bienauree,
>
> .   .   .   .
>
> Devant son autel est venue,
> socors li requiert et aiue:
> O douce mere Jesu Crist,
> dame, ahiez de moi merci;
>
> .   .   .   .
>
> Dame, pries *vostre douz fil*
> *qu'il cest bevrage multiplit.* (49-60) [267]

The distinction between God and the Mediatrix is likewise made in the legend of famine in Jerusalem. The Abbot says to the starving monks:

> Seignor, faisomes oraison
> A nostron seignor *Jhesu Crist*
> *Qui nos dara et blé et vin.*
> La Virge ne porroit soffrir
> Que a ses moines fromenz faillist.
> De virginal ventre saillit
> Li fromenz par que li monz vit. (28-34) [268]

---

[267] *Ibid.*, no. xlix, p. 48.   [268] Paul Meyer, *loc. cit.*, no. ii, p. 66.

They find their barns filled with wheat. When they pray a second time for relief from want, gold is deposited upon the altar by an angel, and the Abbot,

> Bien set c'est dons esperiteus
> Que *al covent a envoié Deus*.
> Graces en rendent Jhesu Crist
> Et a la Virge autresi. (77-80)

They buy the necessary food and the poet remarks:

> Issi *repaissit Nostre Syre*
> Ceuz qui faisoient son servise. (85-86)

The author of this manuscript sees the will of God directing events and drawing good from evil particularly in narratives which concern the welfare of entire cities and which portray a divine vengeance in answer to prayer. The first line of the story of Châteauroux reads: " Per l'escondu *jugement nostron Seignor* nasquit una grant discordi entre lo rei Felipon de France et lo roi Henri d'Engleterre." [269] One division of the English army, composed of " Braimancon, Esquot, Gascon, males genz *qui Jesu Christ non amoient ne temoient,"* take the village of Déols and at the command of their leader proceed to destroy it. The inhabitants gather before an image of Notre-Dame outside the locked church " por *prier Deu* que los conseillet." One of the brigands strikes the statue and falls dead, while blood spurts from the arm of the Christ-child: " Ico *fit nostre Sire* por les enios et por les mescreanz qui ne croient fermament." The writer recalls other miracles

> es ancianes escritures de l'ymage nostre Seignor que li juif feriront d'une lance que li sancs en salli et adonc fu renovellee la passion nostre Seignor, issi con or est. Et einssi reemsit la douce virge Marie s'esglise del sanc de son precios fil, que un avoit comande a avatre, et si co *nostre Sire repetit* la durzia del juex, issi *humiliet nostre Sire* les cuers de ceuz qui eront dur come perre, et *los appella a s'amor*.

The version of the siege of Chartres differs little in theocentric traits from those already considered.[270] When Bishop Galcelun, a very religious man, " Qui Deu amoit et son service," [271] affixes the

---

[269] Mussafia, *Studien*, V, no. ii, p. 21.

[270] Cf. *supra*, pp. 138, 152-53.

[271] Kjellman, *op. cit.*, no. ix, l. 10, p. 271.

Virgin's garment to the end of a lance, the Normans immediately feel the hand of God upon them:

> Li Normant en sont ebahi;
> La veüe tantost perdirent
>
> .   .   .   .   .   .
>
> Quant li Chartain ont entendu
> Que *Jhesu Crist les ha feru.*   (40-50)

However, the slaughter is displeasing to " Jhesu Crist, rois de pidie," and the " douce virge Marie ":

> E *per lo Jhesu Crist plaisir*
> Normant recovrent lo veïr.   (67-68)

The garment disappears because the people of Chartres have offended God who punishes them in this manner for their cruelty:

> Por ço nos fait *Deus* entendant
> Que sus lo *devin jugemant*
> Ne doit neguns humain estendre
> Que tot en poroit pis atendre;
> *Toz crestiains se doit garder*
> *Que por pechier n'offende Deu,*
> De pechié d'orgoil majorment
> Et de cruiauté ensement.   (75-82)

Before beginning the story of the vengeance of God upon Julian the Apostate, the poet takes pains to inform the reader that the Emperor is hardened in sin and an enemy of God.[272]   After a vision in which Basil sees the Virgin Mary order Mercury to deal a death blow to Julian, the saint enters the church where his people are praying:

> De chief en chief conte lor a
> L'avision que veu a.
> Li poples fu liez et joianz,
> *A Deu* en rendent mercis granz.
> L'evesque tantost s'atorna,
> La sainte messe chanté ha;
> Homes et femes *a garni*
> *De cors et del sanc Jhesu Crist.*   (193-200)

Verification is given to his vision by the testimony of Libanius who describes Julian's death:

[272] Paul Meyer, *loc. cit.*, no. iii, ll. 1-12, p. 67.

Bien savent tui ententifment
Fait fu *par devin jugement.*
Li feuz qu'a la terre gisoit
Sa main de son sanc onplisoit,
Raemplis de mal esperit
Fort escria et si a dit:
" *Galileains, tu as vencu !* "
" *Galileains, tu as vencu !* "   (217-24)

Basil is about to return the money which the people had collected
to satisfy the tyrant, when with one voice they protest:

C'al roi mortal o donïons,
Que no destruisist la cite:
Mout o devons nos meuz doner
Jhesu Crist, al roi non mortel,
Qui armes et cors nos gart de mal.   (250-54)

The legend ends with an appeal to Mary Mediatrix that she

Preiet a *son fil Jhesu Crist*
De nos ait pidie et marci.   (269-70)

From these two lines, one may infer that the divine vengeance
which the people recognize to be the judgment of " Damedeu omnipotent," does not obliterate their conception of His mercy.

In the legend of the Pope and the balm it is a punishment of God
that stays the Pope's entry into the church of St. John Lateran.
The realization that God has directly intervened makes him more
conscious of the seriousness of his sin. He has recourse to Mary to
bring about his reconciliation, and while he is reciting her hours,
she appears:

Longemant t'ai oi crier

. . . .

par ma priere *te pardone*
mes fiuz et ta grace te done,
et li apostres ensemant.   (123-28) [273]

In gratitude the pope decrees the recitation of the hours. The poet
promises the joy of the vision of God to him

Qui de bon cuer la priera
et son fil merci criera
si grant guiardon en avra,

---

[273] Mussafia, *Studien,* V, no. vii, p. 30.

> sages qu'en paradis sera,
> *ou il verra Deu en la face;*
> *Jesu Crist nos doint* par sa grace
> que nos puissons chascun jor
> dire les oures a s'onor.   (169-76)

In the Marial legends the grace of sorrow for sin is one which comes directly as a gift from God. The Lord is said to look with pity upon a nun who violated her vow of chastity:

> Nostre Sire non voucit mie
> que longement menast tel vie;
> il la regarda a pidia,
> *car ne la voloit perdre mia.*   (43-46) [274]

Her previous religious life had been one of fervor:

> Une virgine i avoit,
> *que nostre Sire bien amoit,*
>
> .   .   .   .
>
> en jeunes, en aflicions,
> en veziles, en oraisons
> travailloit sa char durement.
> En lermes et en ploremenz
> se travailloit, que elle aut
> *la grace de nostro Seignor.*   (11-20)

But the devil becomes jealous of her virtue and repeatedly tempts her to sin. She loses her virginity, but immediately repents. With the grace of sorrow for sins, comes a great desire to expiate by a life of penance; however, death comes before full atonement has been made. As in other versions the nun later appears to tell the Abbess of the Virgin's visit to her in Purgatory, and of Mary's reprimands:

> Saches que tu me fis iria,
> quant *mon fil aus mespreisia,*
> quar qui mesprise mon douz fil,
> saches qu'il me mesprise ausi.   (201-4)

In MS *818* the nun reveals to the Abbess the prayer which she had said daily and for which she was given the hope of speedy deliverance:

> Sancta et perpetua virgo Maria,
> domina et *advocata nostra.*   (251-52)

---

[274] *Ibid.*, no. lxxiii, p. 60.

A knight who honored only the Blessed Virgin and Saint Michael does not deserve the grace of contrition: " Religion ne Deu n'amoit." [275] One day, while he is reviewing the misdeeds of his life, and is inspired with a dread of death, judgment, and hell, God gratuitously grants him this grace:

> Ala perfin *Deus l'espira*
> et contricion li *dona,*
> que en son cuer dit mout sagement:
> ' Por ce que *Deus* emendament
> *me* doint de ma vie *emender,*
> et por confondre l'aversier,
> en honor de sainte Marie
> ferai fonder une abaie.' (31-38)

He dies before he is able to carry out his good intentions and it is necessary for Saint Michael to wrest his soul from the devils that it may be judged by God:

> . . . '*Davant Deu* soit jugiez;
> nos le volun et vos l'aiez.'
> *Davant le roi de gloire* vindrent,
> et lor plait a derainnier pristrent. (84-87)

Kneeling, Mary makes a plea for him and in this version the Lord does not bid her rise:

> Atant s'est la virge Marie
> davant son fil *agenoillie.* (88-89)

Her will is in accord with the will of God who grants to her the salvation of the knight:

> ' Vostro plaisir tino por mien.
> Dame, reina estes de ciel;
> quant que vos volez et je voil.' (103-5)

Theophilus also receives his first impulsion towards conversion from God:

> Li *sauveres* de tot le mont,
> remenbra li de Theophile,
>
> .   .   .   .
>
> nostre sire no desprisa

---

[275] *Ibid.,* no. xxiii, l. 13, p. 39.

> sa creature, mais *li dona*
> *conversion de penitence*
> et de son pechie remenbrance.[276]

He has a keen sense of the grievousness of his sin but the mercy of Christ inspires hope in the sinner:

> *Jhesus* qui est *misericors,*
> qui le cuer voit dedenz le cors,
> sa creature n'a despit,
> mais quant ele vint la recit,
> *esperance li a done*
> *de revenir a salvete.*[277]

When " Jhesucriz l'ot inspire," Theophilus determines to obtain his reconciliation through the intercession of the Virgin:

> *deus* per sa intercession
> *aura* de moi *verai pardon.*
>
> .   .   .   .   .   .
>
> quar ele soule a poer
> de son fil a toi acorder.[278]

The scene in which Theophilus argues with Mary by citing examples of notorious sinners who were granted forgiveness, places the power of pardon in the hands of God and exalts His attribute of mercy. During the apparition Mary does not seek to dim the glory of God but zealous for His honor demands a profession of faith, assuring Theophilus,

> ' mes fiuz est *mult misericors;*
> tes lermes verra et tes plors,
> la penetence esgardera
> que tes cors de bon gre fera.
> por ce prist deus char en mon cors,
> que *il salvest les pechaors.*' [279]

Moreover, the Virgin promises to place herself at " sos pies " in order to plead for him. When she returns to announce that by her " preieres " the " salvaor de toz " has granted forgiveness, Theophilus exclaims:

> . . . tu es ma proteccions
> *apres deu,* qui est mos patrons.[280]

---

[276] Bartsch-Horning, *La langue et la littérature françaises* (Paris, 1887), no. 58, col. 469.

[277] *Ibid.,* col. 472.   [279] *Ibid.,* col. 479.

[278] *Ibid.,* cols. 472-73.   [280] *Ibid.,* col. 482.

The Bishop's words are also a glorification of God's mercy:

> glorifion tui Jhesu Crist
> et sa pidia et sa merci.
>
> .   .   .   .
>
> seignor, a deu donons grant gloire,
> qui pleins est de misericorde.[281]

Mary's rôle is secondary:

> c'est cele qui porte *a son fil*
> les preieres de nos chaitis
>
> .   .   .   .
>
> qual los, qual gloire vos ferai,
> *a celui qui de toi nasquit,*
> que li traitres Judas vendit!
> *tes ovres sont tant granz, beuz sire,*
> que ma lenge non falt al dire,
> la gloire de *tes meravilles.*[282]

Later the people, looking upon Theophilus' transfigured face, glorify God who alone works miracles:

> *deu* en glorifieront mout
> *qui fait les miracles toz souz.*[283]

In the legend of the thief-monk in which Mary is given the title of Mother of Mercy, the poet concludes:

> Davit dist, qui bien s'i acorde:
> 'Mes *Deus est ma misericorde.*'
> Or prions tuit a une corde
> la mere de misericorde
> que *preiet son glorios fil*
> que nos dont le regne son fil.   (107-12) [284]

In " Love by Black Arts " mercy and justice are made synonomous with God and the Virgin then receives the title of Mother of Mercy and of Justice:

> Li apostoles si nos dit
> que nostre sire Jesu Christ
> est fiuz justice de Deu lo pere,
> et apres trovons el sautere
> que Davit la prophete dit:

---

[281] *Ibid.,* cols. 485-86.   [282] *Ibid.,* cols. 486-87.   [283] *Ibid.,* col. 488.
[284] Mussafia, *Studien,* V, no. xi, p. 33.

> ' Mons deus est ma misericordi.'
> Dont la douce virge Marie,
> qui mere est al roi de pidie
> est verai mere *de justisi*
> et mere *de misericordi.*   (9-18) [285]

In the same legend God's mercy is described as one which encompasses the sinner, not allowing him to be tempted above his strength :

> *O buns Deus,* sire precios,
> ti iugement sont haut sor nos,
> *ta garda est tot'entor nos*
> *et ta misericordi sor nos,*
> quar tu no nos laisses tempter
> outra forci ne outra poer.   (199-204)

Mary's mercy is placed on a par with that of the angels, whose function it is to protect men, and with that of the saints, who are intercessors in Heaven. The poet says that Mary

> . . . nos garde de peril
> et per nos preie son douz fil.   (237-38)

Her rôle is that of one who comforts, and bears no comparison with that of Christ who redeems. One soul seized by the devils after death laments :

> hai, lasse! que me vaut il,
> si Jesu Crist por moi nasquit?
> que me vaut s'*il soffrit* a tort
> en la veraie crois *la mort?*
>
> .   .   .   .
>
> que te valont les oraisons,
> que disies a escondons
> a la douce virge Marie,
> por ce que me feit *aie?*   (119-30) [286]

Salvation is from God ; mere assistance comes from Mary.

Theophilus in his *credo* confesses Christ to be the Good Shepherd who has given His life for sinners :

> je le confesso *verai deu,*
> parfait homen et parfait deu.
> *por nos pechaors deigna soffrir*
> c'um le batist et escopist.

---

[285] *Ibid.,* no. lix, p. 54.   [286] *Ibid.,* no. lxxiv, p. 72.

> crucefiez fu en la croiz,
> mains estendues et batuz,
> *si cum bons pastre pose s'arme*
> *por pechaors* qu'il a en garde.[287]

In the legend "Toledo" such is the testimony of the voice of the Virgin heard on the Feast of the Assumption. The Jews, she says, are again crucifying

> mon cher fil, qui est lumere
> E de fiaus *saluz entere.* (19-20) [288]

He concludes this same legend by appealing to her assistance in obtaining pardon—a pardon which her Son must grant:

> Honorem *por Deu,* bel Seignor,
> La mere Deu, lo Creator;
> Preions per sa virginité
> Nos soit *aiue envers Dé*
> *Que ses glorios fiuz nos dont*
> *Par sa merci verai perdun.* (54-59)

He asks her to intercede further and his confidence in her rôle of Mediatrix is based upon her relation to Christ as God and man:

> Issi ele prit *Jhesu Crist*
> *Que nos gart de l'embrasement*
> *D'enfer* e de trestot torment,
> Ço nos otroit per sa priere
> *Cil qui ses fiuz est e ses pere.* (65-69)

God governs all things and with Him the Virgin Mary has great power of intercession:

> Penseise cum a grant poer
> La douce reïne del cel
> *Vers son fil, qui toz nos governe,*
> *Qui rois est del cel e de terre,*
> E pose jus la mescreance
> Et ait *en Deu* bone esperence;
> La douce virge prist *son fil*
> Que *il nos get* de tot peril. (102-9) [289]

In a secondary sense everything is subject to her will " soz la trinite " (372). It is to be noted, however, that the devil who

---

[287] Bartsch-Horning, *op. cit.,* no. 58, col. 480.
[288] Kjellman, *op. cit.,* no. li, p. 292.   [289] *Ibid.,* no. xxxvi, p. 284.

15

immediately acquiesces to any command of God, refuses to give up a soul when ordered by the Virgin to do so:

> Adonc respondet Sathanas
> a la virge en es lo pas
> que por rien nule nel lairont,
> mais en granz peines lo metront.   (152-55) [290]

Mary then declares that she will appeal to her Son:

> ne savez vos je sui la Virge,
> qui mere soi al criator
> Jesu Crist, al bon salveor,
> qui escote assiduelment
> mes parolles et les entent?
> Ce que jo li quero me done,
> quant que voil fait, co est la summe;
> *poisenz est que il vos abate*
> *en la flame qui est perdurable,*
> et ce fara tot maintenant.
> Si mon moine ne laisiez franc,
> *por lui prierai mon fil poisant,*
> *qui vos metra en grie torment.*   (164-76)

Frightened at this threat, the evil spirit releases the soul of the monk whom Mary comforts with the words:

> . . . n'aies paor, *salvez seras*
> *avoi mon fil*, . . .   (201-2)

When the monk appears to his brothers, he assures them that he has been saved through Christ:

> quar je fusse salvez ausi
> per Jesu Crist et sa marci.   (221-22)

MS *818* contains a passage not usually found in the legend of the "Wife and Mistress," in which the Virgin acknowledges that any power she possesses has been given her by her Son:

> *Mes chiers fiuz m'a doné pooir*
> Sus les choses qui en cel sont,
> En terre, ni en mer parfont.   (56-58) [291]

Her dependence upon God is the burden of the *Magnificat,* one of the three canticles which it is the custom of an Abbess to say:

[290] Mussafia, *Studien*, V, no. lxxiv, p. 72.
[291] Kjellman, *op. cit.*, no. xvi, p. 273.

'M'ame magnifie *mon seignor,*
en cui garde sui nuit et jor,
et *en Deu, qui ma salus est,*
mes esperiz alegrez s'est.' (31-34) [292]

The Abbess falls into dishonor due to slander. She seeks counsel from a recluse who is in alliance with the evil spirit, and is advised to abandon her practice of reciting the three canticles. Whatever devotion the Abbess may have had to Mary, there is no trace that it had dominated her life. In this crisis she declares herself totally resigned to the will of God and makes her decision without any reference or invocation of the Virgin:

Nostre Sire qui tot crea
son bon plaisir de moi fera;
je sui de tot en son pooir,
de moi face tot son voloir. (163-66)

She is firmly determined to lose all honor rather than relinquish her practice, but God chooses to restore her dignities through Mary. The poet concludes:

Cele douce virge Marie,
qui *mere est al roi de pidie,*
deprit le sien glorios fil
que *el nos gart de toz peril.* (189-92)

The title " Mother to the King of Pity " is such a favorite with the author of MS *818* that there are few legends of the collection in which it is not found. Other salutations also contain an indirect praise of the Deity:

La mere *Deu omnipotent* (90) [293]
La mere *lo roi tot poissent* (83) [294]
La mere al *Criator* (62) [295]
la mere *nostron salveor* (307) [296]

The two words, however, which express the status of the Virgin most explicitly, are " après Deu." [297]

* * *

[292] Mussafia, *Studien,* V, no. i, p. 19.

[293] Kjellman, *op. cit.,* no. xxi, p. 279.

[294] Paul Meyer, *Recueil d'anciens textes bas-latins, provençaux et français,* 2 (Paris, 1877), no. 41, p. 349.

[295] Kjellman, *op. cit.,* no. lxiii, p. 299.

[296] Mussafia, *Studien,* V, no. lxxiii, p. 63.

[297] *Ibid.,* no. iv, p. 27; Bartsch-Horning, *op. cit.,* no. 58, col. 482.

A retrospective view of the vernacular legends reveals a theocentrism which does not differ from that of the Latin collections already considered. God alone performs miracles, according to Adgar and the author of MS *818*, for He can do all things. In MS *Old Royal 20 B XIV* God purposely intends to glorify His power and work a miracle through the ministrations of the Blessed Virgin. In the same work and in Gautier de Coincy God performs miracles for His saints, and therefore, He will more willingly do so for His mother. Gautier, in treating of the incredulous attitude of certain individuals toward Mary miracles, accuses such skeptics of disbelief in the existence and power of God. The *Vie des Pères* presents as a moral to the many anecdotes in which the sinner is a protagonist, the truth that God, like the Good Shepherd, sustains and protects those who turn to Him. He is the *Roche fort* and to attain to His love, one must willingly give up all earthly goods. The author's principles of perfection are decidedly theocentric. Jean le Marchant leaves no doubt as to his theocentrism by his repeated assertions that God performs the miracles for His Mother.

The attribute of divine mercy is not in the background. In MS *818* God is the *Roi de pitie* and His mercy encompasses all. Adgar says that God loves all for He has formed all with His hands; no sinner who does good for the love of God is unrewarded. For Gautier de Coincy, God is *débonnaire, miséricors, piteus et douz.* The authors of the *Vie des Pères* portray the warm welcome which Christ gives to the repentant sinner. In MS *818* and in the other vernacular collections it is clear that salvation and pardon are from God; the Blessed Virgin may give protection and assistance, but only in accordance with the divine will.

In the version of "Wife and Mistress," contained in MS *818,* and in the legend of the "Devil in Beast-shapes," considered in this manuscript and in Adgar, Mary definitely attributes all the power which she exercises to her Creator. Her status in the various collections is asserted to be *apres Deu* or *desuz Deu.* The author of MS *Old Royal 20 B XIV* rejoices that she is a Queen, crowned, but of his lineage of flesh and blood, surpassing all creatures but not forgetting her human nature. From such evidence, one may conclude that the vernacular collections considered here are theocentric and accord to the Blessed Virgin the status of a creature.

CHAPTER V

CONCLUSION

In this study the problem of theocentrism and Marial status has not been considered from a theological view point. An attempt has been made to ascertain the correctness of the assertions that Mary was exalted to the height of deification or made equal to God, not from a religious motive, but in order to interpret the philosophy underlying the Marial legend as a literary genre of the Middle Ages.

An investigation of the *miracula* reveals the following facts: the miracles of the twelfth and thirteenth centuries do not differ in the matter of theocentrism from those of the preceding centuries; no collection has been found which does not present the Blessed Virgin in the secondary rôle of suppliant, dependent upon the will of God for the favor she wishes to bestow upon a client.

Medieval writers consistently used a theocentric appeal when they attempt to convince an incredulous reader. They assert that to God all things are possible; for Him nothing is difficult. If God performs miracles for His Saints, He will do more when importuned by His Mother. Gautier de Coincy goes so far as to accuse the skeptic of disbelief in the existence of God and in His power. Moreover, divine omnipotence, manifested in the miracles of the Old Testament, is repeatedly said to be displayed again in those legends in which the Virgin takes an active part.

The theocentric phrase, *divina virtus*, which first appears with Gregory of Tours, recurs six centuries later in the Pez collection, MSS *Phillipps 25142, Cotton Cleopatra C. x., Copenhagen Thott 128, Cornell B. 14* and others. *Deus qui facit mirabilia solus* are words found in the ninth century translations of Paul the Deacon of Naples and later used by Johannes Monachus, Honorius Augustodunensis, Vincent of Beauvais, Caesarius of Heisterbach, Adgar Gilon de Chartres, and the authors of *MSS Copenhagen Thott 128* and *Bibl. nat. fr. 818*. That God performs the miracle or miracles for the Virgin is stated in prologues, epilogues, and in the individual legends of collections.

219

God is depicted as the Creator of Heaven and earth, of angels and men—and what is more significant—of the Virgin Mary. He governs the world, controls the elements, and in His Providence provides for the wants of Man. As the *gentil Saveur,* the *bonus pastor,* He is ready, according to the legendaries, to repeat the Redemption in His love for sinners. Descriptions of the suffering Christ are not wanting in the *miracula* where the one aspect of the Messianic mission, the salvation of sinners, is a predominant theme. The grace of contrition is frequently a direct gift of God, although the Blessed Virgin may later intercede to obtain forgiveness for a soul. The right to pardon, however, is reserved exclusively to the Deity.

Mary's rôle of Mediatrix is founded upon her exalted dignity as Mother of God wherein she is said to surpass the saints and to obtain favors which might be denied them. Her mediation assumes a theocentric aspect since it is specifically stated that God performs the miracles because of her prayers or in her honor, and that the divine power uses her as an instrument or acts through her. Moreover, as a suppliant she is dependent upon the will of God, and therefore, secondary in her subordination to the divine volition. There are few collections which do not depict her in attitudes of prostration, adoration, kneeling, even bowing in reverence to the words of the *Gloria Patri.* Christ maintains a regal dignity. Mary may dispute with the devils; Christ merely commands. The frequency of such expressions as *post Deum* or *desuz Deu,* is noteworthy. It is likewise significant that writers place upon her own lips the acknowledgment that she is the Mother of Him by Whom she was made, and by Whom she can aid her servants. In the light of the four-fold characterization of God's mercies, given in the *Speculum Laicorum,*—the creation, the redemption, the preservation of man, and the bestowal of manifold graces under the New Law—the Blessed Virgin's charity is limited to that of a finite creature dependent upon the will of her Son, even as an Infant Who, according to Peter the Venerable, rules Heaven and earth.

While this study has been based solely upon published collections written earlier than the fourteenth century, the cumulative evidence which it presents points to the theocentrism of the Marial *miracula* and to the Virgin's creature-status during the twelfth and thirteenth. It is true that the statement *tot et tanta mirabilia Christus ad laudem suae matris est dignatus ostendere* or,

> *Mult fait Deu miracles* souent
> Par tut le siecle diuersement,
> *Pur l'amur sa mere chere*

is not repeated in every legend of a collection, nevertheless, these are generalizations and once made, the writer leaves to implication a truth which had become a platitude after centuries of tradition. Inasmuch as the Blessed Virgin Mary is not considered the source of grace or power, it is logical to conclude that charges of mariolatry and deification of the Blessed Virgin in the legends rest upon insufficient evidence. If it is permissible to use a popular phrase to epitomize the rôle of Mary Mediatrix in the *miracula*, we may say that she is not the Power behind the throne, but a power before the throne.

ABBREVIATIONS

Anal. Boll.	Analecta Bollandiana.
BHL	Bibliotheca hagiographica latina.
CFMA	Classiques français du moyen âge.
EETS	Publications of the Early English Text Society.
HLF	Histoire littéraire de la France.
MGH	Monumenta Germaniae historica.
Not. et extr.	Notices et extraits des manuscrits de la Bibliothèque nationale.
PG	Patrologia graeca, ed. Migne.
PL	Patrologia latina, ed. Migne.
Recueil	Recueil des historiens des Gaules et de la France.
RR	Romanic Review.
SATF	Société des anciens textes français.
ZRPh	Zeitschrift für romanische Philologie.

BIBLIOGRAPHY

Adam of Perseigne. *Mariale. PL*, CCXI, 695-744.

Adamnan. *De locis sanctis*. Ed. Paul Geyer. Vienna, 1898. (Corpus Scriptorum Ecclesiasticorum Latinorum, Vol. XXXIX.)

Adams, H. *Mont-Saint-Michel and Chartres*. New York, 1913.

Adgar: see Neuhaus, Carl.

Ahsmann, H. P. J. M. *Le culte de la sainte Vierge et la littérature française profane du moyen âge*. Paris, 1930.

Albe, Edmond. *Les Miracles de Notre-Dame de Roc-Amadour au XIIe siècle*. Paris, 1907.

Anonymi Gesta Francorum et aliorum Hierosolymitanorum. Ed. Beatrice A. Lees. Oxford, 1924.

Anselm of Canterbury. *Orationes. PL*, CLVIII, 855-1016.

Anselm of Gembloux. *Chronica: continuatio. PL*, CLX, 239-58.

" B." *Vita Sancti Dunstani* in *Memorials of Saint Dunstan*, pp. 3-53. Ed. Wm. Stubbs. London, 1874. (Rolls Series, No. 63.)

Barbazan, Etienne. *Fabliaux et contes des poètes françois*. 4 vols. Paris, 1808.

Bardenhewer, Otto. *Geschichte der altkirchlichen Literatur*. 5 vols. Freiburg and St. Louis, 1902-1932.

Bartsch-Horning. *La langue et la littérature françaises*. Paris, 1887.

Bartsch-Wiese. *Chrestomathie de l'ancien français*. 12th ed. Leipzig, 1919.

Batiffol, Pierre. *Histoire du Bréviare romain*. Paris, 1893.

Baumgartner, P. E. " Eine Quellenstudie zur Franziskuslegende des Jakobus de Voragine," *Archivum franciscanum historicum*, II (1909), 17-31.

Becker, Heinrich. *Die Auffassung der Jungfrau Maria in der altfranzösischen Literatur*. Göttingen, 1905.

Becker, Richard. *Gonzalo de Berceos Milagros und ihre Grundlagen mit einem Anhange: Mitteilungen aus der lat. Hs. Kopenhagen, Thott 128*. Strassburg, 1910.

Benrath, Karl. " Zur Geschichte der Marienverehrung," *Theologische Studien und Kritiken*, LIX (1886), 1-95, 197-267.

Berger, E. *Thomas Cantipratensis Bonum universale de apibus quid illustrandis saeculi decimi tertii moribus conferat*. Paris, 1895.

Bernard of Clairvaux. *Ad beatam Virginem Deiparem. PL*, CLXXXIV. 1009-1014.

Bibliotheca hagiographica latina antiquae et mediae aetatis. 2 vols. Brussels, 1898-1901.

Bishop, Edmund. *Liturgica Historica*. Oxford, 1918.

Boman, Erik. *Deux miracles de Gautier de Coinci*. Paris, 1935.

Bouchet, Charles. " Recueil des miracles de la Vierge du XIIIᵉ siècle," *Bulletin de la Société archéologique, scientifique et littéraire du Vendomois,* IX (1870), 187-99.

Caesarius of Heisterbach. *Dialogus miraculorum.* Ed. J. Strange. 2 vols. Cologne, 1851.

―――. *Index in Caesarii Heisterbacensis Dialogum.* Ed. J. Strange. Cologne, 1857.

―――. *Libri VIII Miraculorum.* Ed. Aloys Meister. Rome, 1901. (Römische Quartalschrift für christliche Alterthumskunde, Supplement-Heft 13.)

Carman, J. Neale. *The Relationship of the Perlesvaus and the Queste del Saint Graal.* University of Chicago Dissertation, 1934. Bulletin of the University of Kansas, Humanistic Studies, Vol. V, No. 4 [July, 1936].)

Cartulaire de l'Eglise Notre-Dame. Ed. M. Guérard in *Collection des cartulaires de France.* Vol. IV. Paris, 1850.

Celestine V: See Peter Celestine.

Celidonio, J. *La non-autenticità degle Opuscula Coelestina.* Sulmona, 1896.

Cixila. *Vita Sancti Hildefonsi. PL,* XCVI, 43-48.

Conrad of Everbach. *Exordium magnum Ordinis Cisterciensis. PL,* CLXXXV, 993-1198.

Continuatio Isidoriana Hispana. Ed. T. Mommsen, in *MGH, Auctores Antiquissimi.* Vol. XI. Berlin, 1894.

Coulton, G. G. *Five Centuries of Religion.* Vol. I. Cambridge, 1923.

Crane, Thomas F. *Liber de miraculis Sanctae Dei Genitricis Mariae.* Ithaca, 1925. Reprint from Pez, q. v.

―――. " Miracles of the Virgin," *RR,* II (1911), 235-78.

Dalton, J. N. *Ordinale Exoniense.* 2 vols. London, 1909. (Henry Bradshaw Society, Vol. XXXVIII.)

Delisle, L. V. " Lettre de l'Abbé Haimon sur la construction de l'Eglise de Saint-Pierre-sur-Dive, en 1145," *Bibliothèque de l'Ecole des Chartes,* XXI (1859), 113-39.

―――. " Notice sur un traité inédit du XIIᵉ siècle intitulé Miracula ecclesiae Constantiensis," *Bibliothèque de l'Ecole des Chartes,* IX (1848), 339-53.

Dexter, Elise F. *Miracula Sanctae Virginis Mariae.* Madison, 1927. (University of Wisconsin Studies in the Social Sciences and History, No. 12.)

Dionysius the Areopagite. *Epistola VIII. PG,* III, 1083-1104.

Ducrot-Granderye, A. P. " Etudes sur les Miracles Nostre Dame de Gautier de Coinci," *Annales Academiae Scientiarum Fennicae,* Series B, XXV, 2 (1932), 1-287.

Dudden, F. Homes. *Gregory the Great.* London, 1905.

Eadmer. *Vita Sancti Dunstani* in *Memorials of Saint Dunstan,* pp. 162-223. Ed. Wm. Stubbs. London, 1874. (Rolls Series, No. 63.)

Endres, J. A. "Boto von Prüfening und seine schriftstellerische Thätigkeit," *Neues Archiv der Gesellschaft für ältere deutsche Geschichtskunde*, XXX (1905), 605-46.

Estienne de Fougères. *Livre des manières.* Ed. Josef Kremer. Marburg, 1887. (Ausgaben und Abhandlungen aus dem Gebiete der romanischen Philologie, No. 39.)

Etienne de Bourbon. *Anecdotes historiques, légendes et apologues tirés du recueil inédit d'Etienne de Bourbon.* Ed. Lecoy de la Marche. Paris, 1877. (Société de l'histoire de France.)

Everard de Gateley: See Meyer, Paul.

Faral, Edmond. *La légende arthurienne.* 3 vols. Paris, 1929. (Bibliothèque de l'Ecole des Hautes Etudes, Nos. 255-57.)

Flodoard. *De triumphis Christi Sanctorumque Palaestinae Libri III.* *PL*, CXXXV, 491-550.

Fritzsche, Carl. "Die lateinischen Visionen des Mittelalters bis zur Mitte des 12. Jahrhunderts," *Romanische Forschungen*, II (1886), 247-79; III (1887), 337-69.

Fulbert of Chartres. *Sermones ad populum.* *PL*, CLXI, 317-40.

Funck-Brentano, F. *Le moyen âge.* Paris, 1922.

Galtier, E. "Byzantina," *Romania*, XXIX (1900), 501-27.

Gautier de Coincy. *Les Miracles de la Sainte Vierge traduits et mis en vers.* Ed. Abbé Poquet. Paris, 1857.

Gerald of Barry. *Giraldi Cambrensis Opera.* Edd. Brewer, Dimock, Warner. 8 vols. London, 1861-91. (Rolls Series, No. 21.)

Gerould, Gordon H. *The North-English Homily Collection, a Study of the Manuscript Relations and the Sources of the Tales.* Oxford, 1902.

Gervase of Canterbury. *Opera historica.* Ed. Wm. Stubbs. 2 vols. London, 1879-80. (Rolls Series, No. 73.)

Gesta Romanorum. Ed. Hermann Oesterley. Berlin, 1872.

Graf, Arturo. *Roma nella memoria e nelle immaginazioni del medio evo.* Turin, 1915.

Gregory of Tours. *Liber in gloria martyrum.* Edd. W. Arndt and B. Krusch, in *MGH, Scriptores rerum Merovingicarum.* Vol. I. Hannover, 1885. Pp. 484-561.

————. *Liber Vitae Patrum. Ibid.* Pp. 661-744.

Gregory the Great. *Dialogi libri IV.* Ed. Umberto Moricca. Rome, 1924. (Fonti per la Storia d'Italia, Vol. LVII.)

————. *Moralium libri XXXVI.* *PL*, LXXV, 509-1162; *PL*, LXXVI, 9-782.

Gröber, Gustav. "Ein Marienmirakel," *Beiträge zur romanischen und englischen Philologie: Festgabe für Wendelin Foerster.* Halle, 1902.

Gross, Charles. *The Sources and Literature of English History from the Earliest Times to about 1485.* 2d ed. London, 1915.

Guaiferius Casinensis. *Carmina.* *PL*, CXLVII, 1283-93.

Guibert of Nogent. *De laude Sanctae Mariae.* *PL*, CLVI, 558-78.

Guibert of Nogent. *De pignoribus sanctorum libri IV.* *PL*, CLVI, 607-80.
————. *De vita sua libri III.* *PL*, CLVI, 837-962.
Guiette, Robert. *La légende de la sacristine.* Paris, 1927.
Guiot de Provins. *Œuvres.* Ed. John Orr. Manchester, 1915.
Haimo: See Delisle, Léopold.
Hatto. *Visio Wettini.* Ed. Ernst Dümmler, in *MGH, Poetae latini aevi Carolini.* Vol. II. Berlin, 1884. Pp. 268-75, 301-33.
Helinand of Froidmont. *Chronicon libri XLV-XLIX.* *PL*, CCXII, 481-720.
Herbert of Torres. *De miraculis libri III.* *PL*, CLXXXV, 1273-1384.
Herbert, J. A. "A New Manuscript of Adgar's Mary-legends," *Romania,* XXXII (1903), 394-421.
————. *Catalogue of Romances in the Department of Manuscripts in the British Museum.* Vol. III. London, 1910.
Herman of Tournai. *De miraculis Sanctae Mariae Laudunensis: de gestis venerabilis Bartholomaei Episcopi et Sancti Norberti.* *PL*, CLVI, 962-1018.
Hildebert. *Vita Beatae Mariae Aegyptiacae.* *PL*, CLXXI, 1321-40.
Honorius Augustodunensis. *Liber Sacramentarium.* *PL*, CLXXII, 737-806.
————. *Speculum Ecclesiae.* *PL*, CLXXII, 807-1108.
Hrotsuithae. *Opera.* Ed. Karl Strecker. Leipzig, 1906.
Huebaldus. *Vita Sanctae Aldegundis.* *PL*, CXXXII, 857-76.
Huet, Gédéon. "La légende de la statue de Vénus," *Revue de l'histoire des religions,* LXVIII (1913), 193-217.
Hugo Farsit. *Libellus de miraculis Beatae Mariae Virginis in urbe Suessionensi.* *PL*, CLXXIX, 1778-1800.
Hugo of Saint-Victor. *De sacramentis christianae fidei.* *PL*, CLXXVI, 173-618.
Isnard, H. "Recueil des miracles de la Vierge du XIIIe siècle," *Bulletin de la Société archéologique, scientifique et littéraire du Vendomois,* XXVI (1887), 23-63, 104-49, 182-227, 282-311.
Jacobus a Voragine. *Legenda aurea.* Ed. T. Graesse. 2d ed. Leipzig, 1850.
————. *Mariale sive sermones de Beata Maria Virgine.* Venice, 1497.
Jacques de Vitry. *The Exempla, or Stories from the Sermones Vulgares of Jacques de Vitry.* Ed. Thomas F. Crane. London, 1890. (Publications of the Folk-lore Society, Vol. XXVI.)
————. *Die Exempla aus den Sermones feriales et communes.* Ed. Joseph Greven. Heidelberg, 1914. (Sammlung mittellateinischer Texte, No. 9.)
Jean le Marchant. *Miracles de Nostre-Dame de Chartres.* Ed. G. Gratet-Duplessis. Chartres, 1855.
Jerome. *Epistola XXII ad Eustochium.* *PL*, XXII, 394-425.
Johannes Monachus. *Liber de miraculis.* Ed. Michael Huber. Heidelberg, 1913. (Sammlung mittellateinischer Texte, No. 5.)

John. *Vita Sancti Odonis. PL*, CXXXIII, 43-86.

John of Damascus. *Epistola ad Theophilum Imperatorem. PG*, XCV, 345-86.

John of Jerusalem. *Vita Sancti Johannis Damasceni. PG*, XCIV, 429-504.

John of Salisbury. *Polycraticus. PL*, CXCIX, 585-822.

Kjellman, Hilding. *La deuxième collection anglo-normande des miracles de la Sainte Vierge et son original latin avec les miracles correspondants des manuscrits français 375 et 818 de la Bibliothèque nationale.* Paris and Upsala, 1922.

————. "La légende de Saint Jean Damascène," *Studier i Modern Språkvetenskap*, VIII (1921), 103-20.

————. "Sur deux episodes de Gautier de Coincy," *Romania*, XLVII (1921), 588-94.

————. "Une version anglo-normande inédite du Miracle de Théophile, Avec un appendice: Le miracle de la femme enceinte retirée de la mer par le Sainte Vierge," *Studier i Modern Språkvetenskap*, V (1914), 185-214.

Koehler, Reinhold. "Le Conte de la Reine qui tua son sénéchal," *Romania*, XI (1882), 581-89.

Kölbing, E. "Ueber die englischen Fassungen der Theophilussage," *Beiträge zur vergleichenden Geschichte der romantischen Poesie.* Breslau, 1876. Pp. 1-41.

Krumbacher, Karl. *Geschichte der Byzantinischen Litteratur.* 2d ed. Munich, 1897.

Lacombe, Paul. *Livres d'heures imprimés au XVe et au XVIe siècle conservés dans les bibliothèques publiques de Paris.* Paris, 1907.

Lanfranc. *De nobili genere Crispinorum. PL*, CL, 735-44.

Leroquais, Victor. *Des Livres d'heures manuscrits de la Bibliothèque nationale.* 2 vols. Paris, 1927.

Levi, E. *Il libro dei cinquanta miracoli della Vergine.* Bologna, 1917.

L'Hote, E. *Notre-Dame de Saint-Dié.* Saint-Dié, 1894.

Liber exemplorum ad usum praedicantium. Ed. A. G. Little. Aberdeen, 1908.

Luchaire, Achille. *La société française au temps de Philippe-Auguste.* Paris, 1909.

Ludorff, Franz. "William Forrest's Theophiluslegende," *Anglia*, VI (1884), 60-115.

Lundgren, Hjalmar. *Studier ofver Theophiluslegendens romanska varianter.* Upsala, 1913.

Mabillon, J. *Acta sanctorum Ordinis Sancti Benedicti.* 2d ed. *Saec.* I-VI in 9 vols. Venice, 1733-1740.

Manitius, Max. *Geschichte der lateinischen Literatur des Mittelalters.* 3 vols. Munich, 1911-31.

Maurilius of Rouen: See Anselm of Canterbury.

Méon, D. M. *Nouveau recueil de fabliaux et contes inédits.* Vol. II. Paris, 1823.

Meyer, Paul. "Les manuscrits français de Cambridge," *Romania*, XV (1886), 272-73.

———. "Notice du manuscrit Rawlinson Poetry 241: Miracles de la Vierge par Everard de Gateley," *Romania*, XXIX (1900), 24-47.

———. "Notice sur deux anciens manuscrits français ayant appartenu au marquis de la Clayette," *Not. et extr.*, XXXIII, 1 (1890), 66-71.

———. "Notice sur le recueil de miracles de la Vierge renfermé dans le manuscrit Bibl. nat. fr. 818," *Not. et extr.*, XXXIV, 2 (1895), 57-88.

———. "Notice sur un manuscrit d'Orléans contenant d'anciens miracles de la Vierge en vers français," *Not. et extr.*, XXXIV, 2 (1895), 31-56.

———. *Recueil d'anciens textes bas-latins provençaux et français.* Paris, 1874-77.

———. "Versions en vers et en prose des Vies des Pères." *HLF*, XXXIII (1906), 254-328.

Meyer, Wilhelm. "Radewin's Gedicht über Theophilus," *Sitzungsberichte der königlich bayerischen Akademie* (phil.-philol. und hist. Classe), III (1873), 49-120.

Michel, A. Article "Miracle," in Vacant and Mangenot, *Dictionnaire de théologie catholique.* Vol. X, 2 (Paris, 1927).

Mielot, Jean. *Miracles de Nostre Dame.* Ed. G. F. Warner. Westminster, 1885. (Roxburghe Club.)

"Miracles de Notre-Dame de Chartres": See Thomas, Antoine.

Miracles de Notre-Dame de Roc-Amadour au XIIᵉ siècle: See Albe, Edmond.

Molinier, Auguste. *Sources de l'histoire de France.* 6 vols. Paris, 1901-1906.

Morawski, J. "Mélanges de littérature pieuse," *Romania*, LXI (1935), 145-209, 316-50.

Mussafia, Adolf. "Studien zu den mittelalterlichen Marienlegenden," *Sitzungsberichte der kaiserlichen Akademie der Wissenschaften in Wien* (phil.-hist. Classe), CXIII (1886), 917-94; CXV (1888), 5-93; CXIX (1889), 1-66; CXXIII (1891), 1-85; CXXXIX (1898), 1-74.

———. "Handschriftliches: Zu Wolters Judenknaben," *ZRPh*, IX (1885), 412-13.

———. "Sulle Vies des anciens Pères," *Romania*, XIV (1885), 583-86.

———. "Ueber die von Gautier de Coincy benützten Quellen," *Denkschriften der kaiserlichen Akademie der Wissenschaften in Wien* (phil.-hist. Classe), XLIV (1896), Abh. i, 1-58.

Nalgodus. *Sancti Odonis vita.* *PL*, CXXXIII, 86-104.

Neuhaus, Carl. *Adgar's Marienlegenden.* Heilbronn, 1886. (Altfranzösische Bibliothek, Vol. IX.)

Neuhaus, Carl. *Das Dulwich'er Adgar-Fragment.* Aschersleben, 1887.

―――. *Die lateinischen Vorlagen zu den altfranzösischen Adgar'schen Marienlegenden.* Aschersleben, 1886.

―――. *Die Quellen zu Adgar's Marienlegenden nach der Londoner Handschrift Egerton 612.* Aschersleben, 1882.

Osbern. ˙ *Vita Sancti Dunstani* in *Memorials of Saint Dunstan,* pp. 69-161. Ed. Wm. Stubbs. London, 1874. (Rolls Series, No. 63.)

Ordericus Vitalis. *Historiae ecclesiasticae libri XII.* Ed. Augustus Le Prevost. 5 vols. Paris, 1838-1855. (Société de l'histoire de France.)

Paris, Matthew. *Chronica majora.* Ed. H. R. Luard. 7 vols. London, 1872-1883. (Rolls Series, No. 57.)

Paul of Naples. *Theophilus* in Petsch, *Theophilus, Mittelniederdeutsches Drama.* Heidelberg, 1908. (Germanische Bibliothek, No. 2.)

―――. *De vitis Patrum liber I: Vita Sanctae Mariae Aegyptiacae.* PL, LXXIII, 671-90.

Pelizaeus, Theodor. *Beiträge zur Geschichte der Legende vom Judenknaben.* Halle, 1914.

Peter Celestine. *Opusculum VI, De miraculis Beatae Mariae Virginis* in *Maxima Bibliotheca Veterum Patrum,* XXV (Lyons, 1677), 813-17.

Peter the Venerable. *De miraculis libri II.* PL, CLXXXIX, 851-953.

" Petites pièces de vieille poésie," *Mémoires de l'Académie d'Arras,* XXVIII (1855), 290-97.

Petrus Damiani. *Carmina et preces.* PL, CXLV, 930-86.

―――. *Epistolarum libri VIII.* PL, CXLIV, 205-489.

―――. *Opuscula varia.* PL, CXLV, 19-860.

―――. *Sermones.* PL, CXLIV, 505-924.

Pez, Bernhard. *Venerabilis Agnetis Blannbekin . . . vita et revelationes auctore anonymo . . . Accessit Pothonis Prunveningensis nunc Priflingensis prope Ratisbonam O. S. B. liber de miraculis Sanctae Dei Genitricis Mariae.* Vienna, 1731. See Crane, Thomas F.

Pigeon, E. A. *Histoire de la Cathédrale de Coutances.* Coutances, 1876.

Poncelet, A. " Miraculorum Beatae Virginis Mariae quae saec. VI-XV latine conscripta sunt Index," *Anal. Boll.,* XXI (1902), 341-60.

―――. " Note sur les Libri VIII Miraculorum de Césaire d'Heisterbach," *Anal. Boll.,* XXI (1902), 45-52.

Poquet: See Gautier de Coincy.

Pseudo-Anselm. *Ad Opera S. Anselmi Appendix. Spuria: De Conceptione Beatae Mariae.* PL, CLIX, 319-26.

―――. *Miraculum Sancti Jacobi.* PL, CLIX, 335-340.

―――. *Tractatus de Conceptione Beatae Mariae Virginis.* PL, CLIX, 30˙-318.

Raby, F. J. E. *A History of Christian-Latin Poetry.* Oxford, 1927.

Radbod. *Sermo de Annuntiatione Beatae Mariae Virginis.* PL, CL, 1527-34.

―――. *Vita Sanctae Godebertae Virginis.* PL, CL, 1517-28.

Radbod. *Vita Sancti Medardi. PL*, CL, 1499-1518.

Radewin: See Meyer, Wilhelm.

Radulphus Glaber. *Historiarum libri V.* Ed. Maurice Prou. Paris, 1886. (Collection de textes pour servir à l'étude et à l'enseignement de l'histoire.)

Raynaud, G. "Le miracle de Sardenai," *Romania*, XI (1882), 517-37; XIV (1885), 82-93.

Renclus de Moiliens. *Li Romans de Carité et Miserere.* Ed. A.-G. van Hamel. 2 vols. Paris, 1885. (Bibliothèque de l'Ecole des Hautes Etudes, Nos. 61-62.)

Rigord. *Gesta Philippi Augusti* and *Philippides*, in *Œuvres de Rigord et de Guillaume le Breton, historiens de Philippe-Auguste.* Ed. H. François Delaborde. 2 vols. Paris, 1882-1885. (Société de l'histoire de France.)

Robert of Torigny. *Chronica. PL*, CLX, 411-546.

Roderic Cerratensis. *Vita Sancti Hildefonsi. PL*, XCVI, 47-50.

Rolfs, W. "Die Adgarlegenden," *Romanische Forschungen*, I (1883), 179-236.

Rutebeuf. *Le Miracle de Théophile.* Ed. Grace Frank. Paris, 1925. (*CFMA*, No. 49.)

Sackur, E. *Die Cluniacenser.* 2 vols. Halle, 1892-1894.

Salzer, Anselm. *Die Sinnbilder und Beiworte Mariens in der deutschen Literatur und lateinischen Hymnenpoesie des Mittelalters.* Linz, 1893.

Schaff, D. *History of the Christian Church.* Vol. V, Part 2. New York, 1910.

Schönbach, Anton E. "Studien zur Erzählungsliteratur des Mittelalters, IV and VII: über Caesarius von Heisterbach," *Sitzungsberichte der kaiserlichen Akademie der Wissenschaften in Wien* (phil.-hist. Classe), CXLIV (1902), Abh. ix; CLIX (1908), Abh. iv.

Schwan, Edouard. "La Vie des anciens Pères," *Romania*, XIII (1884), 233-63.

Sedulius. *Elegia. PL*, XIX, 753-64.

Servois, Gustave. "Notices et extraits du Recueil des miracles de Notre-Dame de Roc-Amadour," *Bibliothèque de l'Ecole des Chartes*, XVIII (1856), 21-42.

Sigebert of Gembloux. *Chronica. PL*, CLX, 57-240.

Snavely, Guy E. "Jehan de Vignay and His Influence on Early English Literature," *RR*, II (1911), 323-30.

Strohmayer, Henri. Review of Marius Sepet's "Un drame religieux au moyen âge: Le miracle de Théophile," *Romania*, XXIII (1894), 601-607.

Suger. *Vie de Louis VI le Gros.* Ed. Henri Waquet. Paris, 1929. (Les classiques de l'histoire de France au moyen âge, No. 11.)

Speculum Laicorum. Ed. J. T. Welter. Paris, 1914. (Thesaurus exemplorum, fasc. V.)

Tatlock, John S. P. "The English Journey of the Laon Canons," *Speculum*, VIII (1933), 454-65.

Thomas, Antoine. "Les miracles de Notre-Dame de Chartres," *Bibliothèque de l'Ecole des Chartes*, XLII (1881), 505-550.

Thomas of Cantimpré. *Bonum universale de apibus*. Cologne, ca. 1473.

Tobler, Adolf. "Eine handschriftliche Sammlung altfranzösischer Legenden," *Jahrbuch für romanische und englische Literatur*, VII (1866), 401-36.

Ulrich, J. "Drei Wunder Gautiers von Coincy," *ZRPh*, VI (1882), 325-46.

Ursus. *Vita Sancti Basilii*. *PL*, LXXIII, 293-320.

Vincent of Beauvais. *Speculum Historiale*. Venice, 1494.

Vloberg, Maurice. *La légende dorée de Notre-Dame*. Paris, 1921.

Wace. *The Conception Nostre Dame*. Ed. William R. Ashford. Menasha (Wis.), 1933. (University of Chicago Dissertation.)

——. *Roman de Rou et des ducs de Normandie*. Ed. Hugo Andresen. 2 vols. Heilbronn, 1877-1879.

Waitz, G. "Hermann von Tournai und die Geschichtschreibung der Stadt," *Forschungen zur deutschen Geschichte*, XXI (1881), 431-48.

Walter of Cluny. *De miraculis Beatae Virginis Mariae*. *PL*, CLXXIII, 1379-80.

Ward, H. L. D. *Catalogue of Romances in the Department of Manuscripts in the British Museum*. Vol. II. London, 1893.

Watenphul, Heinrich. *Die Geschichte der Marienlegende von Beatrix der Küsterin*. Göttingen, 1904.

Wattenbach, W. *Deutschlands Geschichtsquellen im Mittelalter bis zur Mitte des dreizehnten Jahrhunderts*. 7th ed. Berlin, 1904.

Weber, Alfred. *Handschriftliche Studien auf dem Gebiete romanischer Litteratur des Mittelalters*. I. Frauenfeld, 1876.

——. "Zu den Legenden der Vie des pères," *ZRPh*, I (1877), 357-65.

——. "Zwei ungedruckte Versionen der Theophilussage," *ZRPh*, I (1877), 522-40.

Welter, J. T. *L'exemplum dans la littérature religieuse et didactique du moyen âge*. Paris, 1927.

William of Malmesbury. *De gestis regum Anglorum*. Ed. Wm. Stubbs. 2 vols. London, 1887-89. (Rolls Series, No. 90.)

——. *Vita Sancti Dunstani*, in *Memorials of Saint Dunstan*, pp. 251-325. Ed. Wm. Stubbs. London, 1874. (Rolls Series, No. 63.)

Wilmart, André. *Auteurs spirituels et textes dévots du moyen âge latin*. Paris, 1932.

Wolter, Eugen. *Der Judenknabe*. Halle, 1879. (Bibliotheca Normannica, No. 2.)

Wright, Thomas. *A Selection of Latin Stories*. London, 1853. (Percy Society, No. 8.)

INDEX

233